# Schweizer Anglistische Arbeiten
# Swiss Studies in English

Begründet von Bernhard Fehr
Herausgegeben von Robert Fricker, Bern, Ernst Leisi, Zürich,
Henri Petter, Zürich

## Band 113

Für Lina

von Annabeth

Dezember 83

Annabeth Naef-Hinderling

# The Search for the Culprit: Dickens's Conflicting Self- and Object-Representations

Francke Verlag Bern

Die vorliegende Arbeit wurde von der Philosophischen
Fakultät I der Universität Zürich im Sommersemester 1983
auf Antrag von Prof. Dr. Henri Petter als Dissertation
angenommen.

A. Francke AG Verlag Bern, 1983
Druck: Juris Druck + Verlag, Zürich
Printed in Switzerland
(ISBN 3-7720-1584-0)

TO WALTER AND MARTINA

# Acknowledgements

I should like to express my sincere gratitude to Professor Henri Petter for his openness to, and tolerance of, views which were not always congenial to him as well as for the untiring patience and encouragement granted me. My warm thanks are due to David Roscoe for his subtle and empathic correcting of my English. I am grateful to my mother, Lina Hinderling-Stöckli, who for more than a year regularly came to St. Gallen once a week to look after Martina, taking her on long outings in all kinds of weather so that I could work at home in peace.

My warmest thanks go to my husband, Walter Naef, who helped me in many ways: by presenting me with a good typewriter, by reading Dickens novels with me, by listening to my as yet unfledged ideas, by being my first reader and critic, by helping me with the proof-reading, and – most of all – by his unfailing moral support and belief in me.

Last but not least, I wish to thank my daughter, Martina, for putting up with a mother who was sometimes preoccupied.

A.N.

# Contents

# List of Abbreviations

F       John Forster, *The Life of Charles Dickens,* 1872-4, reprinted in the Everyman's Library Edition, 2 vols., ed. by A. J. Hoppé, London 1966.

"AF"     "Autobiographical Fragment", in: Forster, *Life,* vol. I, pp. 20-33.

*Letters*   *The Letters of Charles Dickens,* ed. Walter Dexter (the Nonesuch Dickens), 3 vols., 1938.

*PE*     *The Letters of Charles Dickens,* ed. by Madeline House, Graham Storey and Kathleen Tillotson (the Pilgrim Edition), 5 vols. issued so far, Oxford 1965 – .

*The Works*

| | |
|---|---|
| *AN & PI* | *American Notes and Pictures from Italy* |
| *BH* | *Bleak House* |
| *BR* | *Barnaby Rudge* |
| *CB* | *Christmas Books* |
| *CS* | *Christmas Stories* |
| *DC* | *David Copperfield* |
| *DS* | *Dombey and Son* |
| *ED* | *The Mystery of Edwin Drood* |
| *GE* | *Great Expectations* |
| *HT* | *Hard Times* |
| *LD* | *Little Dorrit* |
| *MC* | *Martin Chuzzlewit* |
| *NN* | *Nicholas Nickleby* |
| *OCS* | *The Old Curiosity Shop* |
| *OMF* | *Our Mutual Friend* |
| *OT* | *Oliver Twist* |
| *PI* | See *AN & PI* |
| *PP* | *Pickwick Papers* |
| *RP* | See *UT & RP* |
| *SB* | *Sketches by Boz* |
| *TTC* | *A Tale of Two Cities* |
| *UT & RP* | *The Uncommercial Traveller and Reprinted Pieces.* (This volume includes *George Silverman's Explanation.*) |

If not stated otherwise, the page numbers refer to the Penguin edition of Dickens's works, *OID* is the abbreviation of *The Oxford Illustrated Dickens.*

# Introduction

"It is a devastation!" the late Lionel Trilling is reported to have said about psychoanalytic literary criticism.[1] This is a harsh judgement, coming from one who himself was somewhat of a pioneer in the field. Literary critics who sneer at psychoanalysis as a tool for literary criticism are legion. Scholars who live far apart and work in different fields unite in their rejection of it. The well-known Swiss critic, Emil Staiger, who frowns at psychoanalytically oriented interpretations of *Hamlet* and calls them "eine fragwürdige Illustration einer fragwürdigen Lehre"[2], could join forces with his American colleague, Noffsinger, who contends that an exclusively "psychological" interpretation is necessarily reductive.[3]

The "monster of psychological reductionism"[4] is indeed the most dangerous pitfall for potential critics who are interested in using psychoanalysis as a tool for their interpretation of a text. Reductionism means the critic's attempt to look behind the text, as it were, as if the text itself were unimportant and stood only in the way of its deeper unconscious meaning. Thus a complex text may be reduced to a simple meaning, as if the critic were only able to perceive one thread in one particular colour in a fabric made up of multicoloured and variegated strands. The literary critic who is used to respecting the written word of a writer is bound to react against a treatment of it which disregards so many essential elements. Critics who follow such a line of thought might also be considered arrogant, as has been pointed out by Hewitt[5], if they use such expressions as "the deepest meaning" and "in the last analysis" and link "surface" to "superficial" and "depth" to "profound". An example of this kind of psychoanalytic criticism is Arthur Washburn Brown's study of Dickens's props.[6] Although he has certainly carefully investigated Dickens's text and has found out some interesting connections (see below, p. 64f.), his outlook is rather narrow, so that the reader simply gets bored after some time. We have to bear in mind, however, that psychoanalysts are usually primarily concerned with psychoanalysis; when they want to illustrate particular convictions by turning to literature they by no means claim to be literary critics. Freud himself is one of them with his *Hamlet* interpretation, his remarks on Sophocles' play *Oedipus Rex* and his *Gradiva*.[7] He was cautious in his statements about art[8] and well aware of the fact that he could not account for the

---

1 Alan Roland, "Toward a Reorientation of Psychoanalytic Literary Criticism", *The Psychoanalytic Review* 65 (1978), p. 391.
2 Emil Staiger, *Gipfel der Zeit*. Studien zur Weltliteratur, Zürich 1979, p. 185.
3 John W. Noffsinger, "Dream in 'The Old Curiosity Shop' ", *South Atlantic Bulletin* 42 (1977), p. 34, inverted commas Noffsinger's.
4 Alan Roland, ibid.
5 Douglas Hewitt, *The approach to fiction*, Bristol 1972, p. 136.
6 Arthur Washburn Brown, *Sexual Analysis of Dickens's Props*, New York 1971. Philip Collins says that Brown's study "moved reviewers to unwonted hilarity" (*Victorian Fiction. A Second Guide to Research*, ed. by George H. Ford, New York 1978, p. 66).
7 See also Jean Starobinski, *Psychoanalyse und Literatur*, Frankfurt a. M. 1973. (Translation of the French *La relation critique. L'œuil vivant II*, Editions Gallimard 1970.)
8 Freud writes to Jung: "Gestern im Seminar haben mir einige ganz ungestüme junge Analytiker Dinge gebracht, aus denen nach aller Purifikation doch hervorgehen kann, dass Diktion und Symbolik einer Dichtung eine deutliche Beeinflussung durch die hinter der Dichtung steckenden unbewussten infantilen Komplexe zeigen. Daraus kann sich viel Interessantes entwickeln, *wenn es nur mit Takt und Kritik gemacht wird. Leider sind diese ermässigen-*

"greatness" of a work of art by pointing to its unconscious contents. When talking about Dostoevsky, for instance, he admits: "Leider muss die Analyse vor dem Problem des Dichters die Waffen strecken", i.e. psychoanalysis cannot "explain" such a masterpiece as *The Brothers Karamazov*.[9]. If one were to read the more recent study by Greenacre on Swift and Carroll[10] as psychoanalytic literary criticism, she would be an apt target for attacks from the literature department. If, however, one looks at it as an interesting case history, there is nothing to be said against it. In a perceptive essay Gail Simon Reed points out the different conventions of reading that psychoanalysts and literary critics bring to the reading of a text.[11] He shows that the psychoanalyst often replaces the literary text by a reconstruction of the author's childhood, thus replacing the fictional text by a second book, as it were, by a case history.

We have to bear in mind, however, that psychoanalysis as a science has developed and has given up certain earlier convictions. With the emergence of ego psychology the comparison of the artist with the neurotic – which evoked the literary critics' hostility – has been given up. According to Niederland[12] it is striking how many creative people lost one or both parents in early childhood. The ability to mourn such losses is seen as an essential prerequisite for the mastery of traumatic events by creating something new.[13] Thus the artist's achievement is no longer regarded as an outcome of his neurosis, but is rather indicative of his ego strength. It is victory out of defeat.[14] Thus the still wide-spread fear that our geniuses are reduced to "sordid case histories"[15] does not seem to take note of recent psychoanalytic contributions to the problem of creativity.

There is no doubt, however, that if we only direct our attention to the contents of a piece of literature, so-called "trivial" and "great" literature are alike. The artist's unconscious is not basically different from that of other people. There is probably a limited number of unconscious fantasies which are shared by all human beings. Psychoanalysts meet these fantasies in their daily work. They are used to them and (ideally) do not judge them morally but accept them as they are. Other people have perhaps to learn first that expressions such as "exhibitionism", "masochism", "narcissistic" and so on do not degrade the person they are applied to. Freud himself was ashamed of what he discovered in his self-analysis and talked to his friend Wilhelm Fliess of his "dirtological news" (dreckologische Berichte) and he even wrote the first

*den Eigenschaften selten mit der analytischen Fähigkeit gepaart"*. (Sigmund Freud/C. G. Jung, *Briefwechsel,* Frankfurt a. M. 1974, p. 304 f., emphasis mine.)

9 Sigmund Freud, "Dostojewsky und die Vatertötung", *Studienausgabe,* ed. by Alexander Mitscherlich, Angela Richards, James Strachey, Frankfurt a. M. 1969-75, vol. X, p. 274.

10 Phyllis Greenacre, *Swift and Carroll: A Psychoanalytic Study of Two Lives,* New York 1955.

11 Gail Simon Reed, "Dr. Greenacre and Captain Gulliver: Notes on Conventions of Interpretation and Reading", *Literature and Psychology* 26 (1976), pp. 185-190.

12 Cp. William G. Niederland, "Psychoanalytic Approaches to Creativity", *The Psychoanalytic Quarterly* 14 (1976), pp. 185-212.

13 See Hans Müller-Braunschweig, "Aspekte einer psychoanalytischen Kreativitätstheorie", *Psyche* 31 (1977), pp. 821-43.

14 We might think of Thomas Mann's hero Aschenbach, who contends "dass beinahe alles Grosse, was dastehe, als ein Trotzdem dastehe" (Thomas Mann, *Der Tod in Venedig,* Fischer Bücherei no 54, p. 13).

15 A phrase used by Lawrence Jay Dessner, *"Great Expectations:* 'the ghost of a man's own father' ", *PMLA* 91 (1976), p. 436.

part of "dreckologisch" in Greek letters, so as to distance himself from what he had found.[16]

It is understandable, then, that literary critics feel that, for instance, Shakespeare and Melville are attacked when they are "accused" of homosexuality in *The Merchant of Venice* and *Billy Budd*. One would, however, not dare use the psychoanalytic approach were it not for a number of very good examples by authors who are not reductive, not tedious, and not simplistic. If we think of "psychoanalysis" in its broader sense, i.e. as the science that tries to find out what happens in normal and abnormal psychic human development, there are, of course, many more perceptive studies than if all we understand by "psychoanalysis" is the Oedipus complex, castration fear, penis envy and, perhaps, the death instinct. I would like to mention Steven Marcus, Dianne F. Sadoff, Mark Spilka, Michael Steig, Taylor Stoehr, Warrington Winters, and Alex Zwerdling as a few Dickensian critics who have successfully used the psychoanalytic approach in its wider sense and have impressed me with their insights.[17]

In Chapters Two and Three of this thesis I have endeavoured to listen with care to the text and to take the text itself seriously by reading it repeatedly, just as an analyst can only come to his conclusions by listening very carefully to an analysand's words. Indeed, in one respect the tasks of analyst and literary critic are similar: they both have to be attentive observers and then seek for a meaningful interpretation of the data observed. And much as an analyst does not only pay heed to the content of a patient's tale, but also takes note of the way he says something, the tone of his voice, the choice of words, etc., the critic directs his attention not only to the "what" but also to the "how" of a work of art.[18] In this way the text is not traded for something that lies behind it but is crucial, as it stands, to the critic's interpretation. I do not doubt that I have sometimes fallen prey to psychological reductionism – not too often, I hope. But I wish to point out that I feel I do not at all belittle Dickens or detract from his greatness, if I talk about such things as his disorder of the self or his untempered exhibitionism.

This study tries to show that Dickens's sentimentality, his triteness, his failure to describe women adequately are linked to his neurosis and that, on the other hand, his greatness is coupled with his mastery of his childhood fate. Chapter One will

16 Letter of January 4, 1898, quoted in: Max Schur, *Freud Living and Dying,* London 1972, p. 543. Freud often resorted to Latin or Greek when he felt embarrassed. See also his letter to Fliess of October 3, 1897, in which he speaks of his "libido gegen matrem" which was aroused when he saw her "nudam". (Sigmund Freud, *Aus den Anfängen der Psychoanalyse.* Briefe an Wilhelm Fliess, Abhandlungen und Notizen aus den Jahren 1887-1902, Frankfurt a. M. 1975, p. 189.)

17 Steven Marcus, "Who Is Fagin?" in: *Dickens: From Pickwick to Dombey,* London and New York 1964, pp. 358-378; Dianne F. Sadoff, "Storytelling and the Figure of the Father in *Little Dorrit*", *PMLA* 95 (1980), pp. 234-45; Mark Spilka, "Little Nell Revisited", *Papers of the Michigan Academy of Science, Arts and Letters* 45 (1960), pp. 427-37; Michael Steig, "Dickens' Excremental Vision", *Victorian Studies* 13 (1970), pp. 339-54; Taylor Stoehr, *Dickens. The Dreamer's Stance,* New York 1965; Warrington Winters, "The Death Hug in Charles Dickens", *Literature and Psychology* 16 (1966), pp. 109-115; Alex Zwerdling, "Esther Summerson Rehabilitated", *PMLA* 88 (1973), pp. 429-39.

18 See Harry Slochower, "The Psychoanalytic Approach to Literature: Some Pitfalls and Promises", *Literature and Psychology* 21 (1971), pp. 107-111.

tentatively bridge Dickens's life and his work. Examples are taken from where I could find them, i.e. from all periods of Dickens's literary career. Such a bridging has, of course, been attempted before, for instance by Wilson in his still famous essay.[19] Wilson was the first to point out that Dickens's lifelong obsession with murderes and capital punishment culminated in *Edwin Drood* with Jaspers as a murderer as well as a respected choirmaster in the cathedral town. According to Wilson, Dickens was to explore in this final, unfinished novel "the deep entanglement and conflict of the good and the bad in one man".[20] The basic dichotomy between good and bad is indeed Dickens's problem in his life as well as in his tales. It is surprising that for all the interesting psychoanalytic studies on Dickens (see note 17), Wilson's comments have not yet been taken up and given a new and expanded meaning by psychoanalytic insights on the development of conscious and unconscious images of oneself and of other people. This is precisely the aim of the present study. I shall try to show that Dickens's work can be looked upon as an attempt to deal with his past, as a work of mourning that brought about changes in the author himself as well as in his stories and made possible a partial fusion of the previously rigorously separated spheres of good and bad.

I shall try to show that the writing of *David Copperfield* was a crucial event in Dickens's emotional and literary life. Chapters Two and Three will deal with a pre-Copperfieldian and a post-Copperfieldian novel respectively. I shall attempt to find out whether or not some of the differences in the two novels can be connected with Dickens's personal psychic development.

It is a great help to such a study that Dickens was so prolific a letter writer. The truly admirable Pilgrim Edition of Dickens's letters is very informative. His speeches, his own children's memories of him and various biographies help to delineate the world he lived in.

I am aware of the fact that it is difficult and somewhat arbitrary to impute to Dickens's texts conscious or unconscious motives on the part of the author. If I venture to talk of Dickens's unconscious sympathy for certain characters, for instance, this is done with the knowledge of his professed moral convictions that sometimes contrast with shades of approval of what the author would call immoral behaviour. Some people might feel that I see too much of Dickens and of his own life in his characters and in his books. Before embarking upon our investigation I should therefore like to quote Dickens's daughter Mamie in order to show how much he sometimes identified with the creatures of his imagination:

> It was at Tavistock House that one of his daughters, after an illness, was taken, at his request, to lie on the sofa in the study while he was at work. Of course this was considered a great honour, and of course she lay as quiet as a mouse. For a long time there was no sound but the rapid moving of his pen on the paper, then suddenly he jumped up, looked at himself in the glass, rushed back to his desk, then to the glass again, when presently he turned round and faced his daughter, staring at her, but not seeing her, and talking rapidly to himself, then once more back to his desk, where he remained writing until luncheon time. It was a most curious experience, and it was wonderful to see how completely he threw himself into the character his own imagination had made, his face, indeed his whole body changing, and he himself being lost entirely in the working out his own ideas.[21]

19 Edmund Wilson, "Dickens: the Two Scrooges", in: *The Wound and the Bow,* first published 1941, revised edition, London 1952, pp. 1-93
20 E. Wilson, pp. 88-9.
21 Mary Dickens, *Charles Dickens by His Eldest Daughter,* London 1885, p. 100.

# 1. Hyacinths in Blacking Bottles

## 1.1. Early Experiences

"the greatest mystery ... to me
is how or why the world was
tolerated by its creator through
the good old times, and wasn't
dashed to fragments."

(To Forster, August 1846)

Edgar Johnson entitled his famous biography of Dickens *Charles Dickens: His Tragedy and Triumph.*[1] My own concern with Dickens's works could be phrased similarly. In what way, I ask, is Dickens's personal tragedy connected with his literary work? Is his writing a means of coping with the past, is it a process of working through grief similar to what we should attempt in psychoanalysis, or is it rather a stereotyped re-enactment of his past sufferings? And lastly, is there any link or parallelism between the way he treats his own feelings (accepting them, denying them, or transforming them) and the quality of the literary product? In order to answer such questions, I shall once more investigate Dickens's childhood and I shall then proceed to focus on his way of dealing with his experiences in his life as well as in his fiction.

There seems to exist an established myth among literary scholars about the author's early life: At first little Charles spent a happy time in Kent, but when the family moved to London his father was imprisoned for debt and Charles had to work in a blacking factory. The blissful early days were followed by the so-called "blacking warehouse trauma".[2] Now the blacking warehouse trauma is real enough, and I may be forgiven for repeating the familiar details. In autumn 1822 Dickens's father, John Dickens, was transferred to London and the family had to move into cheap lodgings. Their financial situation deteriorated steadily. Dickens himself had to take various articles to the pawnbroker's, first of all his beloved books *Peregrine Pickle, Roderick Random, Tom Jones, Humphry Clinker, Gil Blas, Don Quixote, The Vicar of Wakefield, The Arabian Nights* and others. Finally, in February 1824, John Dickens was imprisoned for debt in the Marshalsea prison. Charles had to begin work in a blacking factory, two days after his twelfth birthday. His job was to paste pieces of paper on the pots of blacking, tie them with a string and label them. Not only had he to earn his own living but at first he was also separated from the rest of the family, who all moved into the Marshalsea prison. Dickens's autobiographical fragment (probably written after his sister Fanny's death, late in 1848 as part of a planned autobiography – a plan Dickens never carried out) testifies to the intensity of his early sufferings.[3] A few quotations may illustrate his mood:

---

1 Edgar Johnson, *Charles Dickens: His Tragedy and Triumph,* 2 vols., New York 1952; revised and abridged edition, *Charles Dickens,* London 1976.
2 Chapter two of Johnson's biography is headed "The Happy Time", chapter three "The Challenge of Despair".
3 The autobiographical fragment is contained in: John Forster, *The Life of Charles Dickens,* 2 vols., with notes and an index by A. J. Hoppé, London and New York [2]1969, pp. 20-33.

The deep remembrance of the sense I had of being utterly neglected and hopeless; of the shame I felt in my position; of the misery it was to my young heart to believe that, day by day, what I had learned, and thought, and delighted in, and raised my fancy and emulation up by, was passing away from me, never to be brought back any more; cannot be written. My whole nature was so penetrated with the grief and humiliation of such considerations, that even now, famous and caressed and happy, I often forget in my dreams that I have a dear wife and children, even that I am a man; and wander desolately back to that time of my life. ("AF", 22/23)

I (small Cain that I was, except that I had never done harm to anyone) was handed over as a lodger to a reduced old lady ... ("AF", 23/24)

I know that, but for the mercy of God, I might easily have been, for any care that was taken of me, a little robber or a little vagabond. ("AF", 25)

That I suffered *in secret,* and that I suffered exquisitely, *no one ever knew but I.* How much I suffered, it is, as I have said already, utterly beyond my power to tell. No man's imagination can overstep the reality. But *I kept my own counsel, and I did my work.* I knew from the first that, *if I could not do my work as well as any of the rest, I could not hold myself above a slight and contempt.* I soon became at least as expeditious and as skilful with my hands as either of the other boys. ("AF", 25, emphasis added).

My rescue from this kind of existence I considered quite hopeless, and abandoned as such, altogether; though I am solemnly convinced that I never, for one hour, was reconciled to it, or was otherwise than miserably unhappy. I felt keenly, however, the being so cut off from my parents, my brothers, and sisters; and, when my day's work was done, *going home to such a miserable blank* .. One Sunday night I remonstrated with my father on this head, so pathetically and with so many tears, that his kind nature gave way. He began to think that it was not quite right. I do believe he had never thought so before, or thought about ist. ("AF", 26, emphasis added).

A little room was found for Charles in the vicinity of the prison so that he could share breakfast and evening meals with the rest of the family. When his father was released (he had inherited some money from his mother to pay his debts with) Dickens was not at once released from his "drudgery", as he called it, but continued to go to Warren's blacking factory until his father quarrelled with his employer, a relative, and Charles was dismissed from his job. His mother tried to patch up the quarrel and Dickens bitterly remarks: "I never afterwards forgot, I never shall forget, I never can forget, that my mother was warm for my being sent back" ("AF", 32).

We can conjecture that the child's despair was intensified because it was not only a response to the blacking warehouse as such but recalled the sting of earlier wounds or, in other words, that his early childhood had not been entirely happy after all. The following reflections can, of course, be no more than speculations since Dickens himself is not in a position to correct any misinterpretations as a patient in analysis could, but it is to be hoped that the speculations acquire some sort of probability by the circumstantial evidence produced. However, it is patently impossible to take into account the whole complex psychological set-up of the human being called Charles Dickens; emphasis will have to be laid on a few characteristic and conspicuous features.

Charles Dickens was born on 7 February 1812, two years after his maternal grandfather, Charles Barrow, had had to leave the country because he had embezzled nearly £ 6000. Dickens – named after his improvident grandfather – was to become the one member of the Dickens family who was never in debt, who could be relied on, who paid the debts of his father and his brothers as well as those of his sons and supported his brothers' widows and children.[4] It is as if he felt it incumbent upon him to make up to his parents for the failure of his namesake, who had not given them the financial support they had hoped for.

His mother, Elizabeth Dickens, is said to have danced into the small hours of February 7th, the day the future novelist was born.[5] This way of awaiting the arrival of the baby seems characteristic of the Dickens household – the pleasure-seeking of its members having sometimes a somewhat forced quality.[6]

Dickens experienced both his parents as extremely histrionic personalities. Apparently they both craved for admiration and they sometimes reached this goal vicariously through their children. Charles and his elder sister Fanny often had to give little performances for the benefit of their father, i.e. for the enhancement of his self-esteem. They used to sing comical ballads, songs of love between a sailor and his bride, and thus amused John Dickens's friends. Later, Charles Dickens was to repeat the same pattern in his public readings. For a long time he did not permit himself to read for his own benefit – to display himself, so to speak, for himself, but he always read for the benefit of either charitable institutions or of penniless widows and orphans of artist acquaintances.

In various letters Dickens describes his father's verbosity, which must have been confusing to the child. From Genoa he writes to John Forster that their physician has left the city:

> We are very sorry to lose the benefit of his advice – or, as my father would say, to be deprived, to a certain extent, of the concomitant advantages, whatever they may be,

---

4  In 1834 John Dickens was again imprisoned for debt. Charles took charge of the situation, finding cheaper lodgings for the family and paying the father's debts. In later years Dickens granted his parents an annuity but his father – unable to live within his means – approached Dickens's friends and even his publishers for loans (which he never paid back) – often without the novelist's knowledge. In his letters to his friend and lawyer, Thomas Mitton, Dickens often expresses his despair about his father. From America he writes in April 1842: "I am vexed to hear that that father of mine is ['in trou]ble' – again! How long he is, growing up to be a m[an!]" (*PE*, vol. III, p. 191); in 1843 he writes "I quite agree in opinion with you, touching my father who I really believe, as Sam Weller says of some one in Pickwick, 'has gone ravin' mad with conscious willany!' The thought of him besets me night and day; and I really do not know what is to be done with him. It is quite clear that the more we do, the more outrageous and audacious he becomes" (*PE*, vol. III, p. 444); a year later he is even more desperate: "I really think I shall begin to give in, one of these days. For anything like the damnable Shadow which this father of mine casts upon my face, there never was – except in a nightmare." (*PE*, vol. IV, p. 45) When in December 1843 Dickens had overdrawn his account by a few pounds he was horrified and begged Mitton to lend him £ 200 to pay into the account "before I have any notice of my account being overdrawn – which is very important." (*PE*, vol. III, p. 604)

5  See for instance Norman and Jeanne Mackenzie, *Dickens. A Life*, Oxford 1979, p. 6. It is interesting to note that Dickens did not allow his wife Catherine to have much of a social life when she was pregnant, while he himself "commonly sought his entertainment with male friends in bachelor style" (Mackenzie, p. 72).

6  But Dickens always defended the right of the poor to pleasure. See his early paper "Sunday Under Three Heads", *UT & RP, OID*, pp. 637-663, in which he vehemently protests against Sir Andrew Agnew's Sunday Observance Bill (proposing restrictions on travelling facilities, shopping and amusements on a Sunday), which would in fact have allowed the rich to be diverted and denied the poor their right to relaxation.

resulting from his medical skill, such as it is, and his professional attendance, in so far as it may be considered. (*PE,* IV, 243-44)

We recognize, of course, the florid style of the immortal Mr. Micawber, in whom Dickens portrayed his father. When Mr. Micawber, out of work and penniless, learns that there will soon be an additional child in the family, he reacts as follows:

> He gave us to understand that in our children we lived again, and that, under the pressure of pecuniary difficulties, any accession to their number was doubly welcome. (*DC,* 482)

Does he not also imply in these rather unexpected statements that the children have an obligation to their parents – that they must compensate them for "the pressure of pecuniary difficulties"?

Elizabeth Dickens, Dickens's mother, is described by the novelist in the unforgetta-ble Mrs. Nickleby.[7] Mrs. Nickleby is a superbly drawn character who could serve as an illustration for modern textbooks on the psychology of the self. She is not a wicked woman, but she is pathetically in need of adoration, admiration and love. It is exactly this burning desire that makes it hard for people to love her, and her children have long grown accustomed to smiling at her, not taking her seriously, letting their thoughts wander when she embarks upon one of her long monologues. The half-witted Smike is the only one who sits and listens to her for hours "wondering what it was all about" and when he dies, Mrs. Nickleby is really distressed, for she has lost "the best, the most zealous, and most attentive creature, that has ever been a companion to me in my life" (*NN, OID,* 791). She is, furthermore, admired by no-one but the deranged "gentleman in small clothes", who throws vegetable marrows and cucumbers over the garden wall as tokens of his love. Only mad people, Dickens seems to say, will listen to her, and only insane ones will fall in love with her. But she is not even granted this conquest, for, when the said gentleman forces his way into the Nickleby household by way of the chimney, he suddenly turns his attention to Miss la Creevy and heaps abuse upon poor Mrs. Nickleby. Mrs. Nickleby still manages to escape from a sense of dejection and depression by declaring:

> 'I shall never forgive myself, Kate,' said Mrs. Nickleby; 'never! That gentleman has lost his senses, And *I* am the unhappy cause.' '*You* the cause!' said Kate, greatly astonished. 'I, my love,' replied Mrs. Nickleby, *with a desperate calmness.* (650, emphasis added in the last sentence.)

There ist much contempt in the treatment of Mrs. Nickleby by the author as well as by Kate and Nicholas. The implication of the story with the gentleman in small clothes is that not even a madman will love her any more once he has got to know her intimately. Mrs. Nickleby, remembering her son's scorn at the thought that anybody could love her, is set upon the following train of associations:

> 'Kate, my dear,' said Mrs. Nickleby; 'I don't know how it is, but a fine warm summer day like this, with the birds singing in every direction, always puts me in mind of roast pig, with sage and onion sauce, and made gravy.' 'That's a curious association of ideas, is it not, mama?' 'Upon my word, my dear, I don't know,' replied Mrs. Nickleby. 'Roast pig;

---

7 Dickens was highly amused that his mother did not recognize herself in the portrait. See his letters of 27 September 1842 to John Forster (*PE,* vol. III, p. 333), and of 2 January 1844 to Richard Lane (*PE,* vol. IV, p. 5). Mrs. John Dickens is also compared by Angus Wilson to Mrs. Crummles. When the latter wishes to eat, she says, "Let the mutton and onion sauce appear". See Angus Wilson, *The World of Charles Dickens,* Harmondsworth 1972, p. 21.

let me see. On the day five weeks after you were christened, we had a roast – no, that couldn't have been a pig, either, because I recollect there were a pair of them to carve, and your poor papa and I could never have thought of sitting down to two pigs – they must have been partridges. Roast pig! I hardly think we ever could have had one, now I come to remember, for your papa could never bear the sight of them in the shops, and used to say that they always put him in mind of very little babies, only the pigs had much fairer complexions; and he had a horror of little babies, too, because he couldn't very well afford any increase to the family, and had a natural dislike to the subject. It's very odd now, what can have put that in my head! I recollect dining once at Mrs. Bevan's, in that broad street round the corner by the coach-maker's where the tipsy man fell through the cellar-flap of an empty house nearly a week before the quarter-day, and wasn't found till the new tenant went in – and we had roast pig there. It must be that, I think, that reminds me of it, especially as there was a little bird in the room that would keep on singing all the time of dinner – at least, not a little bird, for it was a parrot, and he didn't sing exactly, for he talked and swore dreadfully; but I think it must be that. Indeed I am sure it is. Shouldn't you say so, my dear?' (529-30)

Cruikshank has included this passage in his anthology of humorous Dickens texts[8] ; besides the humour, however, there are other elements embodied in this paragraph. The aggression which is directed against the children is fairly obvious. Not only are the babies compared to pigs, but pigs are definitely preferable to babies: they have a fairer complexion and one can at least eat them.[9] It is also stated quite clearly that children are not wanted, that they are only a financial burden. Even the eating of pigs is associated with unpleasant thoughts: a man has fallen through a flapdoor of an empty (!) house and has been kept there against his will and inclination. The sexual connotations are pretty clear: after intercourse there will be a baby; but a baby cannot be disposed of in the same easy way as one gets rid of roast pig, i.e. by eating it. In this way one would at least get some food. The summer day with the singing birds turns out to be very unpleasant and the warblers are suddenly transformed into a swearing parrot. This interpretation is reinforced if we remember a passage from Dickens's description of his boyhood Chatham in "Dullborough Town":

> … in my very young days I was taken to so many lyings-in that I wonder I ever escaped becoming a professional martyr to them in after-life. I suppose I had a very sympathetic nurse, with a large circle of married acquaintance. However that was, as I continued my walk through Dullborough, I found many houses to be solely associated in my mind with this particular interest. At one little greengrocer's shop, down certain steps from the street, I remember to have waited on a lady who had had four children (I am afraid to write five, though I fully believe it was five) at a birth. This meritorious woman held quite a reception in her room on the morning when I was introduced there, and the sight of the house [when visiting the town in later years] brought vividly to my mind how the four (five) deceased young people lay, side by side, on a clean cloth on a chest of drawers; reminding me by a homely association which I suspect their complexion to have assisted, of pigs' feet as they are usually displayed at a neat tripe-shop. (*UT & RP, OID,* 118-19)

8 R. J. Cruikshank, *The Humour of Charles Dickens,* London 1952.
9 It is possible that Dickens had Swift's pamphlet "A Modest Proposal for preventing the Children of the Poor from being a Burden to their Parents or the Country" in mind, where Swift advocates in savage irony that the tender baby flesh be eaten by the rich. Gottfried Keller, too, compared babies to piglets, for example in his story "Der Schmied seines Glücks" or when congratulating a friend on the birth of her child. See Adolf Muschg, *Gottfried Keller,* München 1977, p. 28.

Again there is the comparison of babies with pigs and again the similarity of their complexions is stressed. We may suspect that Dickens was also reminded of the many "lyings-in" of his own mother, who had six more children after Charles. And we may also ask ourselves whether it is a coincidence that later, in his courtship of Catherine Hogarth, he used to call her "dearest Pig" and "darling Pig", an expression he then playfully changed to "Wig", and that, later still, he used the same term of endearment for his own children.[10]

At any rate, we perceive that there is much mutual hidden aggression between Mrs. Nickleby and her children. Mr. Micawber, too, shows the wish to make away with his offspring when, tearfully comtemplating his financial situation, he states that

> It may be reasonably inferred that our baby will first expire of inanition, as being the frailest member of our circle; and that our twins will follow next in order. So be it! (*DC,* 825)

Need we wonder that the rejected Mrs. Nickleby cannot but be-grudge her children their success? Whenever Kate is admired and courted by a young man, Mrs. Nickleby desperately tries to take her daughter's place, always maintaining that it is she and not Kate who is respected, adored and loved. The fictional representatives of Dickens's parents cannot, of course, be equated with them. Yet there are quite a few affinities between the Micawbers and Mrs. Nickleby on the one hand and Dickens's parents on the other. The following letter, which Dickens wrote in August 1860, is revealing:

> I have been involved in great anxiety and worry by the unexpected death of my brother Alfred. He had had no opportunity of providing for his family, died worth nothing, and has left a widow and five children – you may suppose to whom. Day after day I have been scheming and contriving for them, and I am still doing so, and I have schemed myself into broken rest and low spirits. My mother, who was also left to me when my father died (I never had anything left to me but poor relations), is in the strangest state of mind from senile decay; and the impossibility of getting her to understand what is the matter, combined with her desire to be got up in sables like a female Hamlet, illumines the dreary scene with a ghastly absurdity that is the chief relief I can find in it. (*Letters,* III, 172)

As we shall see later, it is characteristic of Dickens to find relief in the absurdity of the scene.

Both Dickens's parents are unsure of themselves, as we can see from their unswerving aspirations to gentility. Only genteel people seem to be "good enough". They were both ashamed of their own parents – Elizabeth Dickens because of her father's embezzlement, John Dickens because of the social status of his family. His parents had been servants; his father had died before John Dickens was born. Obviously John Dickens's family was socially not equal to the family of his wife and probably never accepted by them. Mrs. Micawber is but one example in Dickens's fiction of wives who plague their husbands with genteel pretensions.[11]

When the Micawbers are about to emigrate to Australia, a sad little scene takes place aboard their ship. They are eagerly talking about their new life in Australia when suddenly Mr. Micawber is called. Mrs. Micawber has a "presentiment" that a member of her family has arrived – at last! – to bid them adieu. But in fact Mr. Micawber is called by an officer who once more arrests him for debt. David then pays the money for him and on the following morning the family depart.

---

10 *PE,* vol. I, pp. 112, 118, 119, 125, 137, 139, 143; and vol. IV, p. 158.
11 Others are, for instance, Mrs. Wilfer in *Our Mutual Friend* and Mrs. Nickleby.

With parents such as Elizabeth and John Dickens there may not be much room for a child. How can a child, for example, who is learning to talk, be quick enough to get in a word or two before the parents rattle off again? How can he display himself if the parents need all the stage to themselves? Dickens's life story suggests that he experienced a serious lack of sufficient mirroring in that important early developmental phase when the child needs to be seen by the mother in order to find himself. Winnicott puts it as follows:

> What does the baby see when he or she looks at the mother's face? I am suggesting that, ordinarily, what the baby sees is himself or herself. In other words the mother is looking at the baby and *what she looks like is related to what she sees there* (emphasis Winnicott's).[12]

If the baby does not see himself in his mother's face he cannot gradually get to know the various facets of his self and eventually integrate them. He does not apperceive himself but he perceives his mother's moods in her face and adapts to them. Thus there develops what Winnicott calls the "false self".[13] If we formulate the psychic development in Kohut's conceptual framework, we can say that the child has two possibilities of making up for the loss of the omnipotence he experienced in a "good enough" symbiotic phase.[14] He develops the conviction that he himself is beautiful, strong, intelligent, etc., i.e. he develops the *grandiose self*. Alternatively he merges with an omnipotent *idealized self-object* – usually father or mother – and can in this way partake of their power. These archaic forms of narcissism are gradually transformed if the child is seen and accepted in his display of his self on the one hand, and, on the other hand, if first the parents can allow him to idealize them and if later the child can give up this idealization *when he is ready for it* and not when gross failures on the part of the parents forces his awareness of their imperfections prematurely upon him. Kohut speaks of the "gleam in the mother's eye" that shows the child that his mother shares his joy in his accomplishments, his developing motor abilities, his acquisition of language, his pride in his healthy body, his exploration of the world. In his more recent book, *The Restoration of the Self,*[15] Kohut has explained his concept of the bipolar nuclear self, which is constituted by ambitions which are related to the grandiose self on the one hand, and ideals which derive from the relation to the idealized self-object on the other and a tension arc between them. The weakness of one of the constituents of the nuclear self can be compensated for by a particularly strong development in the other. A child who has not experienced good mirroring and has not been able to build up self-esteem in the area of his ambitions, can make up for this lack if an empathic self-object responds to his idealization and he can therefore become secure in the pursuance of his ideals. In our society the mirroring self-object is usually the mother, whereas the idealized self-object is very often the father. The mother's failure can, in this case, be compensated for by the father's empathy or vice versa. According to Kohut, then, a child has two chances to obtain a firm nuclear self; only if both parents fail him will there be a serious disorder of the self.

12 D. W. Winnicott, *Playing and Reality,* Penguin Books Ltd., Harmondsworth 1971, p. 131.
13 See also Alice Miller, *Das Drama des begabten Kindes und die Suche nach dem wahren Selbst,* Frankfurt/M. 1979.
14 According to Winnicott a good enough mother can first create in the infant the illusion of omnipotence by being in tune with the baby's wishes and needs and is then able to gradually disillusion the child.
15 Heinz Kohut, *The Restoration of the Self,* New York 1977.

It seems that Charles Dickens experienced faulty mirroring on the part of both his parents, and we have already tried to account for this by describing the personalities of John and Elizabeth Dickens. Apparently, however, the boy Charles Dickens was able to admire his father, with whom he used to take country-walks; and he admired him for his assiduity in his work, for his generosity with his friends, and for his kindheartedness. Later this same father must have appeared very weak to the child in his constant financial struggles and it is possible that the not as yet consolidated psychic structures crumbled again. We can easily imagine, for example, how embarrassed a child will feel who is exposed to scenes similar to the following:

> One dirty-faced man, I think he was a boot-maker, used to edge himself into the passage as early as seven o'clock in the morning, and call up the stairs to Mr. Micawber – 'Come! You ain't out yet, you know. Pay us, will you? don't hide, you know; that's mean. I wouldn't be mean if I was you. Pay us, will you? You just pay us, d'ye hear? Come!' Receiving no answer to these taunts, he would mount in his wrath to the words 'swindlers' and 'robbers'; and these being ineffectual too, would sometimes go to the extremity of crossing the street, and roaring up at the windows of the second floor, where he knew Mr. Micawber war. At these times Mr. Micawber would be transported with grief and mortification, even to the length ... of making motions at himself with the razor; but within half-an-hour afterwards he would polish up his shoes with extraordinary pains, and go out, humming a tune with a greater air of gentility than ever. Mrs. Micawber was quite as elastic. (*DC,* 214)

It seems, however, that all his life Dickens's conflicts centred mainly around his wish to exhibit himself, whereas the pursuance of his ideals did not really pose a problem. In other words, the main damage to his self must have been acquired in his early infancy.

The American psychoanalyst Margaret Mahler argues that there is a period in the toddler's life – roughly between the age of 18 to 36 months – during which the child is particularly vulnerable.[16] He has lost the symbiotic union with his mother and experiences himself already as a separate human being but at the same time he realizes how weak and dependent he still is. During this phase – the "rapprochement" stage of the individuation-separation process – the child particularly needs his mother's emotional availability. He wants to explore himself and his surroundings and he also wants his mother to share in his discoveries. The child no longer fears so much to lose his mother as he fears to lose her love.

It was during this time that Dickens's younger brother Alfred was born.[17] It is natural for a pregnant woman to be narcissistically self-absorbed, and Mrs. Dickens may have been less responsive than before to Charles's needs in consequence of her pregnancy. When the new baby has come the older sibling will usually feel threatened in his rights and sometimes wish to get rid of the pretender to the mother's lap and the mother's attention. These wishes are experienced by the child as something very powerful, and as something very destructive if the baby actually does die – and this is what happened to Charles, for his brother Alfred died when he was six months old.

16 Margaret S. Mahler, Fred Pine, and Anni Bergman, *The Psychological Birth of the Human Infant,* Symbiosis and Individuation, London 1975.

17 Norman and Jeanne Mackenzie in their *Dickens. A Life* tell us that Alfred was born in March 1814 and died in September 1814; Edgar Johnson, *Charles Dickens: His Tragedy and Triumph* states that he was born in 1813 and "died in infancy". Dickens himself speaks in a letter of March 1842 of a brother who "died in infancy some nine and twenty years ago" (*PE,* vol. III, p. 136).

Charles must have felt guilty at the death of his brother. It is probable that his mother – due to her natural mourning reaction – withdrew from him even more. Should this have been the case, he would have attributed it to his own wickedness as a punishment for his murderous aggression.[18]

However, if the mother is not emotionally available, the child will feel that she does not love him, and if she does not love him, there must be a cause for this lack of love. The child will veer from considering his mother all good and himself all bad to regarding himself as all good and his mother all bad and back again. His one question will be: "Who is the culprit, is it mother or is it I?" However, the infant, who is dependent on his mother's care, cannot afford to lose her and will usually shoulder the blame himself. He will perceive himself as the cause of the lack of love he experiences. He is convinced that his parents are sure to love him once he has really become a good child. Meanwhile his deep sense of being unworthy cannot be borne without consolation.

Often the child develops an opposite picture of himself as a child who is full of love and kindness, as somebody who cannot hurt a fly. And he will never be able to integrate these contradictory self-representations[19] if he is not accepted by his love-objects as a child who is both "good" and "bad", as a little person who is full of love and full of aggression, who is insecure, jealous and demanding but who is also eager to help, to accept the other, to give. The child's divided self-representations go hand in hand with contradictory object-representations. In the child's mind there exists the picture of an all-loving holy mother as well as that of a mother who is a threatening monster. The more aggressive the child feels himself to be – and a child whose baby-brother or baby-sister has died will consider himself a monster of aggressiveness – the more he will protect his "good mother" image from being contaminated by his "bad mother" image by keeping the two images as far apart as possible. This splitting mechanism makes it very difficult for the child to realize that his "good mother" and his "bad mother" are one and the same person.

More children were to come into the Dickens family. A sister was born in 1816; another sister, who also died in infancy, was born in 1819.[20] Then there were three more brothers, born in 1820, 1822, and 1827. This experience, too, is reflected in Dickens's fiction. In David Copperfield there is always a twin being nursed at Mrs. Micawber's breast:

> I may remark here that I hardly ever, in all my experience of the family, saw both twins detached from Mrs. Micawber at the same time. One of them was always taking refreshment. (DC, 212)

18 Angus Wilson is convinced that Dickens treated his mother unfairly. But is it not possible that his harsh judgment of her had its roots in early frustrations that could not be remembered but were still felt? See Angus Wilson, *The World of Charles Dickens*, pp. 50 and 59-61.

19 "This term ... refers to our mental concept of the self, i.e., to the unconscious and preconscious images of our body self and of our own personality." Edith Jacobson, "Contribution to the Metapsychology of Psychotic Identifications", *Journal of the American Psychoanalytic Association*, vol. 2 (1954), p. 241.

20 Gladys Storey speaks in *Dickens and Daughter*, London 1939, p. 44 of Harriet "who in childhood died of smallpox in London". She probably died between 1822 and 1824, before Charles's employment at Warren's. This illness was surely a frightening experience to Charles. In *Bleak House* Esther falls ill and the reader is to guess that the illness is smallpox. The unmentionable disease, however, is never called by its name.

The twins do not even have a name; they are just "babies" and as such wholly interchangeable. Any baby, so it seems, can easily be replaced by a new one. In an earlier scene in the novel, David experiences this feeling not only of being replaceable but actually of being replaced when he comes home from school for his holidays and finds his mother singing:

> God knows how infantine the memory may have been, that was awakened within me by the sound of my mother's voice in the old parlour, when I set foot in the hall. She was singing in a low tone. I think I must have lain in her arms, and heard her singing to me when I was but a baby. The strain was new to me, and yet it was so old that it filled my heart brim-full; like a friend come back from a long absence. (*DC*, 162)

And when, shortly afterwards, his mother and the baby die, he wishes to take the latter's place:

> The mother who lay in the grave, was the mother of my infancy; the little creature in her arms, was myself, as I had once been, hushed forever on her bosom. (*DC*, 187)

The wishful thinking of being reunited in death with a loving and good mother was to remain powerful throughout Dickens's literary career.

Little Johnny Tetterby in the Christmas story *The Haunted Man* tells the tale of the older child who, still a child himself, has to take on parental duties and look after a younger sibling whom Dickens aptly calls the "Moloch". Johnny's father admonishes him as follows:

> "Johnny, my child, take care of your only sister, Sally; for she's the brightest gem that ever sparkled on your early brow."
> Johnny sat down on a little stool, and devotedly crushed himself beneath the weight of Moloch.
> "Ah, what a gift that baby is to you, Johnny!" said his father, "and how thankful you ought to be! 'It is not generally known,' Johnny," he was now referring to the screen again, [i.e. the newspaper] " 'but it is a fact ascertained, by accurate calculations, that the following immense per-centage of babies never attain to two years old; that is to say –' "
> "Oh, don't, father, please!" cried Johnny. "I can't bear it, when I think of Sally." (*CB*, II, 281)

Johnny seems only to exist in order to take the load off his parents' shoulders. He must earn "a gem on his brow" by crushing himself before his life is considered worth living. And he not only has to bear the weight but he is also cruelly reminded by his father that many children die in early infancy, and it is implied that if ever such a thing happens to Sally, it will be his fault. We are reminded of Mr. Micawber's bombastic speech, and Johnny's situation seems well described in a letter Dickens wrote about his family when his father was once more in debt:

> He, and all of them, look upon me as a something to be plucked and torn to pieces for their advantage. They have no idea of, and no care for, my existence in any other light. My soul sickens at the thought of them. (*PE*, III, 575)

The oedipal situation cannot but reinforce these early impressions. A child who feels unloved and worthless will experience the rejection of his sexual wishes by the oedipal parent as a rejection of his whole person, of his total self.

Dickens's portrait of Mr. Augustus Moddle in *Martin Chuzzlewit* seems a good example of the fusion of oedipal and pre-oedipal longings. Mr. Moddle, "the youngest gentleman of all" in Mrs. Todgers's establishment, is in love with Mercy Pecksniff. When Mercy gets married to Jonas Chuzzlewit, Augustus is inconsolable. He is forever hanging around the house and weeping for "her who is Another's".

24

Mercy's sister, Charity, is a comfort to him because her "profile in general, but particularly her nose" resembles that of her sister. Charity is informed of the effect her nose has upon our young gentleman and for the rest of the evening she sits presenting her profile to his view. She inveigles him into an engagement but when they are buying furniture and Augustus is bidden to ask the price of some chairs and a table, he says: "Perhaps they are ordered already ... Perhaps they are Another's" and upon Charity's reply that "They can make more like them if they are" he dolefully states "No, no, they can't ... It's impossible." (*MC*, 774)

Mercy cannot be replaced by Charity. On his wedding day Mr. Moddle flees and writes "I love another. She is Another's ... May the furniture make some amends! ... Unalterably, never yours, Augustus" (915). The "Another", so powerful as to receive a capital initial, can refer to the sibling as well as to the parent of the same sex as the child. In a way, this sentence comprises the situation of the oedipal as well as that of the pre-oedipal child. There is, incidentally, a letter by Dickens to his friend Forster which is signed "Moddle". (*PE*, IV, 110)

Dickens also seems to take revenge upon his youngest brother, Augustus, in this character, and in his most cruel treatment of Charity Pecksniff he also punishes the entire female sex for having forsaken him.

If we read the autobiographical fragment once more, we suddenly realize that Dickens expresses his own personal tragedy in the one sentence "It is wonderful to me how I could have been so easily cast away at such an age." (*F*, I, 21) Remembering that Dickens stopped writing his autobiography because he could not bear to recall his unrequited love for Maria Beadnell[21] and bearing in mind that any love relationship will remind the lover of his earliest love-affair, namely that with his parents, there is good reason for stating that the sense of being "so easily cast away at such an age" may well refer to the times of Dickens's infancy. In one sense, then, the blacking factory may have been a blessing in disguise. Without this experience Dickens might have "fogotten" his sense of having once been an abandoned and forlorn child; he might have lost touch with the child in himself. We may speculate that in this case he could well have become for instance a successful business man but hardly the imaginative writer he is.

The speculative reconstruction of the atmosphere of Dickens's childhood suggests to us, then, that he did not experience sufficient mirroring, that the idealized self-object had to be disidealized before the child was ready for this step, that his parents may have been emotionally absorbed by the other children, by the harrowing financial situation and by the death of two of their children. It also suggests that Dickens felt neglected and imputed this neglect to his own "badness", that he felt very powerful and very aggressive because two siblings had died and that the blacking-warehouse trauma simply reinforced and repeated his sense of having been thrown away like dirt.

21 Dickens writes to Maria Beadnell (Mrs. Winter) in 1855: "But nobody can ever know with what a sad heart I resigned you, or after what struggles and what conflict. My entire devotion to you, and the wasted tenderness of those hard years which I have ever since half loved, half dreaded to recall, made so deep an impression on me that I refer to it a habit of suppression which now belongs to me, which I know is no part of my original nature, but which makes me chary of showing my affections, even to my children, except when they are very young. A few years ago (just before Copperfield) I began to write my life, intending the manuscript to be found among my papers when its subject should be concluded. But as I began to approach within sight of that part of it, I lost courage and burned the rest." *Letters*, II, 633.

## 1.2. Dickens's Search for a Self-Object

"She never sees me
when I'm at my best."

(Barnaby Rudge to Hugh)

The fact that Dickens was forever on the look-out for a reliable mirroring self-object can be deduced from various incidents in his life. Quite a few people may have taken on this function, for example John Forster, W. H. Wills, his wife Catherine, his sisters-in-law Mary Hogarth and Georgina Hogarth, his children, particularly his daughter Mamie, and perhaps also his mistress of later years, Ellen Ternan. We could include in this list his readers and the audiences of his public readings, with whom he had his "love affair with the world".[22]

It is obvious that Forster had to encourage his friend and to tell him constantly how good he was.[23] Dickens sent all his manuscripts first to Forster, who helped him greatly in preparing the text for printing by proof-reading, cutting out passages if the manuscript was too long, etc. Whenever Dickens planned a new book or a story it was to Forster that he imparted his ideas and he also sought his advice when he had to decide on the title of a novel or the name of a particular character. "I remain dissatisfied until you have seen and read number three", he wrote to Forster in May 1838, summing up their relationship in this sentence.[24] When Dickens and Forster grew estranged in later years, Wilkie Collins and W. H. Wills fulfilled this mirroring role to a certain extent, though never with Forster's ardent devotion to Dickens. It was Forster, too, who staunchly defended Dickens in all his quarrels with his various publishers.

Dickens apparently also read parts of his books to his wife Kate.[25] There is, furthermore, one telling incident in his life which shows us how much he needed to be seen and admired by her. Dickens had been invited to speak at the inaugural soirée of the Athenaeum in Glasgow on 28th December, 1847. Kate accompanied him to Scotland but was taken ill on the train and could not attend the meeting. The following is Dickens's report to Georgina Hogarth of what had happened:

> The meeting was the most stupendous thing as to numbers, and the most beautiful as to colours and decorations, I ever saw. The Inimitable [i.e. Dickens] did wonders. His grace, elegance, and eloquence enchanted all beholders. *Kate didn't go!* (emphasis Dickens's) having been taken ill on the railroad between here and Glasgow. (...) She is frightfully anxious that her not having been to the great demonstration should be kept a secret. But I say that, like murder, it will out ... (*PE*, V, 217)

22 Phyllis Greenacre uses this phrase to describe the artist's relationships with his environment. See her paper, "The Childhood of the Artist: Libidinal Phase Development and Giftedness" in *The Psychoanalytic Study of the Child,* vol. 12 (1957), pp. 27-72. However, the literary critic Kathleen Tillotson also speaks of Dickens's relations with his readers an "the most interesting love-affair of his life". (Quoted in: Angus Wilson, *The World of Charles Dickens,* p. 12.)

23 Philip Collins has convincingly shown how Forster – in reviewing Dickens's books in *The Examiner* – praised Dickens where the latter most wanted to be praised and was careful not to touch Dickens's sore points. See Ph. Collins, "Dickens' Self-Estimate: Some New Evidence", in Robert B. Partlow (ed.), *Dickens the Craftsman,* Carbondale and Edwardsville 1970, pp. 21-43.

24 *PE*, vol. I, p. 400.

25 ibid., p. 439.

Even if he should have written this in a joking manner, we could not consider his choice of words as fortuitous. One feels uneasy here about Dickens's lack of concern for Kate's illness and his implied reproach: "like murder", Kate's failure will be known. He feels, in other words, that Kate has committed a crime, has murdered him, so to speak, by being ill when he needed her praise and approval. And when we read in a subsequent letter to Dickens's brother, Alfred, that

> Kate was taken very ill on the way from this place to Glasgow, on Tuesday – a miscarriage in short, coming on, suddenly, in the railway carriage (*PE*, V, 221),

Dickens's indifference to Kate's trial seems unbelievable; it can only be explained by his burning desire and compelling need to be reflected or, in other words, by a serious defect in his self.

We know that Catherine Dickens was depressed after the birth of her first child. Her sister, Mary Hogarth, writes about her:

> Kate ... has not gone on so well as her first week made us hope she would. After we thought she was getting quite well and strong it was discovered she was not able to nurse her Baby so she was obliged with great reluctance ... to give him up to a stranger. (...) Every time she sees her Baby she has a fit of crying and keeps constantly saying she is sure he will not care for her now she is not able to nurse him.[26]

Mary, who was an ever-welcome guest at the Dickens establishment, may then have given the author what Kate could not give him in her condition, namely an attentive ear and a great eagerness to admire him. Though I often disagree with Bowen's conclusions about the Dickens family, I think him right when he states that

> Mary Hogarth had one very important element of his ideal. She was an admiring and sympathetic listener. She was for the time being the representative ... of that vast audience of later years which as they listened spellbound gave him an ecstasy of feeling which was the very breath of life.[27]

Apparently, Kate was to suffer from periodic depressions for the rest of her life. Dickens often alludes to her being in low spirits, and in 1851 she went for a water cure to Great Malvern.[28]

Later Georgina Hogarth was to take Mary's place in Dickens's affection. It seems that Dickens could not – until late in life – reconcile his ambivalent feelings in his relationships with women. There was always the splitting into a good and a bad object. His pure, asexual sisters-in-law represented his idealized "good mother", whereas Kate with her pregnancies reminded him of his "bad mother".[29] Dickens resented his wife's pregnancies as if they had nothing to do with him. Again, we see

---

26 "New Letters of Mary Hogarth and Her Sister Catherine", *The Dickensian*, vol. 63 (1967), p. 75.

27 W. H. Bowen, *Charles Dickens and His Family*, Cambridge 1956, p. 113.

28 See for example *Letters*, vol. II, pp. 278, 293, 299, 300, 301.

29 We are reminded of Freud's paper "Über einen besonderen Typus der Objektwahl beim Manne" (1910), *Studienausgabe*, vol. V, pp. 185-195, in which he describes a certain type of man who gives his tender love to women he respects and his sexual love to women he scorns, often to prostitutes. For such men a woman may even become contemptible by the mere fact that she is a sexual being and as such sexually loved – be it in marriage or not. The fantasy to save such "fallen women", which Freud considers an essential element of the condition, is very strong in Dickens. There is no educational or social project he gave so much of his time and energy to as to *Urania Cottage*. Urania Cottage was a home for prostitutes founded by Dickens's friend Angela Burdett-Coutts and largely directed by Dickens himself.

the child who cannot cope with his mother's long period of child-bearing and who later experiences his pregnant wife as somebody who betrays him just as his mother has betrayed him by turning her attention to a younger child. Dickens's remarks about Kate's pregnancies – she bore him ten children and had five miscarriages – are often sarcastic and cutting.[30] In his letters he also gives vent to his dislike of babies. This fact has been mentioned by several scholars but they usually impute it to the growing number of his children, whereas it was there right from the beginning.[31] When his first child was born, he announced this to Cruikshank as follows:

> According to all established forms and ceremonies, I ought to have written on Friday Evening last, to duly acquaint and inform Mrs. Cruikshank that Mrs. Dickens had at a quarter past six o'clock P.M. presented me with a son and heir. But as I know you are not ceremonious people ... I thought I might just as well defer the communication until I had something else to say ...

> What I *have* to say is, that the bustle *et cetera* has rather put me out this month, and that I want you to give me as long a time to prepare the subject in [i.e. for Cruikshank's illustration to the first instalment of *Oliver Twist*], as you can ... (*PE,* I, 221, Dickens's emphasis).

In view of Dickens's later letter in 1852

> My wife is quite well again, after favouring me (I think I could have dispensed with the compliment) with No. 10. (*Letters,* II, 394)

the expression "Mrs. Dickens ... presented me" takes on an ironic quality. Soon after his eldest son was born, Dickens writes to his future brother-in-law:

> I speak most unaffectedly and plainly – when I say, that had I a marriageable daughter (which thank God I have not) of all the young men I know or ever did know, I should delight in seeing her set her cap at you; and *when* I have one (if ever such an event should happen, which Heaven in its mercy postpone) I only hope she may be fortunate enough to meet your exact copy. (*PE,* I, 232)

The fact that he compares his sister Letitia to a possible daughter of his suggests that he had in some way to care for her like a father or to take on a father's responsibility. In August 1840 he writes to a friend:

> A babby is to be christened and a fatted calf killed on these premises on Tuesday the 25th Instant. It (the calf; not the babby) is to be taken off the spit at 6. *Can* you come and gladden the heart of the indignant
>
> BOZ? (*PE,* II, 117)

Many more similar statements were to follow. A last example may be given. To his life-long friend, the actor Macready, Dickens wrote in April 1846:

30  Mrs. Dickens is described as being "in an *un*interesting condition", *Letters,* vol. II, pp. 113, 115, as "hardly presentable", p. 143 and is compared to Joanna Southcot (who was not pregnant but imagined herself to be so) in *PE,* vol. II, p. 204 and vol. IV, p. 416. Dickens who had wanted to "*Eclipse* the Bridegroom" of his adored Christiana Weller with a particularly bright waistcoat, lost interest in her as soon as she got pregnant and called her "a mere spoiled child" (*PE,* vol. IV, p. 604) with "a devil of a whimpering, pouting temper" (ibid., p. 615).

31  Kligermann, for example, contends that Dickens resented his children for the first time when he was in Genoa in Autumn 1844. See Charles Kligermann, "The Dream of Charles Dickens", *Journal of the American Psychoanalytic Association,* 18:4 (1970), p. 790.

I am having engraved on a brass plate to be fixed over the street door, and on another brass plate to be inlaid in the door steps the following words (with a prospective reference) selected from that surprising combination of wit, wisdom, humour, fancy, and pleasantry, The Life and Adventures of Nicholas Nickleby. .

" 'We want no Babbies here,' said Mr. Kenwigs. 'Take 'em away to the Fondling!' " (*PE,* IV, 532)

For all his explicit dislike of babies, however, he would delight his younger children with his conjuring tricks, with his comic songs, and with the theatricals he organized for them. Mamie Dickens describes the scenes that used to take place at bedtime as follows:

But his singing to them of an evening before bedtime was their greatest delight and treat. He generally had a child on his knee, sometimes one on each knee, and the others would stand near, and he would go through no end of songs at their request. They were almost always funny songs, and he would laugh over them quite as much as his small listeners, and enjoy them quite as much, too. He generally would wind up with a favourite one of all, which was about an old man who caught cold while driving in an omnibus, "and rheumatiz as well as a stiff neck", and the poor old man would sing in an old piping voice, and cough, and sneeze, and try to look over his stiff shoulder, until he could hardly be heard for the children's laughter, and the singer often had to stop, and laugh too, but was made to go over the song many times before his listeners could be induced to say goodnight to their father, and go to bed.[32]

Instead of "the gleam in the mother's eye" the gleams in the eyes of his children had to satisfy his craving for being seen while displaying himself. And whereas he used to assign himself several parts in his amateur theatricals, he praised Charley, his eldest son, for not being disappointed when a part which was at first promised him was taken away from him again.[33]

Dickens had a particularly close relationship with his reading public. Most of his novels were published either in monthly or in weekly serial publication, which allowed Dickens to watch the response of his readers to his tales and often to adapt them to their taste. It was his ardent wish to be loved by his readers, to find a place in their hearts and in their homes since he had no home in himself. It was most important to him to secure his readers' affection – even if this meant a sacrifice of his artistic intentions. Walter Gay, for example, was originally planned as a character coming to a bad end, but Dickens changed his plan, because such a career for his hero would have displeased his readers. In the same way he had Edith Dombey leave her husband but not – as he had intended – sexually betray him because judge Lord Jeffrey told him he could not bear Edith to be an adulteress.[34]

And even in *Great Expectations* – in my opinion his most mature book – he changed the sad ending to a moderately happy one at the request of Edward Bulwer Lytton. If he had unwittingly hurt his readers by a book, he tried to make up for it in later chapters of the book or in another tale. In this way he changed Miss Mowcher from a wicked dwarf into a helpful little person in *David Copperfield* and made up for the

---

32 M. Dickens, *Charles Dickens by His Eldest Daughter,* London 1885, pp. 62-3.
33 *Letters,* vol. II, p. 257.
34 "Do you think it may be done, without making people angry?" Dickens asked Forster when he outlined the development of Walter Gay from "one of adventure and boyish lightheartedness, into negligence, idleness, dissipation, dishonesty, and ruin." *F,* vol. II, p. 21. Edith's fate is described on p. 34.

bad Jew Fagin in *Oliver Twist* by the introduction of the benign Riah in *Our Mutual Friend*.

It was his anxious attempt not to "bring a blush to the cheek of the young person" and it was only towards the end of his career that he could ridicule bourgeois respectability, in his chapter "Podsnappery" in *Our Mutual Friend*. Dickens was at least partly aware of his conflict between personal and artistic motives as can be seen from a letter of August 1856 to Forster:

> I have always a fine feeling of the honest state into which we have got, when some smooth gentleman says to me ... how odd it is that the hero of an English book is always uninteresting – too good – not natural ... But O my smooth friend, what a shining impostor you must think yourself and what an ass you must think me, when you suppose that by putting a brazen face upon it you can blot out of my knowledge the fact that this same unnatural young gentleman ... whom you meet in those other books and in mine, must be presented to you in that unnatural aspect by reason of your morality, and is not to have, I will not say any of the indecencies you like, but not even any of the experiences, trials, perplexities, and confusions inseparable from the making or unmaking of all men! (*Letters*, II, 797)

Dickens could not afford to jeopardize his readers' affection; he needed to be shown by them that he was lovable after all. When his indignation about the state of England and the condition of the poor grew, however, and he more and more satirized society as a whole, many of his former admirers found him too disagreeable. Even Forster prefers the genial Dickens of the "Christmas Carol" to the bitter writer of *Bleak House* and the later novels.[35]

But Dickens found a new way of being the centre of attention. Not only did he speak at numerous official dinners and was invariably showered with kindness, but he also started to organize play acting with amateur groups, usually for the benefit of some charity or a friend in need.

The young Dickens had once tried to become an actor and had arranged for an audition with the comedian Charles Matthews and the actor Charles Kemble. But Dickens was "laid up when the day came, with a terrible bad cold and an inflammation of the face."[36] Once more we realize how much his urge to exhibit himself was charged with conflicts. In his later theatrical activities he experienced a feverish excitement when playing which was usually followed by restlessness, sleeplessness, despondency, and despair. In her discussion of the interrelatedness of grandiosity and depression, Alice Miller gives an example which seems the very description of Charles Dickens. She writes:

> So kann sich z.B. ein Schauspieler am Abend des Erfolges in den Augen des begeisterten Publikums spiegeln und Gefühle von göttlicher Grösse und Allmacht erleben. Und doch können am nächsten Morgen Gefühle von Leere, Sinnlosigkeit, ja sogar Scham und Ärger auftreten, wenn das Glück am Vorabend nicht nur in der kreativen Tätigkeit des Spielens, des Ausdrucks, sondern vorwiegend in der Ersatzbefriedigung des alten

35 Forster writes about *Bleak House,* for example, "it is the romance of discontent and misery, with a very restless dissatisfied moral, and is too much brought about by agencies disagreeable and sordid. The Guppys, Weevles, Snagsbys, Chadbands, Krooks, and Smallweeds, even the Kenges, Vholeses, and Tulkinghorns, are *much too real to be pleasant;* and the necessity becomes urgent for the reliefs and contrasts of a finer humanity. These last are not wanting; yet it must be said that we hardly escape, even with them, into the old freedom and freshness of the author's imaginative worlds ...", vol. II, p. 115, emphasis mine.

36 Quoted in E. Johnson, *Charles Dickens,* p. 51.

Bedürfnisses nach Echo, Spiegelung, Gesehen- und Verstanden-werden wurzelt. Ist seine Kreativität von diesen Bedürfnissen relativ frei, so wird unser Schauspieler am nächsten Morgen keine Depression haben, sondern sich lebendig fühlen und schon mit anderen Inhalten beschäftigt sein. Diente aber der Erfolg am Vorabend der Verleugnung der kindlichen Frustration, so bringt er – wie jeder Ersatz – nur eine momentane Stillung. (...)

*Die alte Wunde kann* wiederum *nicht heilen, solange sie in der Illusion, d.h. im Rausch des Erfolges verleugnet wird* (emphasis Alice Miller's).[37]

After the performances of Wilkie Collins's *The Frozen Deep* in 1857, Dickens's depression was particularly evident. Dickens writes to Wilkie Collins, his friend and collaborator in his periodical *Household Words,* of his mental state:

Partly *in the grim despair and restlessness of this subsidence from excitement,* and partly for the sake of Household Words, I want to cast about whether you and I could go anywhere – take any tour – see anything – whereon we could write something together. (...) We want something for Household Words and *I want to escape from myself.* For when I do start up and stare myself seedily in the face, as happens to be my case at present, my blankness is inconceivable – indescribable – my misery amazing (emphasis mine). (*Letters,* II, 873)

Not only was he painfully aware of his broken marriage but he once more fell in love with a girl who had a sister. The girl was Ellen Ternan, the sister Maria Ternan, who had played in *The Frozen Deep* together with Dickens and who had cried over the fate of the character whom Dickens played.[38] Dickens writes about Maria Ternan:

... perhaps Mr. Wills has not told you how much impressed I was at Manchester by the womanly tenderness of a very gentle and good little girl who acted Mary's part. (...) At night when she came out of the cave [i.e. during the performance] and Wardour [Dickens's part] recognised her, I never saw anything like the distress and agitation of her face ... But when she had to kneel over Wardour dying and be taken leave of, the tears streamed out of her eyes into his mouth, down his beard, all over his rags – down his arms as he held her by the hair. At the same time she sobbed as if she were breaking her heart, and was quite convulsed with grief. (...) I told her on the last night that I was sure she had one of the most genuine and feeling hearts in the world ...[39]

In Dickens's mind Maria Ternan wept for him, for the wronged child who – like Richard Wardour in the play – is "not so bad as he seems". Dickens – whose acknowledged aim it was to make his readers cry[40] – was deeply touched. It seems that by turning his attention to the younger girl Ellen, he allowed himself to experience

---

37 Alice Miller, *Das Drama des begabten Kindes,* pp. 74-75.
38 Nomen est omen! There existed various "Maries" who all admired Dickens. Mary Hogarth appeared to Dickens in a dream as the Virgin Mary. The spirit was "so full of compassion and sorrow for me ... that it cut me to the heart" and when the dreamer – in reality a staunch anti-Catholic – asked whether the Roman Catholic church was good for him, the spirit answered "full of such heavenly tenderness for me, that I felt as if my heart would break; 'for *you,* it is the best!' " *F,* vol. I, p. 337. Dickens's daughter Mamie, who was named after her dead aunt Mary Hogarth, was to become the daughter who never criticized him in the least but admired him whole-heartedly. There was also a friend, called Mary Boyle, who did the same.
39 To Angela Burdett Coutts, September 5, 1857, *Letters,* vol. II, p. 877.
40 About *The Chimes* he writes to Lady Blessington: "I am in great hope that I shall make you cry, bitterly, with my little book ..." (*PE,* vol. IV, p. 227) and to Angela Burdett Coutts "though I am not malicious, I am bent on making you cry, or being most horribly disappointed" (ibid., p. 236).

this compassion by proxy, so to speak, as if it were not for him to receive it directly in a love-relationship, or as if, once more, he had to remove himself from the source of goodness in order to protect it against his ambivalence.

It is well known how much gratification Dickens derived from his public readings. He adapted scenes from his novels to the stage and was obviously a remarkably gifted reader who held his audiences spellbound. He clearly enjoyed his power. He acquired his first taste of what it was like to move his audiences from a reading of *The Chimes* to a select group of friends in 1844. Dickens, who was spending a year in Genoa at that time, travelled to London expressly to act the story before them and he wrote to his wife:

> If you had seen Macready [the famous actor] last night – undisguisedly sobbing, and crying on the sofa, as I read – you would have felt (as I did) what a thing it is to have Power. (*PE*, IV, 235)

No longer a neglected child, he could now make people laugh and make them cry; they responded to him during the readings exactly as he wanted them to; they were like members of his own body whose movements he could control.

Kohut says that the relationship of a small child to his self-object can be made understandable if we use the above-mentioned simile. Early in life every child should experience relief of tensions by having the feeling that he is just as capable of galvanising his self-objects into action as he is the members of his own body. Kohut says that people who suffer from brain injuries, for example, and suddenly cannot move their limbs any more or cannot utter the word they try to pronounce, experience the same kind of rage which the child feels when he realizes that the self-object is not directed in his or her actions by him. There is a large admixture of helplessness to this so-called narcissistic rage.[41] Some people experience a similar feeling when their car suddenly breaks down. If – consciously or unconsciously – the car represents an extension of their body, the machine which does not function behaves like the limbs of the brain-damaged people.

The child in Dickens seems to have said by way of his readings: if you do not give your love willingly, I shall force it from you. How much he had to force himself in order to attain this goal can be imagined if we look at his American reading tour in 1867/68.

Dickens travelled across the country in railway carriages. The stifling heat in them was insupportable to him and he used to stand outside in the open and expose himself to the bitter cold, the rain and the snow. In this way he actually prevented his abominable cold from healing and he suffered greatly from it as well as from sleeplessness and lack of appetite and taste. We know from Dickens's children Mamie and Henry that after the railway accident at Staplehurst in 1865 Dickens was always apprehensive when travelling by train. Possibly he had to stand outside because he feared that otherwise he might not get off the train in time if there should be an accident. Dickens, who had shown remarkable presence of mind at Staplehurst in helping "the dying and the dead" (a sentence which recurs like a refrain in all his letters about the accident), was later shaken with fear. Mamie gives us the following description:

41 Cp. Heinz Kohut, "Thoughts on Narcissism and Narcissistic Rage", *The Psychoanalytic Study of the Child,* vol. 27 (1972), pp. 360-400.

... we have often seen him, when travelling home from London, suddenly fall into a paroxysm of fear, trembly all over, clutch the arms of the railway carriage, large beads of perspiration standing on his face, and suffer agonies of terror. (...) Sometimes he would suddenly get better, and sometimes the agony was so great, he had to get out at the nearest station and walk home.[42]

Dickens's death on 9 June 1870, five years to the day after the accident may be the ultimate indication of how much he was agitated by this event. It is possible that Dickens somehow (consciously or unconsciously) believed this accident to be a punishment for his illegal relationship with Ellen. (Ellen was with him in the carriage *1)* when it happened.) Be that as it may, Dickens's time in America was certainly like being in hell for him. He was separated from Ellen and, although he had hoped that she would be able to join him, he soon saw that it was impossible to travel incognito and he told her in a coded telegram to stay at home.[43]

His cold, however, may be viewed as a form of incessant weeping – Dickens himself often describes his colds in these terms:

> I have got *such* a cold! I have been crying all day ...   or

> I am ornamented with one of my most intensely preposterous and utterly indescribable colds. If you were to make a voyage from Cape Horn to Wellington Street, you would scarcely recognise in the bowed form, weeping eyes, rasped nose, and snivelling wretch you would encounter here, the once gay and sparkling & c., & c...

> I am writing with a cold, too ridiculous to be more particularly referred to in its weeping and gasping intensity...[44]

One more letter must be quoted since it tells us how much Dickens had to undergo in order to gain what he needed so much:

> That afternoon my "catarrh" (quotation marks Dickens's!) was in such a state that Charles Sumner, coming in at five o'clock and finding me covered with mustard poultice, and apparently voiceless, turned to Dolby and said: "Surely, Mr. Dolby, it is impossible that he can read tonight." Says Dolby: "Sir, I have told the dear Chief so four times today, and I have been very anxious. But you have no idea how he will change when he gets to the little table." After five minutes of the little table, I was not (for the time) even hoarse. The frequent experience of this return of force when it is wanted saves me a vast amount of anxiety; but I am not at times without the nervous dread that I may some day sink altogether ... (*Letters*, III, 619)

Did he have to pay this awful price for the gratification of the wish to be seen by "thousands upon thronging thousands"[45] in every aspect of his personality: in his grief, his joy, his humanity, his care and compassion for the poor, his sarcasm, his bitterness, his aggression? The wish was so ardent that in spite of the cold he could muster his voice when he needed it, but only at the price of misery for the rest of the time. As Dickens himself once put it, he was riding over himself "like a dragoon".

---

42  *Charles Dickens by His Eldest Daughter,* pp. 114-115.
43  Ada Nisbet discovered in Dickens's notebook the following entry: Tel.: all well means/ *you come*/ Tel.: safe and well, means/ *you don't come*. See Ada Nisbet, *Dickens and Ellen Ternan,* Berkeley 1952, p. 54.
44  November 1840, *PE,* vol. II, p. 150; October 1852, *Letters,* vol. II, p. 425; September 1860, *Letters,* vol. III, p. 176 respectively.
45  Emlyn Williams reading Charles Dickens, "I, Charles Dickens".

It seems to me that the first time Dickens read from his works to an audience he dealt with the old question: who is the bad one? Trotty Veck in *The Chimes* is led to believe that the poor are "born bad" by such people as the Alderman Cute, who is going to "Put suicide Down", i.e. to punish severely anybody who has attempted to kill himself. Trotty is shown in his dream that his own daughter Meg could not help being crushed by her miserable situation, her lack of employment, her want of bread as well as of a bed to sleep in, by her having not a single friend. When she tries to drown herself and her child, Trotty exclaims:

> "Have mercy on her! ... Think what her misery must have been, when such seeds bear such fruit!" (*CB*, I, 240)

Trotty is taught, in other words, not to forsake himself and his kind any longer by believing that they "have no business on the face of the earth" and that they are "intruding".

Dickens might well have needed the response to this tale from his friends in order to feel certain that nobody, not even he himself, is "born bad".

The piece of writing he included last in his reading repertoire was the murder of Nancy by Sikes from *Oliver Twist*. For a long time he did not dare to read this scene, fearing that its effect might be too horrible, but in the end he could not resist the temptation.

In his letters we find numerous references to this reading, such as:

> Come early in January and see a certain friend of yours do the murder from Oliver Twist. It is horrible like, I am afraid! I have a vague sensation of being "wanted" as I walk about the streets

and

> I do not commit the murder again in London until Thursday

or

> I begin to doubt and fear on the subject of your having a terror of me after seeing the murder. I don't think a hand moved while I was doing it last night, or an eye looked away. And there was a fixed expression of horror of me, all over the theatre, which could not have been surpassed if I had been going to be hanged to that red velvet table. It is quite a new sensation to be execrated with that unanimity; and I hope it will remain so![46]

One gets the feeling that in displaying the murderous aggression against the woman who had wanted to send him back to Warren's Blacking, just as Nancy had pulled Oliver forcefully away from his happier existence at Mr. Brownlow's, he hoped to obtain absolution. It seems as if he was experimenting to see whether they could really see him the way he felt himself to be and still accept him. However, as he only perceived horror on the faces of his listeners, he had to try again and again. "Look at me," he seems to have said, "in my heart of hearts I am a murderer. But I want you to understand me and to know that I was not born bad." I shall come back to this example when discussing the conscious and unconscious images Dickens had of himself.

Since the wish to be accepted the way he was may be traced back to his childhood, or, in other words, to the past, its fulfilment in the present could not adequately satisfy it. Dickens seems to have felt this somehow when writing to a photographer:

46 November 1868, *Letters,* vol. III, p. 602; January 1869, ibid., p. 700; April 1869, ibid. pp. 718-19 respectively.

It is a melancholy fact, – but I don't see the remotest chance of my interesting countenance being ever photographed, of my own knowledge and consent, again. If I were to begin, I could never leave off. (*Letters*, III, 11)

Consciously Dickens means that he would be plagued by photographers requesting to take a picture of him, but unconsciously he acknowledges at the same time the fear that being photographed might become some sort of addiction for him. Again, he would not be able to leave off, since the ultimate goal, namely a change of the mirroring object of the past, could not be reached.

Let us once more turn to the blacking-warehouse trauma. Dickens writes about himself and another boy at the warehouse:

Bob Fagin and I had attained to great dexterity in tying up the pots. I forgot how many we could do in five minutes. We worked, for the light's sake, near the … window … and we were so brisk at it, that the people used to stop and look in. Sometimes there would be quite a little crowd there. I saw my father coming in at the door one day when we were very busy, and I wondered how he could bear it. ("AF", 32)

In this situation Dickens could not enjoy his skill and the admiration of the passers-by. He only felt exposed in his degradation, namely his being cast away by his parents. How could his father bear to see him displayed in this shameful condition to the eyes of the world? How could he indeed bear it – the son's shame being necessarily his own, too, for was it not, so Dickens thought, something to be ashamed of, to dispose of a child in this way?[47]

John Dickens and James Lamert, Charles's employer, quarrelled and the quarrel brought about the son's release. Bowen comments on this event as follows:

It may be argued in favour of John Dickens that it was he who liberated Charles from the blacking warehouse; but it is clear when the facts are analysed that he acted from wounded vanity. There is little doubt from what is known of these two men that Lamert had lent money to John Dickens and had vainly asked for its return. Knowing that he had come into money and that verbal appeals were useless, the probability is that he wrote to him and was severely critical. In return, John Dickens was abusive, and for this reason Lamert told Charles that he could not have him back.[48]

If this conjecture be true, Dickens's own fantasy that his father quarrelled with Lamert because of him, Charles, is pathetic. This is Dickens speaking:

At last, one day, my father and the relative so often mentioned quarrelled; quarrelled by letter, for I took the letter from my father to him which caused the explosion, but quarrelled very fiercely. It was about me. It may have had some backward reference, in part, for anything I know, to my employment at the window. ("AF", 32)

Dickens's search for a reliable self-object can also be inferred from his behaviour as it is described by his daughter Mamie. Apparently Dickens had "a passion for

---

47 It is hardly surprising that Dickens, too, sometimes forsook his children. When he and his wife went to America in 1842 they left behind their four children, aged between one and five years, with their friend Macready. Dickens felt that Kate was behaving hysterically when she at first wanted to stay with them. The children were intensely unhappy in Macready's gloomy house. When they returned after five months, Charley fell into convulsions which were interpreted as a sign of his too great joy at his parents' return. When the Dickens family moved to Italy for a year in 1844/45 they at first wanted to leave the baby behind with Catherine's mother.

48 W. H. Bowen, *Charles Dickens and His Family,* p. 69.

X looking-glass" and there were "looking-glasses placed in every possible corner of the house".[49]

Dickens also had five mirrors installed in his study in the "Swiss chalet" which was across the road from his home at Gad's Hill. He had them placed in such a way that they reflected for him the foliage of the nearby trees, the fields, the changing sky and the "sail-dotted river" (*F*, II, 211-12). For many people nature is the embodiment of the "good mother" and in seeing nature with his mirrors all around him, Dickens enveloped himself, so to speak, with his self-object; he was supported by it like the embryo who is held by the amnionic fluid and could merge with the elements around him.[50]

The fact that nature indeed represented for Dickens the good aspect of his mother image is also evident in the following episode: Dickens was much impressed with the beauty of the Niagara Falls. At the end of chapter 14 in *American Notes* we find the following description of the feelings he had when contemplating the roaring waters:

> Then, when I felt how near to my Creator I was standing, the first effect, and the enduring one – instant and lasting – of the tremendous spectacle, was Peace. Peace of Mind, tranquillity, calm recollections of the Dead, great thoughts of Eternal Rest and Happiness; nothing of gloom or terror. Niagara was at once stamped upon my heart, an Image of Beauty; to remain there, changeless and indelible, until its pulses cease to beat, for ever.
> Oh, how the strife and trouble of daily life receded from my view, and lessened in the distance, during the ten memorable days we passed on that Enchanted Ground! What voices spoke from out the thundering water; what faces, faded from the earth, looked out upon me from its gleaming depths; what Heavenly promise glistened in those angels' tears, the drops of many hues that showered around, and twined themselves about the gorgeous arches which the changing rainbows made! (*AN & PI, OID,* 200)

Is it not striking that for Dickens the water stood for "angels' tears" which were being wept by the dead, possibly by the immortal, angelic Mary Hogarth who – we have seen it above – represented for him the "good" object? How much he felt this good object was in danger of being contaminated is evident from Dickens's reaction to the entries of other visitors in a guide book in a near-by cottage. Dickens was appalled by their lack of awe and he wrote to a friend:

> My wrath is kindled, past all human powers of extinction, by the disgusting entries in the books which are kept at the Guide's house; and which, made in such a spot, and preserved afterwards, are a disgrace and degradation to our nature. If I were a despot, I would force these Hogs to live for the rest of their lives on all Fours, and to wallow in the filth expressly provided for them by Scavengers who should be maintained at the Public expense. Their drink should be stagnant ditch, and their food the rankest garbage; and every morning they should each receive as many stripes as there are letters in their detestable obscenities. (*PE*, III, 239)

Dickens's extreme reaction to these entries can be explained by the intense fear those writings must have evoked in him. It is as if he panicked because he felt that by their unseemly jokes they could possibly destroy his blissful experience. And as the remembrance of the peace and the rest he had experienced there was so dear to him, he must have felt as if he were being robbed of his most treasured possession when he

---

49 M. Dickens, op. cit., p. 103.
50 Argelander's patient acted out a similar merger fantasy with nature as an idealized self-object in his gliding. See H. Argelander, *Der Flieger,* Frankfurt/M. 1972.

36

read what to him were obscenities. He therefore indulged in his fantasies of revenge – the punishment he assigned to the writers of these lines was proportionate to the wound he had received by them, and the wound could only have been so great because it touched a sore point.


## 1.3 Dickens's Self-Representations

"I am not a dragon,
but a villified lamb"

(To Wills, February 1857)[51]

It has been mentioned above that such contradictory object-representations go together with a divided image of the self. Dickens was to himself both the most beautiful and intelligent child but also just dirt or refuse, to be thrown away; he felt a saviour of mankind as well as a murderer.

In his letters he often gives himself epithets such as "the Inimitable", "the National Sparkler", "our illustrious novelist", "what an amazing man!", "the cheerful Dick", "my illustrious person", "an Intrepid", "the pride of Albion and the admiration of Gaul", and later "Wenerables" (i.e. "Venerables" for "grandfather"). Most frequent is the use of "the Inimitable" and sometimes this is expanded to "the only real Inimitable", "my inimitable self", "the inimitable Dick" and, of course, "the Inimitable Boz". The defensive nature of these beautiful names, however, is evident when we look at the origin of the appellation "the Inimitable Boz". Dickens's early writings, namely *Sketches by Boz* and *Pickwick Papers,* were published under the pen-name "Boz". *Oliver Twist* was the first of Dickens's novels to appear under his own name. Johnson tells us that Dickens had given his youngest brother Augustus the nickname "Moses" after the boy Moses in *The Vicar of Wakefield*. The child had mispronounced it as "Boses" which was then shortened to "Bose" and "Boz".[52] In *The Vicar of Wakefield* Moses is a likeable simpleton who means well but is often laughed at. He is once sent to the fair to sell a colt and buys in exchange for it a gross of green spectacles because he assumes their copper rims to consist of silver. "Marry, hang the idiot, ... to bring me such stuff" is his mother's reaction to his business transaction.

In large families the younger children are often envied by the older ones, who take their revenge in ridiculing them, in laughing at them and giving them the impression not of being children (and therefore not yet able to perform certain feats) but of being idiots. This is what Dickens did when he assigned his younger brother this name. However, in calling himself "Boz", he also clearly expressed his belief that Augustus's position was enviable: he wanted to be in his brother's place; he wanted to bear his brother's name; he wanted to be his brother. However, in adding the adjective "Inimitable" to the nickname, he seemed to say: "I am the real baby; I am, or should have been, the youngest child. I cannot be replaced for I am inimitable, I am unique." Dickens used the combined name "the Inimitable Boz" first for signing his "Answers

---

51 Dickens adds in parenthesis: "(Note. An L too many in the last word but one.)" The assonance to "villain" is obvious.
52 Edgar Johnson, *Charles Dickens,* p. 73.

to Correspondents" in *Bentley's Miscellany*. Soon afterwards he was given a silver snuff-box inscribed "to the inimitable Boz" by William Giles, his former schoolmaster at Chatham. From then on, Dickens referred to himself constantly as "the Inimitable Boz".

His identification with the youngest child, his simultaneous wish to replace him and his reaction-formation to this wish is striking in Dickens's relationship with his youngest son (the No. 10 of p. 28), Edward Bulwer Lytton Dickens, later called "Plorn" by his father. In his letters to his friend, the philanthropist Angela Burdett-Coutts, Dickens often refers to the "inimitability" of the baby:

> I think that must be all a mistake about that Suffolk baby your nephew, because (it is a remarkable fact) we have in this house the only baby worth mentioning; and there cannot possibly be another baby anywhere, to come into competition with him. I happen to know this, and would like it to be generally understood.

A little later he writes of the "Baby who defies competition" and is "unapproachable by any baby whomsoever" or, in another letter, he mentions that the "baby sends his pity (for the pretended baby), his forgiveness, and respects". The following is another of his playful and yet serious eulogies:

> You will be sorry to hear that the
>       Beauty,
>       Size,
>       and
>       Vigor
> of the
>       Baby
> are the admiration of the entire population of Boulogne ...[53]

Apparently, Dickens had not experienced that he – like anybody else – was a unique, non-replaceable human being; he had to offer proof of it with his books, to himself as well as to the world. Consciously he seems to have experienced himself mainly as the successful writer, the Inimitable, the child who is so great that he really defies competition. The reverse side of the coin, however, was present as well, although it was on the whole much more repressed. Dickens always had to ward off a deep-seated feeling of being dirty. We are told by his children how they suffered from his excessive love of order of which Dickens himself once said that it was "almost a disorder". He inspected the rooms of his children at least once a day, checked their drawers and pinned messages on their cushions if he was not satisfied. He himself was often accused of being dandified – his clothes being very important to him.

When Dickens travelled to England from Italy in 1844 in order to read *The Chimes* to his friends, he wrote to his wife:

> I arrived here at half past five tonight, after 50 hours of it, in a French coach. I was so beastly dirty when I got to this house, that I had quite lost all my sense of identity, and if anybody had said 'Are you Charles Dickens?' I should have unblushingly answered 'No. I never heard of him' (*PE,* IV, 230).

In other words, he could not tolerate the thought of being dirty. It was not he who was dirty, it was another person. Charles Dickens was always clean. Any person who travelled as he did would have become dirty. Yet Dickens could not feel this but only experienced it as being somehow his fault – being dirty was, in his unconscious,

---

53 *Letters from Charles Dickens to Angela Burdett-Coutts 1841–1865,* selected and edited by Edgar Johnson, London 1953, pp. 225, 227, 229 and 237 respectively.

equated with being unwanted, being unlovable. During his first visit to America, Dickens was tortured by the Americans' spitting habits, for, he declared, "I can bear anything but filth" (*PE,* III, 119).

A fixation to the anal phase of psychosexual development – corresponding in time more or less to the above-mentioned rapprochement stage (p. 22) – seems obvious. Dickens's cleanliness, his love of order, his compulsive behaviour (for example his compulsive street-walking at night, or his compulsive patterning of his pencils before starting to write), his concern with money and with power[54] and his testiness – all these character traits correspond to Freud's descriptions of the anal character.[55]. Freud also mentions the by now familiar equation of dirt/faeces with money/gold in the unconscious. It is hardly necessary to point out that in *Our Mutual Friend* the dust mounds (which contained human faeces in the Victorian age) are the central symbol for money and that the characters are correlated by their various attitudes towards a false value system.

Dickens's excited accounts in his letters to Forster and Miss Coutts of how much money he earned at a single reading can be understood as his triumphant feeling at having mastered his fate. He was no longer the helpless child who had to witness the family's various breakdowns but he was powerful now, he had money to spare, he could not only support himself but also numerous friends and relations. He may unconsciously have fostered their sponging attitude since it made him feel strong to reverse his childhood situation. The deep anxiety of suddenly being exposed to the old dangers, however, was always present and made him write to his wife: "keep things in their places, I can't bear to picture them otherwise" (*PE,* IV, 216). His wish to control the situation at home may have sprung from his memory of the pawnbroker's shop. He could not stop checking the position of the tables and chairs, for example, because he was never free from the apprehension that they would suddenly disappear.

At the end of his first American tour Dickens was looking forward to returning home and said: "How I busy myself in thinking how my books look; and where the tables are; and in what position the chairs stand, relatively to the other furniture" (*PE,* III, 244). In der last analysis this fear of losing his furniture might well go back to the early dread of the infant of losing his mother forever.

Just as he felt beautiful, gay and sparkling on the one hand and dirty and repulsive on the other, Dickens experienced himself as a member of the Holy Family as well as a murderer and an outcast. Once more the positive image, that of the Holy Family is defensive and more conscious than its opposite, the deep-seated dread of being a criminal.

I have already mentioned the various Maries Dickens became infatuated with, and it is interesting that even his beloved Maria Beadnell – who did not admire him as the

---

54 I am not only thinking of Dickens's theatrical power over his audiences, but also of his hypnotic skills. He mesmerized not only the ailing Mrs. de la Rue but also his wife Catherine and his sick friend John Leech besides various other persons. See Fred Kaplan, *Dickens and Mesmerism,* Princeton 1975.

55 See for example "Charakter und Analerotik", in: Sigmund Freud, *Studienausgabe,* ed. by Alexander Mitscherlich, Angela Richards, James Strachey, vol. 7, Frankfurt/M. 1973, pp. 24-30.

others did – can be added to this group. In his letters to Mary Boyle, Dickens often signs himself as "Joseph" or "Joe" or "the humble Jo".[56]

Furthermore, a child who is needed to protect his parents from a psychic collapse is in a way pushed into the role of the saviour. By sacrificing himself, by not getting a chance of establishing his true identity and by building up a false self such a child is killed on the cross in order to give life to others.[57] Dickens once laughingly told the story of the charity boy who said to the school inspector that "Our saviour was the only forgotten son of his father, and that he was forgotten ... before all worlds ..."[58]. We can only guess what bitter laughter this must have been.

In his *Pictures from Italy* Dickens describes how he found many people lounging about on the staircase at the Piazza di Spagna in Rome. The people seemed strangely familiar to him and suddenly it dawned upon him that he had met them before in various paintings and that they were models waiting for artists to engage them. There was "the venerable or patriarchal model", "the assassin model", "the scornful model", etc. Dickens proceeds:

> As to Domestic Happiness, and Holy Families, they should come very cheap, for there are lumps of them, all up the steps; and the cream of the thing is, that they are all the falsest vagabonds in the world, especially made up for the purpose... (*AN & PI, OID*, 379)

However, Dickens was obviously not aware of the fact that he was selling cheap domestic happiness to his readers, too, in the depiction of all his unconvincing, saccharine, angelic heroines.

Even after his separation from his wife and his official explanation in *Household Words,* which only bred scandal, he seriously considered calling his newly founded periodical "Household Harmony" after the lines in Shakespeare's *Henry VI* where the captive King, who is treated gently by his keeper, says to him:

> I'll well requite thy kindness,
> For that it made my prisonment a pleasure;
> Ay, such a pleasure as incaged birds
> Conceive when, after many moody thoughts,
> At last by notes of household harmony
> They quite forget their loss of liberty.[59]

In this simile, the household harmony is again only a compensation for what has been lost; it is not a good that is striven after for itself. When Forster called Dickens's attention to the inherent irony in this title, Dickens was "at first reluctant even to admit the objection when stated to him". (*F,* II, 227-28)

Dickens's main symbol for expressing "household harmony" and the love between parents and children as well as between husband and wife is, of course, Christmas. With the *Christmas Carol* in 1843 Dickens started his habit of giving his readers a

---

56 Dickens and Mary Boyle had played together in the farce *Used Up,* playing the characters of Mary and Joseph.

57 There is a moving example of such a fatal tie between a father and his son in H. E. Richter, *Der Gotteskomplex,* Reinbek bei Hamburg 1979. When the son frees himself in his analysis from his father's possession of him, the latter collapses and finally dies in a psychiatric hospital.

58 *Letters,* vol. III, p. 230.

59 *III Henry VI,* 4.6., ll. 10-15.

particular story as his Christmas present. The *Christmas Carol* is the best of these stories; *The Chimes* carries a particular social appeal, but *The Cricket on the Hearth*, *The Battle of Life* and *The Haunted Man* are less satisfactory from a literary point of view. The Christmas stories of his later years vary greatly, *Going Into Society*, and part of *Mugby Junction*, namely *The Signalman*, being among the best.

Often Dickens felt weary when thinking of the Christmas number but he was convinced that he owed his readers a special story for Christmas. When writing *Dombey and Son* in 1847, Dickens hesitated to embark upon another Christmas story, since the novel sapped his strength, but he wrote to Forster that he was "loath to ... leave any gap at Christmas firesides which I ought to fill" (*Letters*, II, 55).

His ambivalence with regard to this Christmas duty is visible in a letter of March 1868:

> ... after I have rested – don't laugh – it is a grim reality – I shall have to turn my mind to – ha! ha! ha! – to – ha! ha! ha! (more sepulchrally than before) – the – The CHRISTMAS NUMBER!!! I feel as if I had murdered a Christmas number years ago (perhaps I did!) and its ghost perpetually haunted me. (*Letters*, III, 630)

In the same year he was to write to his sub-editor, W. H. Wills:

> I have been, and still am – which is worse – in a positive state of despair about the Xmas No. I cannot get an idea for it which is in the least satisfactory to me, and yet I have been steadily trying all this month. I have invented so many of these Christmas Nos. and they are so profoundly unsatisfactory after all with the introduced stories and their want of cohesion and originality, that I fear I am sick of the thing. I have had serious thoughts of abandoning the No.! There remain but August and September to give to it (as I begin to read in October), and I CAN NOT see it. (*Letters*, III, 659-60)

Dickens seems to have noticed at last how superficial and even harmful the sort of cheerfulness was which he called "Carol Philosophy" and had advocated in his stories, praising it as the highest virtue in women as well as in children. In 1847, for example, he had proudly written about his children: "They never cry, but go into corners to be convulsed, and come out cheerful."[60]

The fact that Dickens somehow felt he had a gospel to preach can also be surmised from his thrill when he was asked during his reading-tour in America to read in a chapel, with the listeners sitting in pews.[61]

The opposite self-image, namely the conviction of being a murderer, crops up from time to time in his letters. In May 1834 Dickens apologizes for not having given back a. coat which was lent to him:

> 'Appearances are against me, I know' – as the man said when he murdered his brother, but it really is not my fault that it has not been returned (*PE*, I, 39).

And after finishing *The Chimes*, he confesses that he felt "as haggard as a Murderer" (*PE*, IV, 224). A little later he compares himself to a murderer in a play whose preoccupation is not guilt, however, but regret at having to leave his friends. The servants at Gad's Hill were once frightened by strange sounds and everybody went ghost-hunting. Dickens threatened that he would blow off the head of anybody who might be playing tricks. After this threat, Dickens said, his new groom was evidently convinced that he had "entered the service of a bloodthirsty demon" (*Letters*, III, 189). (The ghost turned out to be an asthmatic sheep!)

---

60 *Letters to Angela Burdett-Coutts*, p. 94.
61 See his letter to Mamie of 26 December 1867 and his letter to Forster of 5 January 1868.

Dickens was also much interested in penal reform[62], and he strongly attacked the Solitary System of imprisonment. In chapter VII of *American Notes* Dickens movingly describes the horrible fate of the prisoners of the famous Eastern Penitentiary:

> I believe that very few men are capable of estimating the immense amount of torture and agony which this dreadful punishment, prolonged for years, inflicts upon the sufferers; and in guessing at it myself, and in reasoning from what I have seen written upon their faces, and what to my certain knowledge they feel within, I am only the more convinced that there is a depth of horrible endurance in it which none but the sufferers themselves can fathom, and which no man has a right to inflict upon his fellow-creatures. (*AN & PI, OID,* 99)

He describes his impressions in a letter to a friend and says: "I never in my life was more affected by anything which was not strictly my own grief" (*PE*, III, 111). Dickens may not have realized that he was so much affected by the prisoners' fate because it might easily have been his own, too, or even that his inner isolation was akin to theirs. One would like to see Dickens always as compassionate, understanding himself as well as others. The contrary is, in fact, the case. The older he grew, the more reactionary his views became. His unfeeling attitude towards himself, his horror at, and shame about, his own aggression are reflected in his attitude towards offenders. He identified with them[63] and, because he tried so hard to suppress and castigate these forbidden emotions in himself, he had to do the same to the real lawbreakers. He advocated the tread-mill, for example, although he is also reported to have looked at it and exclaimed: "My God! If a woman thinks her son may come to this, I don't blame her if she strangles him in infancy." (*PE*, III, 503, footnote)

Nor did he realize the cruelty of the Silent System he so highly praised. To be imprisoned under the Silent System meant working in the same room and side by side with fellow-prisoners without being allowed to exchange even one word with them. Any transgression of this rule was severely punished. We might ask ourselves whether Dickens did not see the cruelty of this system because he had grown accustomed to this particular kind of suffering. The system seems to be a symbol of a family whose members live together in the same place but are emotionally estranged from one another and cannot talk to each other any more. Dickens wished to be protected against his own aggression much as a child needs his parents to set limits to his (imagined) destructiveness, and he therefore admired the police force who kept lawbreakers in check. In his identification with the murderer, he was also frightened of the mob and wanted the police to control it as well. The following letter is revealing:

> You have no idea what the hanging of the Mannings really was. The conduct of the people was so indescribably frightful, that I felt for some time afterwards almost as if I were living in a city of devils. (*Letters,* II, 195)

It seems that Dickens's advocation of "private" hanging within the prison walls partly originated in his wish to protect the person who was going to be executed against "the devils". Although he reasoned that anybody who was going to be hanged

---

62  I am much indebted in the following paragraph to Philip Collins's excellent study *Dickens and Crime,* London ²1965.

63  There exists one letter by Dickens to his friend Tracey, a prison governor, in which Dickens assumes the character and writing of an imaginary prisoner and signs with a cross (*PE*, vol. III, p. 503).

could attain to a fearful dignity and display himself before a crowd of witnesses, he was also shocked at the brutality of the onlookers. From a beheading in Rome, Dickens reports:

> There was no manifestation of disgust, or pity, or indignation, or sorrow... It was an ugly, filthy, careless, sickening spectacle; meaning nothing but butchery beyond the momentary interest to the one wretched actor. (*AN & PI, OID*, 391)

Children who feel neglected often indulge in day-dreams about getting killed or killing themselves. "If I were dead, my parents would feel sorry for me. They would regret having treated me so badly. They would finally realize how good a child I was." There may be some traces of such fantasies in Dickens's obsession with capital punishment. If only the spectators could have cared. Even disgust or indignation would have been better than the utter lack of interest Dickens witnessed.

As he repudiated his desire to exhibit himself, he had to fight an acting out of the disguised wish as well. There is a playful reference to such fantasying in Dickens's letter to Maclise, in which he talks about being in love with the Queen:

> What is to be done. Heavens my friend, what is to be done! What if I murder Chapman and Hall [his publishers]. This thought has occurred to me several times. If I did this she would hear of me; perhaps sign the warrant for my execution with her own dear hand. What if I murder myself. (*PE*, II, 28)

Again we are reminded of children who will do anything to gain attention, who will gladly accept punishment if only they are noticed. The psychoanalyst Charles Kligerman has analyzed Dickens's dream of Mary Hogarth which has been mentioned above. Dickens dreamt that his dead sister-in-law visited him and that her face was full of compassion and tenderness for him. He wanted to keep her by his bedside as long as possible and when he was allowed to form a wish he decided to be good and not to think of himself – this would drive the spirit away. Instead he wished that his mother-in-law (whom he detested in reality) might be helped. Kligerman says:

> In sum, the dream represents the disguised breakthrough of an infantile memory in which the dreamer, in a state of great excitement (partly somatized) [since Dickens suffered at that time from severe neuralgic pains], calls his mother or nurse to his bedside and tries to detain her by various artifices. Rebuked for some advance, he tries to regain her good graces by sharing her high aims; or turns to altruistic do-goodism to offset the rage of his wounded narcissism.[64]

Whether it be by behaving particularly well or by behaving particularly badly, the aim is the same – namely to gain the mother's (the Queen's) attention. In Dickens's letter about the Queen there are clearly some sexual undertones too, if we consider that hanged men often have an erection. But the letter mainly conveys to us a child's feeling that only when dying will he be heeded. It is sad to see how little understanding Dickens had for his natural wishes which – in his despair – had taken on this distorted form of wish-fulfilment. So little, in fact, was his understanding that he engaged in a life-long battle to fight them on the issue of capital punishment. It is true that there was often some acting in front of the gallows. Hollingsworth describes it thus:

---

64 Charles Kligerman, "The Dream of Charles Dickens", p. 789. The dream itself is already given in Forster, vol. I, pp. 336-337.

There was an opportunity for him [i.e. the doomed man] to speak last words to the clergyman and officials on the platform – and to address the spectators if he wished. This was a moment of glory, drama on a grand scale, a part to be played once and never repeated.[65]

Dickens was intensely irritated by these little shows and he persisted in his demand for the abolition of public execution in order to prevent the murderers from exhibiting themselves. Had their acting not reminded him of some of his own wishes and fantasies, he probably would have pitied the poor devils and he would not have grudged them this last miserable display of themselves.

Collins draws our attention to the story *Five Points in Criminal Law* in which Dickens "reiterated his favourite jibe that 'the real offender is the Murdered Person'."[66] This shows us once more that we are dealing with Dickens's childhood problem. What he so jokingly mentions and so lightly dismisses is an inkling of the conviction that any child who wants to kill his parents must have good reasons for his hatred. We are thrown back upon the old question, "whose fault is it?"

In his fiction, Dickens could gradually attain to a more sympathetic attitude towards his portrayed murderers. Edmund Wilson was the first to point out that in Dickens's late novels, *Our Mutual Friend* and *The Mystery of Edwin Drood*, he created two criminals who no longer belong to an out-group like Magwitch and Sikes but who are respectable members of society, the one a schoolmaster, the other a choirmaster. The murderous aggression is no longer a state of mind which belongs only to lower class people or, in other words, to people who live an entirely different life from his, but to his next-door neighbour and thus to himself.[67]

In the person of the dissolute Sidney Carton, who is beheaded in someone else's place, Dickens was able to combine the divergent aspects of his self-image. Christ and criminal are reunited in this character. And, as Wilson has pointed out, the Christmas season itself, which Dickens has upheld to his readers as the time for expressing mutual love, becomes "the appointed time for the murder by an uncle of his nephew".[68]

There is yet another link between the two spheres – the sphere of Christmas on the one hand and that of crime on the other: both worlds are peopled with ghosts.

After visiting another solitary confinement prison in Pittsburgh, Dickens wrote to Forster:

> A horrible thought occurred to me when I was recalling all I had seen, that night. *What if ghosts be one of the terrors of these jails?* I have pondered on it often, since then. The utter solitude by day and night; the many hours of darkness; the silence of death; imagine a prisoner covering up his head in the bedclothes and looking out from time to time, with a ghastly dread of some inexplicable silent figure that always sits upon his bed, or stands (if a thing can be said to stand, that never walks as men do) in the same corner of his cell. The more I think of it, the more certain I feel that not a few of these men (during a portion of their imprisonment at least) are nightly visited by spectres. I did ask one man in this last jail, if he dreamed much. He gave me a most extraordinary look, and said – under his breath – in a whisper – "No." (*PE*, III, 181)

65 Keith Hollingsworth, *The Newgate Novel, 1830–1847,* Detroit 1963, p. 4.
66 Ph. Collins, *Dickens and Crime*, p. 190.
67 Edmund Wilson, "The Two Scrooges", in: *The Wound and the Bow,* first published in 1941, revised edition 1952, p. 74 f.
68 E. Wilson, *The Wound and the Bow*, p. 91.

44

This reminds us of the hallucinations of patients. Sometimes it is easier to hear persecuting, threatening, mocking or belittling voices than to become aware of one's utter solitude. Many of Dickens's Christmas Books and Christmas Stories deal with lonely people who converse with a ghost, much as Dickens imagined the prisoners to be in the habit of doing. Sometimes the ghost stands for the irretrievable past, for instance in *The Haunted Man* or *The Haunted House*. Not always are the ghosts in these stories benevolent; the signalman, for example, is haunted to death by the phantom he sees. But wherever they turn up they indicate that there is a person who is isolated, withdrawn, and lonely, who has no close relations with other people. In his tale *Nurse's Stories* Dickens muses on the fate of Robinson Crusoe and pictures "the hut where Robinson lived with the dog and the parrot and the cat, and where he endured those first agonies of solitude, which – strange to say – never involved any ghostly fancies; a circumstance so remarkable, that perhaps he left out something in writing his record" (*UT & RP, OID,* 149). In other words, Dickens cannot imagine a solitude which is not relieved by ghosts. Does Christmas, then, the celebration of love, remind Dickens of the love he had not received? It is common knowledge that the suicide-rate is particularly high at this time of the year; Dickens apparently belongs to the vast group of people who, never so keenly as at Christmas time, feel the discrepancy between what should be and what is.

Dickens's divided image of himself, his deep dread of being found wanting, made him very intolerant. In his conflicts with his publishers, with the American press and, most importantly, with his wife Catherine, Dickens revived his old search for the guilty party. In order to override his inner voice which told him that he was the villain, he had to blame the other, to prove that the other was bad. Unfortunately, Dickens could never break free of this pattern of thinking. Even the originally planned title for *Little Dorrit, Nobody's Fault,* is no sign of his awareness that this search for a culprit is futile, that, for instance, his parents could not help being the way they were, that it was neither his fault nor theirs. The title *Nobody's Fault* meant for him that dreadful things happened and that nobody wanted to be responsible for them.

The biblical saying "he, that is not with me, is against me" applies to Dickens. People who helped Catherine could not be his friends any more. Even such an old friend as Mark Lemon suddenly became his mortal enemy. If they did not condemn her, this meant that they accused him.

Ada Nisbet is right when she says:

> The total impression after reading through Dickens's correspondence during the months before and after the separation is that Dickens was seized by a sense of panic that the discovery of the real skeleton in his cupboard would destroy him.[69]

The real skeleton in his cupboard was nothing else but his childhood misery. It seems to me that Dickens not only tried to keep up appearances in holding Catherine back. Although he was aware of their estrangement, he probably felt betrayed when Catherine – almost forced to the step by her relations – left him. Dickens intuitively felt the connection between his childhood suffering and the failure of his marriage when he wrote to Forster in 1862:

> I must entreat you to pause for an instant, and go back to what you know of my childish days, and to ask yourself whether it is natural that something of the character formed in me then, and lost under happier circumstances, should have reappeared in the last five

69 Ada Nisbet, *Dickens and Ellen Ternan*, p. 46.

years. The never to be forgotten misery of that old time, bred a certain shrinking sensitiveness in a certain ill-clad, ill-fed child, that I have found come back in the never to be forgotten misery of this later time (*Letters,* III, 297).

## 1.4 Dealing With the Past

There are various ways of dealing with painful childhood experiences. The importance of mourning has been mentioned. By being sad about what has gone wrong and by thus accepting the fact that the past cannot be changed, one ceases to attempt to correct it in a repetition compulsion. Instead of walking the old paths in endless variations and searching for unattainable goals, one can then find new ways of being and relating to people. However, there is always the temptation to glorify the past. Very often, for instance, we hear people declare that the beatings they received as children did them good. We are probably more apt to view the past through rose-coloured spectacles if the covered-up emotions are very intense and very painful.

Another form of dealing with the past – often combining denial and mourning – may be a mastery by creating a work of art. But – as Müller-Braunschweig and Auchter have shown[70] – the ability to mourn is a prerequisite of creativity and therefore, with Dickens as with others, creativity cannot be equated with productivity.

"How is mourning possible?"[71] we might ask with Martha Wolfenstein. This is such a complex and complicated question that I can only hazard a few remarks which seem relevant to an understanding of Dickens. Wolfenstein contends that only after adolescence is a human being capable of mourning. A child who has lost a parent cannot as yet fulfil this grief work. Wolfenstein understands the separation of the adolescent from his parents as a "trial mourning" which enables him to face later losses of loved persons with the mourning reaction. However, this developmental task becomes impossible if there is too large an admixture of hatred in the attachment between parents and child.

Freud and Abraham described the mourning reaction after the death of a loved person.[72] An introjection and temporary overcathexis of the loved object takes place and is followed by a gradual decathexis which Freud describes thus:

> [Die Aufgabe, alle Libido aus ihren Verknüpfungen mit dem Objekt abzuziehen,] wird nun im einzelnen unter grossem Aufwand von Zeit und Besetzungsenergie durchgeführt und unterdes die Existenz des verlorenen Objektes psychisch fortgesetzt. Jede einzelne

70 Hans Müller-Braunschweig, "Psychoanalyse und Kreativität", in: *Psyche,* vol. 31 (1977), pp. 821-843; Thomas Auchter, "Trauer und Kreativität", *Psyche,* vol. 32 (1978), pp. 52-77. Auchter says: "Kreativität ist eine Form des Umgangs mit der Versehrtheit menschlichen Lebens, eine Trauerarbeit, ausgelöst durch das Leben als Sterben. ... Das kreative Individuum aber ist begabt mit einer *spezifischen 'Fähigkeit zu trauern'* "; ibid. p. 74, emphasis Auchter's.
71 Martha Wolfenstein, "How Is Mourning Possible?", *The Psychoanalytic Study of the Child,* vol. 21 (1966), pp. 93-123.
72 Sigmund Freud, "Trauer und Melancholie", *Studienausgabe,* vol. III, pp. 194-212; Karl Abraham, "Versuch einer Entwicklungsgeschichte der Libido auf Grund der Psychoanalyse seelischer Störungen", in: *Psychoanalytische Studien I,* Frankfurt/M. 1971 (originally 1924), pp. 113-183.

der Erinnerungen und Erwartungen, in denen die Libido an das Objekt geknüpft war, wird eingestellt, übersetzt und an ihr die Lösung der Libido vollzogen.[73]

Similar processes take place in an adolescent's mind. If, however, the relationship between parents and child was a highly ambivalent one, an introjection and overcathexis of the introjected object results not only in a temporary enhancement of the love for, but also of the hatred of, the love object. This transient emphasis of aggression can be very threatening and therefore may be avoided so that a real separation never takes place. It seems that Dickens was not able to face his own aggression and that he therefore created his sickly sweet heroines. They have to be so saintly and angelic in order to cover up his deep distrust of womankind. In their idealization they express the warded-off aggression as well as Dickens's deep longing for motherly tenderness and affection.

Sometimes Dickens very nearly makes this connection explicit. Consider, for example, the following incidents in *Little Dorrit:*
Coming home from China, the autobiographical hero Arthur Clennam meets his former fiancée, Flora Finching. He hasn't seen her for many years and instead of finding the slender and beautiful girl he used to know, he is confronted with a fat and garrulous woman and is deeply disappointed.

> When he got to his lodging, he sat down before the dying fire, as he had stood at the window of his old room looking out upon the blackened forest of chimneys, and turned his gaze back upon the gloomy vista by which he had come to that stage in his existence. So long, so bare, so blank. No childhood; no youth, except for one remembrance; that one remembrance proved, only that day, to be a piece of folly.
> It was a misfortune to him, trifle as it might have been to another. For, while all that was hard and stern in his recollection, remained Reality on being proved – was obdurate to the sight and touch, and relaxed nothing of its old indomitable grimness – the one tender recollection of his experience would not bear the same test, and melted away (206).

It is well known that in this episode with Flora Finching Dickens is describing the meeting between Maria Winter, née Beadnell, and himself many years after their separation. Against all reason Dickens had ardently hoped and expected to find his lovely young maiden again or, in other words, to regain the past, only alas, to meet the middle-aged, matronly Maria who made it perfectly clear to him that he was no longer a youth, either. Arthur Clennam, however, is comforted in his sorrow:

> That he should have missed so much, and at this time of life should look so far about him for any staff to bear him company upon his downward journey and cheer it, was a just regret. (...) (...) 'From the unhappy suppression of my youngest days, through the rigid and unloving home that followed them, through my departure, my long exile, my return, my mother's welcome, my intercourse with her since, down to the afternoon of this day with poor Flora', said Arthur Clennam, 'what have I found!'
> His door was softly opened, and these spoken words startled him, and came as if they were an answer:
> 'Little Dorrit.' (207)

Dickens, too, needed the comfort of his Little Dorrits, his impeccable, all-giving, all-loving heroines who are called Rose Maylie, Little Nell, Florence Dombey, Esther Summerson, Agnes Wickfield, Little Dorrit, Ruth Pinch, Lucie Manette or Kate

73 Sigmund Freud, "Trauer und Melancholie", p. 199.

Nickleby. Even Dickens lovers agree that Dickens's major shortcoming as a writer lies in this area and that he has been productive but not creative in this field. Owing to his inability to face his ambivalence conflict he had to resort to splitting mechanisms and he could never entirely move away from the angel/witch pattern. For this "great defect of the Dickensian universe", Angus Wilson says, "the absence of any real sympathy with, or understanding for, women, I can see no compensation".[74] Wilson considers Dickens's unhappy love of Maria Beadnell the source of Dickens's "imaginative failure" and he even connects this frustrating love-affair with the way Dickens experienced his mother during his work at the blacking factory. When, however, he goes on to defend the real Mrs. Dickens and demonstrates how 'good-natured' and 'commonsensical' she was, this is off the point. Parents are incomprehensible to, and unempathic with, their children not because they are "bad" but because they have suffered themselves and, as Mrs. Miller has argued, the skeleton in the cupboard – i.e. the parents' unconscious wishes and needs – is felt by their own children and not by other people.[75]

We have talked about Dickens's divided self-representations. In his fiction, in which he pictured himself in all his forsaken and lonely children, he portrays the "child of grace" on the one hand and the "child of wrath" on the other. The child of grace is "the principle of Good surviving through every adverse circumstance, and triumphing at last",[76] to quote the description of little Oliver, whose inherent goodness remains unscathed. Although he has never been loved, has not even been given enough to eat, is beaten and abused, he can constantly return good for evil. "All's well that ends well", as we see once he is taken care of by Mr. Brownlow or the Maylies; no permanent harm has been done. As Zwerdling aptly puts it:

> Dickens characteristically resorts to fantasy whenever his sharp eye for human suffering has uncovered more than he can bear to contemplate.[77]

and

> Dickens's vision of society depends on the idea of victimization, on the absolute separation of the oppressors from the oppressed. That the oppressed ones can go on to become oppressors in their turn is an example of the sort of pessimistic conclusion his fantasy exists to deny.[77]

The host of his saintly, incorruptible children seem to tell us the story of the victimized, innocent little Dickens time and again. And yet, we can also discern another message, namely his conviction that, had he been good enough, as good as little Oliver or little Dick (!) in his first child-novel, he would have been rewarded like them by love – be it the love of a parental figure (such as that of the Maylies, Mr. Brownlow, the Cheeryble brothers or Mr. Jarndyce) or the love of a marital partner (such as that of Allan Woodcourt or Agnes Wickfield). But even these saintly children can often obtain the longed-for tender care only by dying. They are reunited

---

74  Angus Wilson, *The World of Charles Dickens*, p. 59.
75  Alice Miller, *Das Drama des begabten Kindes und die Suche nach dem wahren Selbst* says on p. 48: "Jeder Mensch hat wohl in sich eine mehr oder weniger vor sich selbst verborgene Kammer, in der sich die Requisiten seines Kindheitsdramas befinden. Vielleicht ist es sein geheimer Wahn, seine geheime Perversion oder ganz schlicht der unbewältigte Teil seines Kinderleidens. Die einzigen Menschen, die mit Sicherheit Zutritt zu dieser Kammer bekommen werden, sind seine Kinder."
76  Charles Dickens, "Preface", *Oliver Twist*, p. 33.
77  Alex Zwerdling, "Esther Summerson Rehabilitated", *PMLA*, vol. 88 (1973), p. 438.

in death with a loving person who is awaiting them. As in the fantasy of suicides,[78] death is not a frightening experience in the Dickens world but a happy reunion with kind and affectionate people. Little Dick dreams before his death "of Heaven and Angels and kind faces" (*OT,* 97), Little Nell and Paul Dombey are reunited with their dead mothers, Jo with "OUR FATHER WHICH ART IN HEAVEN" and the protagonist in *A Child's Dream of a Star* with mother, sister, brother and daughter. Even Smike dies contentedly because he will be buried near the spot where the little girl Kate Nickleby once fell asleep and he thus feels united with her.

There are also the children of wrath – frightening little monsters devoid of any humanity such as the nameless boy in *The Haunted Man* or Deputy Winks in *The Mystery of Edwin Drood*. This is Dickens's description of Deputy:

> John Jasper ... is brought to a standstill by the spectacle of Stony Durdles ... and a hideous small boy in rags flinging stones at him as a well-defined mark in the moonlight. Sometimes the stones hit him, and sometimes they miss him, but Durdles seems indifferent to either fortune. The hideous small boy, on the contrary, whenever he hits Durdles, blows a whistle of triumph through a jagged gap, convenient for the purpose, in the front of his mouth, where half his teeth are wanting; and whenever he misses him, yelps out 'Mulled agin!' and tries to atone for the failure by taking a more correct and vicious aim. 'What are you doing to the man?' demands Jasper ...
> 'Making a cock-shy of him,' replies the hideous boy.
> 'Give me the stones in your hand.'
> 'Yes, I'll give 'em you down your throat, if you come a-ketching hold of me,' says the small boy, shaking himself loose, and backing. 'I'll smash your eye, if you don't look out!' 'Baby-Devil that you are, what has the man done to you?' 'He won't go home.' 'What is that to you?' 'He gives me a 'apenny to pelt him home if I ketches him out too late,' says the boy. And then chants, like a little savage, half stumbling and half dancing among the rags and laces of his dilapidated boots:
> > 'Widdy, widdy wen!
> > I-ket-ches-Im-out-ar-ter-ten,
> > Widdy, widdy wy!
> > Then-E-don't-go-then-I-shy-
> > Widdy, Widdy Wake-cock warning!'
> – with a comprehensive sweep on the last word, and one more delivery at Durdles. (*ED,* 71-72)

The "Baby-Devil", the "hideous small boy", the chanting "little savage" who throws stones at a man as if he were a doorpost, is aggression personified. His task of pelting Durdles to his house is a caricature of the parental responsibility to offer the child a home. And his chanting song endows him with the magical powers of a ✗ Music medicine-man. His is the untamed aggression of an infant. That is why he is called a "*Baby*-Devil" just as the boy in *The Haunted Man* is referred to as a "baby savage" (emphasis mine).

We can understand that Dickens's holy children have to be protected against such aggression. Only rarely does Dickens show in a symbolic way that the savage is an integral part of ourselves and should be accepted as such. An inkling of this conviction emerges in *The Haunted Man,* where Redlaw at first abhors the boy and is then moved to cover him compassionately with a blanket.

78 Cp. Heinz Henseler, "Die Suizidhandlung im Lichte der psychoanalytischen Narzissmus-theorie", *Psyche,* vol. 28 (1974), 203.

The two sets of children are by no means unconnected. In his highly sensitive essay, "Esther Summerson Rehabilitated", Alex Zwerdling points out how Dickens portrays in the coy, virtuous Esther the maimed child to whom love does not come naturally but who has to earn it by being "industrious, contented, and kind-hearted" (*BH*, 65). As Zwerdling rightly points out, Esther is convinced of her basic unworthiness and is even ready to marry the elderly Mr. Jarndyce as she has no right to a lover, for "her romantic nature is much more completely crushed than her intelligence".[79] The happy end, namely Esther's marriage to Woodcourt, is not convincing; it is not the logical outcome of Esther's inner situation. To quote Zwerdling once more:

> Everything in her narrative has stressed the potent nature of her conflicts and the feebleness of her own will in dealing with them. Indeed, she must not even allow herself to acknowledge them. Such a situation demands a tragic ending – or a deus ex machina. Dickens chooses the latter. Esther's decision is made for her by Jarndyce, who surrenders her to Woodcourt without even consulting her. The whole scene is dominated by magical and fantastic elements inherent in the situation. Where conflict was, there harmony shall be.[80]

It seems that the child of grace is a child of wrath, after all. Dickens, who has so plausibly portrayed Esther in her struggles, cannot free her from the long-term effects of her childhood deprivation in any convincing way.

In *George Silverman's Explanation,* the last story he completed, Dickens is better able to grasp the fate of a child who considers himself utterly bad. George Silverman remembers his childhood as one series of reproaches:

> Whether I cried for that I was in the dark, or for that it was cold, or for what I was hungry, or whether I squeezed myself into a warm corner when there was a fire, or ate voraciously when there was food, she would still say, "O you worldly little devil!" (*UT & RP, OID*, 730)

The most natural strivings of the child are condemned as "worldly" or "selfish" and the child has no alternative but to accept this judgement and condemn himself, too. The tragedy is that it is precisely because of this early harsh accusation that he does indeed become preoccupied with himself. His parents die of an infectious fever and the surviving little boy is "camphored and vinegared and disinfected in a variety of ways" and sent into the country "to be purified" (*UT & RP, OID,* 733). Unlike Esther, who is "happy ever after", George Silverman is permanently wounded. His fear of being found "a young vampire" or "a rat" makes him willingly renounce not only his inheritance but also the woman he loves and who loves him. George Silverman, we hear, is "always in the shadow looking on" (*UT & RP, OID,* 746).

After the completion of the story Dickens wrote to his sub-editor Wills:

> Upon myself, it has made the strangest impression of reality and originality!! And I feel as if I had read something (by somebody else) which I should never get out of my head!! (*Letters*, III, 533)

It is not surprising that Dickens experienced this story as being written by somebody else. In his fiction he found an access to his feelings which was denied to him otherwise. What happened to his characters was close enough to move him and remote enough to protect him against being overwhelmed. The most repressed part of his self-representations could only gradually emerge and find its lasting expression in

---

79 Alex Zwerdling, "Esther Summerson Rehabilitated", p. 433.
80 Alex Zwerdling, "Esther Summerson Rehabilitated", p. 437.

Deputy. And only towards the end of his career could Dickens face the fact that permanent harm can be done to a child. We could say, then, that by describing his childhood tragedy in various ways Dickens found an outlet for his mourning but that there were limitations to what he could achieve in this respect. He wrote eight novels with children as heroes and heroines, namely: *Oliver Twist, The Old Curiosity Shop, Dombey and Son, David Copperfield, Bleak House, Hard Times, Little Dorrit* and *Great Expectations. Hard Times* stands apart from the rest of these novels: its difference from them is recognized. Critics disagree, however, as to whether it is superior or inferior to the remaining seven.[81] It is rather obvious that these seven novels deal with Dickens's own sufferings, thinly disguised, and that by weeping over the sad lot of his children Dickens weeps about himself. *Hard Times,* on the other hand, is not primarily a repetition of his childhood but – as Warrington Winters has shown – a reversal of it. Mr. Gradgrind, who crams his children and his pupils with hard facts can in no way be compared with Dickens's volatile father. This is not to say that Dickens has freed himself from his childhood experiences. On the contrary; even here they are crucial. Winters puts it thus:

> Dickens set out in *Hard Times* to show that the home of the entertainer is the special source of the happy childhood. That he failed is hardly surprising. After all, he himself had observed precisely the opposite phenomenon: that an entertaining father is an unreliable father and the sponsor not of a happy childhood, but of a lost childhood.[82]

Winters also draws attention to the similarities between Bounderby and Dickens himself. In view of this resemblance it is highly revealing that at the end of the book Bounderby is exposed as a fraud. He is the "Bully of humility", priding himself on having risen from the gutter:

> 'I hadn't a shoe to my foot. As to a stocking, I didn't know such a thing by name. I passed the day in a ditch, and the night in a pigsty. That's the way I spent my tenth birthday. Not that a ditch was new to me, for I was born in a ditch.' (*HT,* 59)

After telling Mrs. Gradgrind that he "was born with inflammation of the lungs, and of everything else, I believe, that was capable of inflammation" and that he was therefore always "moaning and groaning" and that he was so ragged and dirty that she "wouldn't have touched him with a pair of tongs" he declares:

> 'How I fought through it, I don't know ... I was determined, I suppose. I have been a determined character in later life, and I suppose I was then. Here I am, Mrs. Gradgrind, anyhow, and nobody to thank for my being here but myself!' (*HT,* 59)

Bounderby's fantasy is not too different from Dickens's own. It is true that Dickens was not brought up in the gutter, in the literal sense of the term; yet he did feel as if he had been thrown away as if, indeed, he were a dirty and repulsive object, as has been shown. The absence of shoes and stockings in Bounderby's account stand for the lack of protection against the cold. And indeed, Bounderby feels that he was born with inflammation, that he was sore all over. Dickens, too, was sickly as a child and in his attacks of kidney spasms was "moaning and groaning", and, like Bounderby, he determined to fight his way through and felt that he owed no thanks to his parents. In

81 For the different views of the critics see Edward Hurley, "A Missing Childhood in *Hard Times*", *Victorian Newsletter* 42 (1972), pp. 11-16.
82 Warrington Winters, "Dickens' *Hard Times*. The Lost Childhood", *Dickens Studies Annual*, vol. 2 (1972), p.235.

*Hard Times,* however, we get to know Bounderby's mother, Mrs. Pegler. When she is charged with having forsaken her son when he was a child, she indignantly answers:

> '*I* deserted my Josiah!' cried Mrs. Pegler, clasping her hands. 'Now, Lord forgive you, sir, for your wicked imaginations ... 'Josiah in the gutter? ... No such a thing, sir. Never! For shame on you! My dear boy knows, and will give *you* to know, that though he come of humble parents, he come of parents that loved him as dear as the best could, and never thought it hardship on themselves to pinch a bit that he might write and cipher beautiful, and I've his books at home to show it! Aye, have I!' (*HT,* 280)

In a wishful fantasy Dickens endows Mrs. Pegler with the very qualities he wished his parents would have possessed. She is devoted to her son and "pinches" so as to be able to afford an education for him. The pension Bounderby has granted his mother is "more than I want, for I put by out of it"; Mrs. Pegler keeps out of her son's way when she is not wanted and comes regularly to his house to look at him in silent and secret admiration.

It is as if Dickens tried to wipe away his psychic realities. Whereas he complained in the autobiographical fragment that

> no one had compassion enough on me ... to suggest that something might have been spared, as certainly it might have been, to place me at any common school. Our friends, I take it, were tired out. No one made any sign. My father and mother were quite satisfied. They could hardly have been more so, if I had been twenty years of age, distinguished at a grammar-school, and going to Cambridge ("AF", 21),

he now creates a mother who sacrifices some of her comfort to the education of her son. His own parents could not live with the money he gave them but always wanted more, Mrs. Pegler, however, can even save from her pension. And, in contrast to Elizabeth and John Dickens, who objected to being sent off to Devon, Mrs. Pegler does not disturb Bounderby with her presence.

Dickens expresses here the natural egoism of the infant who wants his mother to be with him when he nees her and to disappear when she is not longer wanted.[83] Mrs. Pegler even gives Bounderby the adoration Dickens so much craved for. In the character of Bounderby Dickens is expressing the hope that his trials were only "wicked imaginations".

In *Hard Times* Dickens accuses Gradgrind – the opposite image of his own father – on the one hand and on the other puts the blame on the son Bounderby, who cannot appreciate his wonderful mother.

The old conflict of "Who is the guilty one?" has found a new solution. However, having been raised by the loving Mrs. Pegler, how could Bounderby have become a Bounderby? Taking the blame upon himself is one way of expressing the glorification of the past that we have talked about.

Dickens, in other words, can deal with the past in two different ways. He can either deny and reverse it, as in *Hard Times,* or he can re-live and weep about it as in the other child novels.[84] The division of the critics into the Leavis-group (i.e. those who with Leavis consider *Hard Times* Dickens's best book) and the anti-Leavis-group (i.e.

83 See Alice Balint (1939), "Liebe zur Mutter und Mutterliebe", in: Michael Balint, *Die Urformen der Liebe und die Technik der Psychoanalyse,* Stuttgart 1966, pp. 116-135.
84 This generalization is made for the sake of clarity. If they were analysed in detail we could find in all of Dickens's novels both the acknowledging and denying attitude, but in varying proportions.

those who prefer Dickens's other novels to *Hard Times*) might well be connected with this basic difference in Dickens's approach. In *Hard Times* he was, so to speak, further removed from his own fate. This may have reduced his spontaneity but at the same time furthered his artistic control over his subject matter. He was therefore less apt to utter the sentimentalities he is so often accused of. The following is a typical comment on Dickens, standing for many similar verdicts:

> It needs only half an eye to detect the sentimentalities, especially towards children, to discern the poor little drudge of the blacking factory, corroding his feelings in torrents of self-pity. He is there on almost every other page. But it is the other page, between, that deserves its due attention.[85]

Covenay's opinion seems to contradict our emphasis on the importance of mourning as a prerequisite for creativeness. However, if we apply to "sentimentality" the definition given by Steven Marcus, the concepts of literary criticism come close to those of psychoanalysis.

Marcus says about the conditions which generate sentimentality:

> One of these conditions, I suggest, is the presence, consciously or unconsciously, of a memory around which a large reservoir of painful feelings has accrued, feelings charged with the antipathies and suppressions of the experience from which the memory grew. Whenever, therefore, its recollection takes place, or whenever situations occur which call forth the memory for whatever reason and in whatever form, the floodgates of all this accumulation of feeling are forced open, and one might seem in danger of being overwhelmed, were it not for that faculty of the mind to repress and distort whatever feelings it finds too unpleasant to know – though it cannot, in natures such as Dickens's, repress altogether the feelings themselves. The result of this process we call sentimentality when what we allow ourselves to *believe* we are feeling is shaped somehow to what we want to feel, to what we ought to feel, to what we think we deserve to feel – to a kind of self-deception.[86]

This "large reservoir of painful feelings" is exactly what Dickens has brought along from his childhood and the sudden opening of the floodgates is liable to occur if there has been no working-through process, no gradual remembrance and emotional experience of the original suppressed feelings.

Dickens's stilted prose, the atrocious blank verse he adopts when he is particularly moved lends itself to a channelling of these floods into the regular rhythms of his language. Dickens calls his involuntary blank verse ("I run into it, involuntarily and unconsciously, when I am very much in earnest. I even do so, in speaking", *PE,* IV, 113), "a very melodious and agreeable march of words" (ibid.), thus expressing his desire for structuring his emotions; his verse serves as a kind of dirge. To Forster he writes: "If in going over the proofs you find the tendency to blank verse ... too strong, knock out a word's brains here and there" (*PE,* IV, 656). By personifying his words he endows them with some sort of magical power.

When thinking of Marcus's definition that "we call sentimentality when what we allow ourselves to *believe* we are feeling is shaped somehow to what we want to feel", we might ask ourselves what Dickens does want to feel and what feelings he avoids. In the pathetic death scenes of his novels, for example, Dickens wants to convey to the

---

85 Peter Covenay, *Poor Monkey*. The Child in Literature, London 1957, p. 72.
86 Steven Marcus, *Dickens: From Pickwick to Dombey,* London 1965, pp. 159-160, emphasis Marcus's.

reader a sort of dignified, elevated, solemn sadness about the death of a child. This child, – as we have seen – has either been loved or will be clasped to a loving bosom and serves as a symbol of the love between human beings and an admonition to the surviving relatives and friends to keep up that love between them. In *The Old Curiosity Shop* the schoolmaster preaches to Nell the moral that "There is nothing, ... no nothing innocent or good, that dies, and is forgotten. Let us hold to that faith, or none" (*OCS*, 503). And yet, Dickens confesses the following feelings when he has to "kill" Nell (as he expresses it):

> Nobody will miss her like I shall. It is such a painful thing to me, that I really cannot express my sorrow. Old wounds bleed afresh when I only think of the way of doing it: what the actual doing will be, God knows. I can't preach to myself the schoolmaster's consolation, though I try. (*PE*, II, 181-82)

The obvious interpretation, namely that Dickens refers here with the "old wounds" to the death of his sister-in-law Mary Hogarth, whom he idealized much as he did Little Nell, is not quite adequate. Much earlier in his life he had to bear the death of two close relations, of a little brother and a little sister. It seems evident that Dickens's emotions at their deaths could not have been so self-forgetful as he describes them in his fiction. It is, of course, impossible for us to know them. What one would expect are feelings of fright (at his supposed power), of guilt (about his aggression and about the fact that he survived), of anger (at their leaving him behind by dying, at his parents' preoccupation with them), of loneliness (there was nobody to take care of his feelings). In his fiction the fantasied merger of the dead child with a loving mother figure might reflect what he felt had happened, namely that his mother was in her thoughts with his dead brother and sister and not with him. But the hostility such an experience could have aroused is warded off by turning the dying child as well as the mother figure into angels. Angel comes home to angel, and angels are no apt butts for the release of aggression. In this way Dickens could in the death scenes re-live the earlier experiences and at the same time deny their emotional impact.

If, in other words, Dickens tries to relieve the suffering of his fancy children (and thus of himself) either by making them "incorruptible", i.e. making them possess and retain an (inborn) capacity for love, whatever be done to them, or by uniting them with an all-loving mother figure, he becomes unconvincing and sentimental. If, however, he succeeds in facing the consequences of a deprived childhood, he is capable of an extraordinary identification with the outcast. Innumerable examples of this Dickensian faculty could be quoted; the image of the bewildered Affery who, in her confusion, throws her apron over her head in order to protect herself against unknown dangers; of Magwitch eating ravenously like a dog on the marshes; of the "infant phenomenon" who is stunted in her growth by being "kept up late every night and put upon an unlimited allowance of gin and water from infancy, to prevent her growing tall" (*NN, OID,* 290); or of Bradley Headstone's helpless rage at the superciliousness of Eugene Wrayburn and Mortimer Lightwood. The following is Dickens's attempt to step into the shoes of Jo, the crossing-sweeper in *Bleak House:*

> It must be a strange state to be like Jo! To shuffle through the streets, unfamiliar with the shapes and in utter darkness as to the meaning, of those mysterious symbols, so abundant over the shops, and the corner of streets, and on the doors, and in the windows! To see people read, and to see people write, and to see the postman deliver letters, and not to have the least idea of all that language – to be to every scrap of it, stone blind and dumb!

(...) To be hustled, and jostled, and moved on; and really to feel that it would appear to be perfectly true that I have no business here, or there, or anywhere; and yet to be perplexed by the consideration that I *am* here somehow, too, and everybody overlooked me until I became the creature that I am! It must be a strange state, not merely to be told that I am scarcely human ... but to feel it of mine own knowledge all my life! (*BH*, 274)

We feel that the identifying "I" Dickens suddenly uses is not fortuitous, and the following scene, in which Jo is caught by a policeman, makes it clear that Dickens knew what it meant to be always in the way and to have nowhere to go:

'This boy,' says the constable, 'although he's repeatedly told to, won't move on –'
'I'm always a-moving on, sir,' cries the boy, wiping away his grimy tears with his arm. 'I've always been a-moving and a-moving on, ever since I was born. Where can I possibly move to, sir, more nor I do move!'
'He won't move on,' says the constable, calmly, with a slight professional hitch of his neck involving its better settlement in his stiff stock, 'although he has been repeatedly cautioned, and therefore I am obliged to take him into custody. He's as obstinate a young gonoph [i.e. pickpocket] as I know. He WON'T move on.'
'O my eye! Where can I move to!' cries the boy, clutching quite desperately at his hair, and beating his bare feet upon the floor of Mr. Snagsby's passage.
'Don't you come none of that, or I shall make blessed short work of you!' says the constable, giving him a passionless shake. 'My instructions are, that you are to move on. I have told you so five hundred times.'
'But where?' cries the boy. (*BH*, 319-20)

Dickens, however, is not only known for his pathos but also for his wit and humour. His humour and his pathos are intimately connected. It has often been noted, for instance, that Dickens ridicules in his minor characters the very character traits he praises in his heroes and heroines. In *Martin Chuzzlewit* we find the following description of the lovely Ruth Pinch:

Pleasant little Ruth! Cheerful, tidy, bustling, quiet little Ruth! (...) To be Tom's housekeeper. What dignity! (...) Well might she take the keys out of the little chiffonier which held the tea and sugar; and out of the two damp cupboards down by the fire-place, where the very black beetles got mouldy, and had the shine taken out of their backs by envious mildew; and jingle them upon a ring before Tom's eyes when he came down to breakfast! Well might she, laughing musically, put them up in that blessed little pocket of hers with a merry pride! (*MC*, 672)

Charity Pecksniff, on the other hand, fulfilling her household duties, is described thus:

Truly Mr. Pecksniff is blessed in his children. In one of them, at any rate. The prudent Cherry – staff and scrip, treasure of her doting father – there she sits, at a little table white as driven snow, before the kitchen fire, making up accounts! See the neat maiden, as with pen in hand, and calculating look addressed towards the ceiling, and bunch of keys within a little basket at her side, she checks the housekeeping expenditure! (*MC*, 397)

Though this may not be obvious, the aggression which Dickens has suppressed in dealing with the adorable Ruth Pinch is displaced on the anti-heroine, the shrewish Charity, and there released in his wit. The same verbal style serves in one instance to praise and in the other to ridicule. Words like "blessed", "cheerful", "white as driven snow", as well as the jingling of the housekeeping keys are stock properties in Dickens's description of young women. And it is curious to note that the mocking phrase "the neat maiden" could be inserted by Dickens in one of his sentimental passages in full earnest and without any alteration. Only the adjectives "prudent" and "calculating" in the description of Charity are indications of Dickens's irony: Charity is not really charitable or cherry-lipped but only seems to be so. She displays her feminine virtues with a definite aim, namely that of capturing a husband.

Another example of Dickens's mocking of himself is the description of Mrs. Chirrup in *The Nice Little Couple*. This is Dickens talking:

> Mrs. Chirrup is the prettiest of all little women, and has the prettiest little figure conceivable. She has the neatest little foot, and the softest little voice, and the pleasantest smile, and the tidiest little curls, and the brightest little eyes, and the quietest little manner, and is, in short, altogether one of the most engaging of all little women, dead or alive. She is a condensation of all domestic virtues, – a pocket edition of the young man's best companion, – a little woman at a very high pressure, with an amazing quantity of goodness and usefulness in an exceedingly small space. (*SB, OID,* 584)

Dickens's humour allows him a relatively "guilt-free release of aggression".[87] He allows himself the mocking disdain of Charity because he feels justified in attacking such a cunning and artful creature. What has been left out in his pathetic scenes, namely his bitterness, comes to the fore with a vengeance. In describing Dickens's comedy, Carey provocatively states that "Dickens has stopped feeling and has started to write well",[88] thus pointing to the fact that Dickens's comic scenes are often superior to his sad and lofty comments on the fate of his deprived children. In his comedy Dickens gives us an unparalleled richness of images, of speech mannerisms, of gestures, and even of clothes coming alive, as is the case with Mrs. Gamp's dresses which, although put on a peg, still show their inhabitant's silhouette. As Carey has pointed out, the prerequisite for creating such comedy is the writer's aloofness or – to speak with Bergson –

> *l'insensibilité* qui accompagne d'ordinaire le rire. Il semble que le comique ne puisse produire son ébranlement qu'à la condition de tomber sur une surface d'âme bien calme, bien unie. L'indifférence est son milieu naturel. Le rire n'a pas de plus grand ennemi que l'émotion.[89]

It is, however, the lack of a particular feeling, namely the feeling of sympathy with, or concern for, the ridiculed person which enables Dickens to laugh. We can only laugh at the mishaps of another human being if we adopt the oberserver's stance. Watching somebody stumble, for example, can give us a feeling of superiority. We did not stumble – the other one did. We saw it happen, but *it* happened to the stumbler. We can also laugh at ourselves by dividing into an observing and an observed part. The lack of concern is in both cases essentially the same. We know from Dickens himself that early in life he developed his powers of observation. In his autobiographical fragment he tells Forster that his father drew up a petition on the part of the prisoners, asking permission to drink "His Majesty's health on His Majesty's forthcoming birthday" (Forster's words not Dickens's, *F*, I, 30). This is Dickens speaking:

> I mention the circumstance because it illustrates, to me, my early interest in observing people. When I went to the Marshalsea ... and when I heard of this approaching ceremony, I was so anxious to see them all come in, one after another ... that I got leave of absence on purpose, and established myself in a corner, near the petition. (...)

87 Martin Grotjahn, *Beyond Laughter,* New York 1957, p. ix.
88 John Carey, *The Violent Effigy*. A study of Dickens' imagination, London 1973, p. 71.
89 Henri Bergson, "Le rire" (1900), in: *Œuvres,* Paris 1959, p. 388, emphasis Bergson's.

Whatever was comical in this scene, and whatever was pathetic, I sincerely believe I perceived in my corner, whether I demonstrated or not, quite as well as I should perceive it now ("AF", 30).

In this scene – comical and pathetic as Dickens's books – he was with his father and the other prisoners but was not involved in the situation as they were; he was looking on from a safe distance. To gifted people, such as Dickens, the observer's position offers an invaluable opportunity of mastering difficult and potentially traumatic events.

But Dickens's humour was also often of another kind. It isn't simply characterized by the absence of sympathy but – as we have seen in the example of Charity – by the release of aggression against the ridiculed person.[90]

Kincaid and Carey have carefully analysed Dickens's text and have shown that very often Dickens encourages us to laugh at his victims[91], for example at the starving children in the workhouse in *Oliver Twist* or at the neglected boys at Dotheboys Hall in *Nicholas Nickleby*. In these instances our "comfortable aloofness" as Kincaid renders Bergson's "insensibilité", turns into the vice of callousness. We can laugh at little Oliver, who is told to "bow to the board" of the workhouse and "seeing no board but the table, fortunately bowed to that". But when he is described as crying and being hit by the beadle, we feel ashamed of our laughter and suddenly realise the isolation of this little boy, who is not even addressed in a language that he can understand. Thus, Kincaid contends, Dickens cleverly traps us into laughter to make us aware of our own callousness. He then takes advantage of our ensuing feelings of guilt:

> Our laughter is a necessary part of the proper reaction to the novel, but in the end it is used against us, undercutting the comfortable aloofness we had originally maintained and forcing us into the dark world of the lonely and terrified orphan.[92]

However, Kincaid's reaction to Dickens's humour is only one of several possible responses. Carey reacts differently:

> The result of the irony is not to make social criticism more bitter. On the contrary the pity or anger we would normally feel at the sufferings of the little victims is extinguished in laughter.[93]

His example is the scene at Dotheboys Hall where the pupils are fed with treacle and brimstone, a nourishment that fills their bellies and is very cheap at the same time. This is Dickens's description:

> Mrs. Squeers stood at one of the desks, presiding over an immense basin of brimstone and treacle, of which delicious compound she administered a large instalment to each boy in succession: using for the purpose a common wooden spoon, which might have been originally manufactured for some gigantic top, and which widened every young gentleman's mouth considerably: they being all obliged, under heavy corporal penalties, to take in the whole of the bowl at a gasp. (*NN, OID,* 88-89)

90  I cannot understand at all how Cruikshank comes to the conclusion that "Dickens had in him the springs of divine laughter" and that his "humour is never mean, never spiteful. He never sniggers." It seems to me that Dickens also had in him the springs of devilish laughter. See R. J. Cruikshank, *The Humour of Dickens,* London, n.d., pp. vi, viii.
91  James R. Kincaid, "Laughter and Oliver Twist", *PMLA,* vol. 83 (1968), pp. 63-70, and *Dickens and the Rhetoric of Laughter,* Oxford 1971; John Carey, *The Violent Effigy.*
92  James R. Kincaid, "Laughter and *Oliver Twist*", p. 63.
93  John Carey, *The Violent Effigy,* p. 71.

Clearly the aggressive element of his humour is turned against the children themselves, who are no longer respected as human beings. Like inanimate objects, they consist of mouths which are being forced open. One can very well visualize the scene. In endless succession boy after boy appears before Mrs. Squeers. Wooden spoon is filled with the "delicious compound", boy's mouth forced open, spoon taken out again, filled again, next boy's mouth forced open and so on. Mrs. Squeers repeats the same few movements, as if she were standing at a conveyor-belt, an impression which is confirmed by Phiz's illustration of the scene. We can only laugh at the boys because they have become dehumanized, resembling objects, rather than human beings. As Bergson puts it:

> Ce qu'il y a de risible ... c'est une certaine *raideur de mécanique* là où l'on voudrait trouver la souplesse attentive et la vivante flexibilité d'une personne.[94]

Although Mrs. Squeers, too, resembles a machine, we cannot laugh at her, since she is a frightening, nightmarish apparition. Our feelings are too much involved with her and the laughter is directed against the children. The children are multiplied and therefore no individual beings; there is only one Mrs. Squeers and she smothers every kind of laughter at her. In this way Dickens undermines his own sympathy with the downtrodden children; Carey even accuses him of being corrupted by his disdain of human beings.[95] This scorn, however, is in the last analysis a scorn of himself. We know how much Dickens identified with his child-heroes; his disregard of their needs, his contemptuous, supercilious attitude towards them is a reflection of his lack of concern for the child in himself or of the child he once was.

In two ways, then, Dickens uses his laughter to divert the aggression from the love object: first he displaces it from the idealized heroine onto a minor figure and releases it in his ridicule of this character and secondly he undermines the reader's and his own sympathy for the victims by creating them as lifeless dummies whose mouths (in our example) can be opened by some sort of mechanical contrivance. This turning of the aggression from the object onto the self is a very frequent psychic mechanism. It seems to me that this kind of self-destructive humour is intimately connected with Dickens's urge to be wept over. People who can take care of themselves do not expect to be taken care of by others. People, however, who have not learned to look after themselves and to take their own feelings seriously will at some point rebel against this form of masochism and will expect others to make up for it. Dickens's pathetic scenes can thus be interpreted as a vindication of the same lonely little beings whom he forsakes in his laughter. A vicious circle is established. The more aggressive the attack, the holier and saintlier and more pathetic does the child become so as to compensate for it. The more the child is represented as a young saint, the less can his needs be felt, since he ultimately stands above them.

Dickens's humour, then, allows him to give vent to his anger, his scorn, and disdain, which is directed either against parental or child figures or, particularly in his later novels, against institutions and society as a whole. This aggression, which is covered up and denied by Dickens in his pious and solemn scenes, can at least be felt in this ego-syntonic form – ego-syntonic because only by using his great talent for observation can Dickens express his indignation in so brilliant a form.

94 Henri Bergson, "Le rire", p. 391.
95 John Carey, *The Violent Effigy,* p. 76.

There is, however, still another function of Dickens's humour. Very often, when intensely moved, Dickens tries to escape into a facetious tone, in order to run away from his painful feelings. To my mind it is unjust to accuse Dickens of trying to soften things down with a view to the sales of his books. It seems to me that he did not primarily fear the reaction of his public but that he himself could not stand the intensity of the feelings which were aroused in him. Hearing of the "abdication" of his friend, the actor Macready, Dickens writes:

> With the same perverse and unaccountable feeling which causes a heartbroken man at a dear friend's funeral to see something irresistibly comical in a red-nosed or one-eyed undertaker, I receive your communication with ghastly facetiousness. (*PE*, I, 539)

Dickens also describes the funeral of the radical author and publisher Hone as "a scene of mingled comicality and seriousness ... which has choked me at dinner-time ever since." Dickens drove to the funeral together with Cruikshank. After recalling that it was "muddy, foggy, wet, dark, cold, and unutterably wretched in every possible respect" his laughter surges up when he comtemplates Cruikshank's "enormous whiskers which straggle all down his throat in such weather, and stick out in front of him, like a partially unravelled bird's nest." The anticipated sadness of the funeral and the depressing weather made him feel acutely ill at ease. In this situation he lighted upon any external idiosyncrasy of a person (the whiskers, as in the example above the red nose), centred his interest on this detail and found in his laughter a way of escaping from his sadness. He even shed tears – tears of laughter instead of tears of grief: "I really cried with an irresistible sense of his comicality, all the way." They met the funeral party, which is described by Dickens:

> God knows it was miserable enough, for the widow and children were crying bitterly in one corner, and the mourners – mere people of ceremony, who cared no more for the dead man than the hearse did – were talking quite coolly and carelessly together in another; and the contrast was as painful and distressing as anything I ever saw.

Once more Dickens escaped from his feelings – this time by focussing his thoughts upon the vanity of the clergyman. He concludes his account with: "I felt that nothing but convulsions could possibly relieve me" (*PE*, III, 453-4).

We see, then, that Dickens uses his laughter as well as his tears partly to experience his own feelings once more and thus to find himself and partly to ward off those emotions which he could not bear. His books allowed him a regression similar to what a patient experiences in treatment. However, since he had to face his experiences by himself, there could only be a partial change in his psychic structures. Although he attained to a greater understanding of human beings in his fiction, he could not benefit from it in his life. His restlessness, his insomnia, his depression, his somatic symptoms grew worse, the older he became.

What is striven after in art as well as in therapy is a "regression in the service of the ego".[96] This kind of regression – i.e. a return to earlier forms of psychic experience without being overwhelmed by them – was certainly partly possible for Dickens in his writings. It is not neurosis with its repetition compulsion and its resulting repetitiveness that makes for creativity but the being open to one's own unconscious and its rich affective life. Thus Dickens could create an unparalleled intensity of atmosphere in his novels. In his own life, however, the regression was no longer in the service of his ego and he became more and more governed by it.

96 An often quoted statement by Ernst Kris, *Psychoanalytic Explorations in Art,* New York 1952.

I have mentioned that the novels *Oliver Twist, The Old Curiosity Shop, Dombey and Son, David Copperfield, Bleak House, Little Dorrit* and *Great Expectations* are variations on the fate of the forsaken child. It is a curious fact that these novels form a kind of bilateral symmetry, *David Copperfield* being the axis:

> *Oliver Twist*
> *The Old Curiosity Shop*
> *Dombey and Son*
> *David Copperfield*
> *Bleak House*
> *Little Dorrit*
> *Great Expectations*

*Oliver Twist* and *Great Expectations* deal with the growing up of a young boy; Little Nell and Little Dorrit are both devoted girls, the one to her elderly father, the other to her grandfather; Florence Dombey and Esther Summerson share their ardent striving for love and recognition. At the same time, there is a marked difference between Dickens's early and his late novels. One could even go so far as to speak of pre-Copperfieldian and post-Copperfieldian Dickens novels. Something must have happened to Dickens, some sort of inner change must have taken place when he wrote this novel, which he calls his "favourite child", feeling "as if he were dismissing some portion of himself into the shadowy world".[97] Dickens probably achieved with this novel a partial self-analysis, although – as Manheim and Manning have shown – he concealed as much as he revealed.[98] Dickens could also paint the portrait of the child-wife Dora, who is inexpressibly charming and yet vexing him, too, with her inability to run the house. When Dora dies, David is deeply affected. For the first time Dickens describes a deep and tender love for an imperfect woman and a sincere mourning reaction on the part of the hero when she dies. I think that this work of mourning enabled Charles Dickens to integrate some of his ambivalence. In his post-Copperfieldian novels he did not resort quite so often and quite so indiscriminately to those splitting mechanisms which he needed to prevent the "good" self-image and the "good" object-image from being contaminated by the "bad" one. How far did Dickens succeed in this development and where were his limits? We shall try to find out more about it by looking closely at two corresponding novels, namely *The Old Curiosity Shop* and *Little Dorrit*. Where are the parallels in Dickens's treatment of the interrelatedness of persons, where are the divergences? Can we connect them with what we have learned about Dickens up to now? In order to find answers to these questions let us first turn to Little Nell and the other characters in *The Old Curiosity Shop*.

---

97 "Preface to the Charles Dickens Edition (1969)", Penguin edition, p. 47.
98 Leonard F. Manheim, "The Personal History of David Copperfield", in: Leonard Tennen-house, ed., *The Practice of Psychoanalytic Criticism*, Detroit 1976, pp. 75-95 and Sylvia Manning, "Masking and Self-Revelation: Dickens's Three Autobiographies", *Dickens Studies Newsletter* 7 (1976), pp. 69-74.

# 2. The Old Curiosity Shop

## 2.1. Looking Through Keyholes

When reading Dickens we sometimes come across episodes that have all the signs of undisguised fantasies. Look, for instance, at the passage from *Sketches by Boz* where he tells the gruesome story of a baker who "murdered his son by boiling him in a copper". The baker, we hear, was often drunk and maltreated his wife, "half-killing her while in bed, by inserting in her mouth a considerable portion of a sheet or blanket." This can be understood as a rather outspoken fellatio fantasy, which is followed by this passage:

> "It appears in evidence, gentlemen," continued Mr. Bolton, "that on the evening of yesterday, Sawyer the baker came home in a reprehensible state of beer. Mrs. S., connubially considerate, carried him in that condition up-stairs into his chamber, and consigned him to their mutual couch. In a minute or two she lay sleeping beside the man whom the morrow's dawn beheld a murderer! (Entire silence informed the reporter that his picture had attained the awful effect he desired.) The son came home about an hour afterwards, opened the door and went up to bed. Scarcely (gentlemen, conceive his feelings of alarm), scarcely had he taken off his indescribables, when shrieks (to his experienced ear *maternal* shrieks) scared the silence of surrounding night. He put his indescribables on again, and ran down-stairs. He opened the door on the parental bed-chamber. His father was dancing upon his mother. What must have been his feelings! In the agony of the minute he rushed at his male parent as he was about to plunge a knife into the side of his female. The mother shrieked. The father caught the son (who had wrested the knife from the paternal grasp) up in his arms, carried him down-stairs, shoved him into a copper of boiling water among some linen, closed the lid, and jumped upon the top of it, in which position he was found with a ferocious countenance by the mother, who arrived in the melancholy wash-house just as he had so settled himself.

The mother calls the police, who carry the body of the boiled son to the station-house "with a promptitude commendable in men of their station". Afterwards the father is arrested "while seated on the top of a lamp-post in Parliament Street, lighting his pipe." (*SB, OID,* 684-85)

It is not very far-fetched, I think, to connect this tale with a primal scene fantasy. The primal scene, as Freud saw it, is the coitus between the parents which is witnessed by the child and misinterpreted as some sort of brutality usually inflicted on the mother by the father.[1] In our passage there are the familiar elements of the intensely charged scene between the parents, the child's being left out of it, the imagined brutality, the fantasy of saving the mother by attacking the father and the fear of his revenge. However, what is particularly Dickensian in this paragraph is the intensity of

---

1 See, for instance, Sigmund Freud, *Aus der Geschichte einer infantilen Neurose,* Studienausgabe, Bd. VIII, pp. 149-165. In his old age the patient considered Freud's interpretation of his dream artificial (Karin Obholzer, *Gespräche mit dem Wolfmann,* Reinbek bei Hamburg 1980, p. 51). While Obholzer convincingly shows how much the Wolfman suffered in his old age, her attacks on Freud and psychoanalysis via his old patient are not always fair. We know how much – owing to transference – analysands may unwittingly distort an analyst's remarks or intentions.

the terror it embodies[2] and the attempt at reducing it by a grotesque sort of humour. Dickens's interjections "Entire silence informed the reporter ...", "gentlemen, conceive his feelings of alarm", "what must have been his feelings" serve as reminders to the reader that all this is only a story, not a scene we are actually witnessing. It is, in fact, three times removed from the original place of action: Mr. Dickens tells the reader a story he has heard from Mr. Bolton. Mr. Bolton comments on the story, Dickens describes the reaction of the audience and the reader mentally notes what he has read. There is a stale joke at the unexpected promptitude of the police and the picture of the surprisingly collected father, who is smoking his pipe on top of a lamp-post, who – in other words – is not castrated despite the son's attack. But the humour cannot really mitigate the horror of the scene. The son who has interrupted the coitus is not only punished by death but by a shameful death. He is put among dirty linen – his rottenness is being boiled out of him. But now the son seemed so strong (he could wrench the knife from his father's hand), and suddenly he is caught up in his father's arms like a baby and shoved away. It is the scene which is indescribable, not the underwear to which this quality is transferred.

There can be found many fantasies of primal scenes in the novels and stories of Dickens. I shall simply remind the reader of Steven Marcus's brilliant essay "Who Is Fagin?"[3], in which he cleverly connects various passages from *Oliver Twist* with a paragraph of the autobiographical fragment which he interprets as a screen memory of a primal scene experience or fantasy. In *The Old Curiosity Shop* Quilp is angry with his wife for chatting with her neighbours about the rights of women and decides to punish her by keeping her awake all night while indulging himself in drinking and smoking. This is the description of the scene:

> 'Now, Mrs. Quilp,' he said; 'I feel in a smoking humour, and shall probably blaze away all night. But sit where you are, if you please, in case I want you.'
> His wife returned no other reply than the customary 'Yes, Quilp,' and the small lord of the creation took his first cigar and mixed his first glass of grog. The sun went down and the stars peeped out, the Tower turned from its own proper colours to grey and from grey to black, the room became perfectly dark and the end of the cigar a deep fiery red, but still Mr. Quilp went on smoking and drinking in the same position, and staring listlessly out of the window with the dog-like smile always on his face, save when Mrs. Quilp made some involuntary movement of restlessness or fatigue; and then it expanded into a grin of delight. (*OCS,* 82-83)

Gabriel Pearson calls this description "the closest we get to downright copulation in early-Victorian fiction",[4] a copulation, however, we might add, conceived of in terms of the left-out child: a sado-masochistic affair, the subjection of one parent by the sheer physical power of the other. (Mrs. Quilp is often pinched and beaten by her husband and complies to his wishes out of fear.)

Eavesdropping to be sure is a common literary device. Still, the number of scenes in the novel in which somebody is either looking through a keyhole, or spying on others, or overhearing a conversation, is striking. What, in the infantile view, makes up the

2 The terror reminds me of Jerry Cruncher, Jr. in *A Tale of Two Cities,* who spies on his father, a resurrection man, and is afterwards pursued by a coffin. This event could be interpreted among similar lines.
3 Steven Marcus, "Who Is Fagin?" in: *Dickens: From Pickwick to Dombey,* pp. 358-378.
4 Gabriel Pearson, "The Old Curiosity Shop" in: *Dickens and the Twentieth Century,* ed. by John Gross and Gabriel Pearson, London 1962, p. 84.

scene, namely the loneliness of the observing child on the one hand and the brutality of the act on the other, is separated by Dickens into two kinds of settings: the eavesdropping and spying either reveals to the listener and spy how somebody is tormented by another person or it is an attempt by him or her to overcome a basic loneliness and to find some sort of contact with other human beings. The following is only a selection of such scenes – many more examples could be quoted:

An obviously violent scene is the one between the Marchioness and Sally Brass witnessed by Dick. Sally enters the kitchen with a cold leg of mutton and taking up a carving knife makes "a mighty show of sharpening it upon the carving fork" (351). But the small starving servant is only allowed to eat two inches of cold mutton and "a dreary waste of cold potatoes, looking as eatable as Stonehenge" (351). Like Oliver, the child must on no account confess her hunger. On the contrary, she is trained to say "no" when asked whether she wants any more. Dickens then goes on:

> It was plain that some extraordinary grudge was working in Miss Sally's gentle breast, and that it was that which impelled her, without the smallest present cause, to rap the child with the blade of the knife, now on her hand, now on her head, and now on her back, as if she found it quite impossible to stand so close to her without administering a few slight knocks. (353)

The "few slight knocks" suddenly expand into "some hard blows with her clunched hand".

The conversation between Nell's grandfather and the gamblers is another instance of a scene of rough treatment witnessed during which the

> utter irresolution and feebleness of the grey-haired child, contrasted with the keen and cunning looks of those in whose hands he was, [and] smote upon the listener's heart. (399-400)

The helplessness of the old man is ruthlessly exploited by the gamblers, just as the Marchioness is exploited and has to do all the housework and the cooking without even being given enough to eat. Nell has unexpectedly come upon the gipsies' tent where they try to get the old man's money by fraud. It is as if in these scenes a door or window suddenly opened, letting Nell see what is happening within. We may remember that she actually sees her bedroom-door open when her grandfather slinks in to rob her and she silently witnesses the wrong that is being done to her.

When she and her grandfather flee from the gamblers and come to the Black Country, it is Nell who opens the door of a poor cottage, intending to beg for some bread – only to look upon a scene of misery. She learns from an overheard conversation that there are two families living together and that the two boys of these families have each committed a robbery. Whereas one of them has been pardoned because he is deaf and dumb, the other one is being transported as he is "in possession of all his senses" (428). His mother pleads that her son is "deaf and dumb in ... [his] mind" (428) because he has never been taught anything. He is, as Dickens points out, a victim of society's cruelty.

Quilp becomes involved in Kit's arrest and transportation to prison by suddenly leering at him from the window of a tavern, enjoying his enemy's downfall and "being swoln with suppressed laughter ... into twice his usual breadth" (548). A little later, Sampson Brass peeps through Quilp's window at the wharf and is shocked to hear his chant: "The worthy magistrate, after remarking that the prisoner would find some difficulty in persuading a jury to believe his tale, committed him to take his trial at the approaching sessions; and directed the customary recognizances to be entered into for the pros-e-cu-tion" (563) – all the time knowing that Kit has been wrongly accused. More is to come, for when Brass enters, Quilp shows him a huge figure-head which serves as an image of Kit and begins to batter it with all his might.

It is interesting, however, that Sampson is not sure at first whether the figure-head is supposed to resemble Quilp himself. There seems to exist a basic similarity between Quilp and Kit. Both of them, as Dyson has it,[5] are freaks. They both fight feelings of loneliness and they both often watch other people and listen to their conversations in order to be among them.

Kit watches Nell's window every evening and only returns home when she has put out her light. In addition to his conscious motive, which is to protect her, he finds a kind of companionship in the light of her room and is sadly disappointed when her grandfather stays home one evening and he does not see her at her window.

Quilp, on the other hand, often spies on people out of his deep-seated conviction that they intend to harm him.

Nell, in turn, often spends her time at the window, watching

> the people as they passed up and down the street, or appeared at the windows of the opposite house, wondering whether those rooms were as lonesome as that in which she sat, and whether those people felt it company to see her sitting there, as she did only to see them look out and draw in their heads again. (120)

When she and her grandfather stay at Mrs. Jarley's, Nell makes the acquaintance of a compassionate girl called Miss Edwards, whom she afterward sees in the company of her little sister. When they go for a walk she follows them at a little distance "stopping when they stopped, sitting on the grass when they sat down, rising when they went on, and feeling it a companionship and delight to be so near them" (316).

Later in the story, when Nell and her grandfather arrive in the industrial city, she again falls back on that habit of watching people without being seen: "It was like being in the confidence of all these people to stand quietly there, looking into their faces as they flitted past" (413). The observer's stance – which we have already met with as one of Dickens's own attitudes – helps the child to bear her own misery.[6]

One of the most moving examples of a lonely child seeking company by looking through a keyhole is, of course, the Marchioness. To pass the time, Dick is playing cribbage with a dummy. Suddenly he hears a snorting noise coming from the door and catches the servant-girl looking through the keyhole. Arthur W. Brown contends, after having traced the associations of 'cribbage' in Dickens, that playing cribbage is a symbolic expression for sexual intercourse.[7] If his interpretation is correct, Dick's solitary games can be looked upon as acts of masturbation which are then superseded by a sexual relationship with the Marchioness when he teaches her to play the game. The "many hundred thousand games of cribbage" (669) they play together in their

---

5 A. E. Dyson, "*The Old Curiosity Shop*. Innocence and the Grotesque" in: *Dickens. Modern Judgements*, ed. by A. E. Dyson, London 1968, p.67.

6 Master Humphrey, who was originally meant to be the narrator of the tale, finding the manuscript of the story in his clock, and who disappears after chapter 3, tells us: "Night is generally my time for walking (...) I have fallen insensibly into this habit ... because it affords me greater opportunity of speculation on the characters and occupations of those who fill the street. (...) a glimpse of passing faces caught by the light of a street lamp or a shop window is often better for my purpose than their full revelation in the daylight" (43).

7 Arthur Washburn Brown, *Sexual Analysis of Dickens' Props*, New York 1971, pp. 21 ff.

married life are thus love's counterbalance to the destructive games of Nell's grandfather.[8]

By looking through the keyhole, the Marchioness commits something similar to what the Baker's son in *Sketches by Boz* commits, and she, too, fears retaliation:

> 'Oh! I didn't mean any harm indeed. Upon my word I didn't,' cried the small servant, struggling like a much larger one. 'It's so very dull downstairs. Please don't you tell upon me; please don't.' (526)

Being seen becomes dangerous and is often replaced by its opposite: seeing. Quilp is the character who, more than anyone else, fears to be seen or, as he puts it, to be spied upon. His main reason for moving to the wharf is his need to "be secure from all spies and listeners" (465). He hates Kit but he is also afraid of him, regarding him as "a prowling prying hound; a hypocrite; a double-faced, white-livered, sneaking spy" (478). Since the very thought of being observed and found wanting makes him vulnerable, he tries to protect himself by spying on others. Thus he tells his wife: "I'll be a spy upon you, and come and go like a mole or a weazel" (464).

However, he finds his mistrust confirmed time and again – either because people really show their disgust of him ("I'm a little hunchy villain and a monster, am I, Mrs. Jiniwin? Oh!" (85)), or that he is tortured by imaginary slights:

> ... very sharp was the look he cast on his wife to observe how she was affected by the recognition of young Trent. Mrs Quilp was as innocent as her own mother of any emotion, painful or pleasant, which the sight of him awakened, but as her husband's glance made her timid and confused, and uncertain what to do or what was required of her, Mr Quilp did not fail to assign her embarrassment to the cause he had in his mind, and while he chuckled at his penetration was secretly exasperated by his jealousy. (241)

Not only is he often described as "leering" at people but he also believes in the magical power of his sight. When little Jacob screams at the unexpected apparition of the dwarf, the latter looks "sternly at him" and says threateningly: " 'Mind you don't break out again, you villain ... or I will make faces at you and throw you into fits, I will' " (223). Similarly, when meeting the Marchioness for the first time "it ... occurred to him as a pleasant whim to stare the small servant out of countenance" (473-74). Returning from the country after the vain search for Nell and her grandfather, Quilp terrifies Mrs. Nubbles with his monkeyish gymnastic feats "staring in[to the coach] with his great goggle eyes, which seemed in hers the more horrible from his face being upside down" (454), and when Kit reproaches him for this behaviour

> Quilp said not a word in reply, but walking up so close to Kit as to bring his eyes within two or three inches of his face, looked fixedly at him, retreated a little distance without averting his gaze, approached again, again withdrew, and so on for half-a-dozen times, like a head in a phantasmagoria (455).[9]

However, the power is obviously not so impressive, for Kit "finding that nothing came of these gestures, snapped his fingers and walked away" (455). On his way home Quilp pictures to himself

8 This has been pointed out by James R. Kincaid, "Laughter and Pathos: The Old Curiosity Shop" in: Robert B. Partlow (ed.), *Dickens the Craftsman*, Strategies of Presentation, Carbondale and Edwardsville 1970, p. 92.

9 The editor of the Penguin edition explains *phantasmagoria* as follows: "In 1802 Philpstal produced a magic-lantern of this name to show optical illusions, which by use of lenses gave the impression of moving and mingling" (*OCS*, 707).

the fears and terrors of Mrs Quilp, who, having received no intelligence of him for three whole days and two nights, and having had no previous notice of his absence, was doubtless by that time in a state of distraction, and constantly fainting away with anxiety and grief. (456)

This wishful thinking, however, is disappointed, for when Quilp arrives at Tower Hill he is informed by his boy that he is supposed to be drowned: " 'You was last seen on the brink of the wharf, and they think you tumbled over' " (457). With a "grim laugh" Quilp decides to spy on the mourning party "disappointing them all by walking in alive" (457). Far from "constantly fainting away with anxiety and grief" his wife preserves "a very decent and becoming *appearance* of sorrow" (458, emphasis added), whereas his mother-in-law, Mrs. Jiniwin, openly rejoices at his death and Sampson Brass hypocritically feigns sadness:

'It would be a comfort to have his body; it would be a dreary comfort.' 'Oh, beyond a doubt,' assented Mrs Jiniwin hastily; 'if we once had that, we should be quite sure.' (459)

They are all drinking his punch, even the presence of the waterside men, who have been searching for his body, "rather increased than detracted from that decided appearance of comfort, which was the great characteristic of the party" (458). Quilp's conviction that they wished him dead is psychologically convincing, although Dickens tries to deny this by stating that

Mrs Quilp did seem a great deal more glad to behold her lord than might have been expected, and did evince a degree of interest in his safety which, all things considered, was rather unaccountable. (458)

Dickens is telling us, in other words, that a person such as Quilp cannot possibly be loved. When he returns from the dead his wife faints away and Quilp is described as "looking at his insensible wife like a dismounted nightmare" (462).[10] How, we might ask ourselves, can a dismounted nightmare be accepted?

He is thus not welcomed with glad faces when he comes home; the only response he gets from the party is fear (the women shriek, Brass retreats backwards towards the door, Mrs. Jiniwin flees, Mrs. Quilp faints, the watermen speedily leave the room). And after having witnessed their comfortable drinking and listened to their unloving description of his bodily appearance,[11] he can only console himself by drinking off the contents of every single glass in the room and by hugging his case-bottle. This comic

10  In a letter to Miss Burdett-Coutts Dickens writes: "A kind of daymare comes upon me sometimes ... of your supposing me ... a species of moral monster with the usual number of legs and arms, a head, and so forth, but no heart at all." (*Letters from Charles Dickens to Angela Burdett-Coutts,* ed. by Edgar Johnson, London 1953, p. 31.)
11  We must bear in mind, however, that Dickens meant Quilp to be sexually attractive. Thus Mrs. Quilp contends that "if I was to die to-morrow, Quilp could marry anybody he pleased – now that he could, I know" (76). When interrogated about this statement, Dickens answered in a letter: "Mr. Charles Dickens presents his compliments to Mr. Synge and begs to say, in reply to Mr. Synge's letter, that he thinks Mrs. Quilp must have had good reasons for bearing witness to the attractive qualities of her husband. Mr. Dickens cannot speak quite confidently of any lady's reasons for anything, but he is inclined to believe that Mr. Quilp could easily have provided himself with another pretty wife, in the event of Mrs. Quilp's decease; it being generally observable that men who are very hideous and disagreeable are successful in matrimonial ventures" (*PE,* vol. IV, p. 540). Quilp's insistence on his nose being aquiline and his contempt for Kit's flat nose may point to his pride in his sexual potency.

scene, furthermore, is a rehearsal for Quilp's death. Towards the end of the novel Quilp really does fall off the wharf and is drowned in the river. Just before his death, his wife has brought him a letter from Sally Brass urging him to flee because Brass has confessed their plot. Quilp sends his wife away and bids his boy accompany her, since the night is dark and foggy and since there are many stumbling blocks on the wharf. His wife, however, frightened of him but not aware of his despair, questions him – of all things – about "dear little Nell" and wants to know whether she has harmed the girl by letting Quilp secretly share in their conversation.

> The exasperated dwarf returned no answer, but turned round and caught up his usual weapon with such vehemence, that Tom Scott dragged his charge away by main force and as swiftly as he could. It was well he did so, for Quilp, who was nearly mad with rage, pursued them to the neighbouring lane, and might have prolonged the chase but for the dense mist which obscured them from his view, and appeared to thicken every moment. (617)

He then closes and bars the gates and his revenge fantasy, namely to drown Sampson, let him come to the surface three times and watch him go down without stirring, is turned literally against him. He trips, falls into the dark and cold water, struggles and dies while his wife and Tom Scott – the two people on earth he loves with his curious kind of love – who have lost their way, are knocking at the barred gate:

> they were all but looking on while he was drowned; ... they were close at hand, but could not make an effort to save him; ... he himself had shut and barred them out. (620)[12]

It seems that in any triangular relationship someone has to die – be it the child as in *Sketches by Boz* or be it one of the marital partners as in our scene. It is interesting to note, moreover, that Quilp is a doubly cathected character – he can be viewed as a parental figure (he is married to Mrs. Quilp and the father of the Marchioness) while at the same time serving as a double to Nell and embodying the "bad child". In psychoanalytic terms Quilp's janus-like position might point to a fusion of self- and object-representations in the author. The fusion of self- and object-representations is prevalent in infancy but may well be experienced even in adult life. It may be fleeting and enable us to understand other people or it may be concomitant with any kind of regression – for instance with the creative regression in the service of the ego. We shall also have to deal with Quilp's special position in 2.2.

## 2.2 Giants and Dwarfs

When travelling with Codlin and Short Nell and her grandfather make the acquaintance of various circus people, among them Mr. Vuffin, the "proprietor of a giant" (203). Their conversation is about giants who are "going at the knees" because of old age. Old giants, we learn, are of no use to business; they must not show themselves in the street because people must not get used to the sight of giants:

12 When Nell is buried, the two people who have loved her most – her grandfather and the little boy – are excluded from the burial service and are not allowed to take leave of her. This is one of many parallels between Nell and Quilp. See 2.2.

Once make a giant common and giants will never draw again. Look at wooden legs. If there was only one man with a wooden leg what a property he'd be! (204)

Thus the old giants have to remain indoors in the caravans, and to "wait upon the dwarfs." Mr. Vuffin remembers

> the time when old Maunders as had tree-and-twenty wans ... had in his cottage in Spa fields in the winter time when the season was over, eight male and female dwarfs setting down to dinner every day, who was waited on by eight old giants in green coats, red smalls, blue stockings, and high-lows: and there was one dwarf as had grown elderly and wicious who whenever his giant wasn't quick enough to please him, used to stick pins in his legs, not being able to reach up any higher. (204-206)

This seems a symbolic picture of what goes on in many people's lives. At first, as a child, one is subjected to parental power. The parents, like giants, seem omniscient and almighty. However, the child pictures himself grown up and the parents weak with old age with an ensuing reversed balance of power. The tables are turned, "many that are first shall be last and the last first." Or, as we often experience in life, the wronged and humiliated will wrong and humiliate in turn once they get the opportunity. Aging parents may have to depend partly on their children, just as the children used to depend on them. The younger generation becomes potent, the older comparatively impotent.[13] The oedipal situation is reversed. As Grotjahn has pointed out, this is a common theme of comedy – in comedies the sons triumph over their fathers, in tragedies they succumb to them.[14] It is also, of course, the subject of many myths. In *The Old Curiosity Shop,* however, the reversal of power does not primarily take place on an oedipal level. Spilka contends that the "psychic clue" to the novel is its "flight from sexuality".[15] I agree with this statement but wish to modify it: it is a flight from genital sexuality and a predominance of preoedipal, mainly anal forms of sexuality. In 2.1 we were mainly concerned with oedipal longings; we shall now move back in time and talk about emotions which can be connected with the anal (2.2) and the oral (2.3) phases of psychosexual development.

Grunberger has pointed out that the child – in losing his prenatal paradise – suffers a narcissistic wound and that in the anal phase of development he tries to recover his narcissistic integrity by dominating his object.[16] In our novel there are numerous characters who relate to others either by subduing them or by being themselves subdued, by trying to gain power over others and force them to give attention and love or by masochistically submitting to them, thus securing their love in an indirect way. As examples of such relationships among the minor characters one could mention Jerry and his dogs, Mr. Grinder and his children, Codlin and Short (and even Punch and Judy), Mr. Vuffin and his giant, Miss Monflathers and Miss Edwards, the single gentleman and the people at his service (for instance Mrs. Nubbles), and perhaps even – though to a much lesser degree – Mrs. Jarley and George, the driver.

---

13  Otto F. Kernberg states in an unpublished paper on "Normal and Pathological Narcissism in Middle Age" that "the unconscious experiences of oedipal rivalry and incestual strivings have powerful reactivators throughout various points of adulthood, including the children's adolescence, [and] the middle-aged adult's rivalry with a newly established social and power structure of the younger generation."

14  Martin Grotjahn, *Beyond Laughter,* New York 1957, pp. 86f.

15  Mark Spilka, "Little Nell Revisited", *Papers of the Michigan Academy of Science, Arts and Letters,* vol. 45 (1960), p. 428.

16  Béla Grunberger, *Vom Narzissmus zum Objekt,* Frankfurt/M. 1976, passim.

Among the major characters we find sadomasochistic relationships between Sally Brass and her brother, Sally and the Marchioness, the grandfather and Little Nell, the gamblers and the grandfather, Fred and Dick and, of course, Quilp and his various victims, namely Mrs. Quilp, Nell's grandfather, Sampson Brass, Mrs. Jiniwin, Kit and Tom Scott. Quilp's subjugation of a helpless creature can best be seen in the scene where he worries a chained dog. Quilp has just found out that Dick intends to get married to Little Nell in order to become rich. Knowing himself that Nell is poor, he pictures to himself with infinite glee Dick's disappointment on finding out that he has married a penniless girl. Dickens then goes on:

> In the height of his ecstasy, Mr Quilp had like to have met with a disagreeable check, for, rolling very near a broken dog-kennel, there leapt forth a large fierce dog, who, but that his chain was of the shortest, would have given him a disagreeable salute. As it was, the dwarf remained upon his back in perfect safety, taunting the dog with hideous faces, and triumphing over him in his ability to advance another inch, though there were not a couple of feet between them.
> 'Why don't you come and bite me, why don't you come and tear me to pieces, you coward?' said Quilp, hissing and worrying the animal till he was nearly mad. 'You're afraid, you bully, you're afraid, you know your are.'
> The dog tore and strained at his chain with starting eyes and furious bark, but there the dwarf lay, snapping his fingers with gestures of defiance and contempt. When he had sufficiently recovered from his delight, he rose, and with his arms akimbo, achieved a kind of demon-dance round the kennel, just within the limits of the chain, driving the dog quite wild. Having by this means composed his spirits and put himself in a pleasant train, he returned to his unsuspicious companion ... (228)

Quilp has been frightened in the first instance by the dog's sudden appearance and threatening attitude. He has been reminded of his own smallness and vulnerability and he must prove his own power to himself. By tormenting the animal he can display his superiority; yet he is probably frightened of the dog's (albeit restrained) violence and thus has an even greater need to render him helpless and impotent. We remember the enormous size of the figure-head (which is brought out in Phiz's illustration, too) which indicates how large Kit looms in Quilp's mind.[17]

If Nell stands for the "good" child and Quilp stands for the "bad" child,[18] their partners assume reversed roles: Nell's grandfather is an exploiting parent, whereas Mrs. Quilp is called tender-hearted and loving: the good child is coupled with a bad parent, the bad child with a good parent. The old search for the culprit has been resumed by the author. The two conflicting self-representations ("I am good/I am bad") and object-representations ("the other is good/the other is bad") are separately described in the relations of Nell and her grandfather on the one hand and Quilp and

17 The scene reminds me of an episode which is told by Sir Henry Dickens. Dickens's raven used to place his food in front of a big dog who used to strain his chain in his attempt to reach it, but the bird always placed it just a little bit too far away so that the dog could not get at it. The raven teased the dog now with the meat, showing it to him perhaps burying it or eating it with great relish itself. "It was a rare treat," Henry Dickens says, "to see how that bird dominated over Turk, the mastiff. This used to afford my father and myself intense amusement, I remember." (Henry Fielding Dickens, *Memories of My Father,* London 1928, p. 27.)
18 Steven Marcus was the first to point out the psychological relationship between Nell and Quilp: "Nell is purity incarnate ... Quilp, her antithesis, is pure carnality. But he is more than her antithesis – he is her other half", *Dickens: From Pickwick to Dombey,* p. 151.

Mrs. Quilp on the other. What, then, makes up the good and the bad child, the good and the bad parent in Dickens's view?

Nell ist the "stay and comfort" of her grandfather's life (249), just as Kit – another paragon of a child – has been "a comfort" to his mother "from the hour of his birth" (560). Like Kit, who comforts his mother when he is ill ("don't cry ... I shall soon be better"), Nell has the obligation to cheer her grandfather up.[19] During their wanderings she always contrives to walk behind him so as to keep from him the fact that her feet are sore and her whole body full of pain. She also has to assume cheerfulness and gaiety in order to dispel his depression: "When he could for a moment disengage his mind from the phantom that haunted and brooded on it always, there was his young companion with the same smile for him, the same earnest words, the same merry laugh, the same love and care ..." (119).

This pattern is carried through right to the end of the tale. When Nell swoons at the schoolmaster's feet

> her grandfather, standing idly by, wrung his hands, and implored her with many endearing expressions to speak to him, were it only a word. (429)

Even in her fear of the grave, Nell gets no support except from the words of the schoolmaster, in which – as we have seen – Dickens himself did not believe. However, she has to pacify her grandfather, who fears that she might "steal away alone" and promises to be good: "Indeed, I will be very true, and faithful, Nell." Her answer is revealing:

> 'I steal away alone! why that,' replied the child, with assumed gaiety, 'would be a pleasant jest indeed. See here, dear grandfather, we'll make this place our garden'. (505)

In thus consoling her grandfather Nell denies what she knows to be the truth: she will have to steal away alone – not in jest but in earnest – she is dying. She is frightened of the grave; she calls Dickens's symbol of it – the old, dried-up well in the church – a "black and dreadful place" (511). And yet, she must not show her terror, let alone any rage or rebellion against her fate of an early death. She has to deny its reality to her grandfather as well as to herself, and so the churchyard is to become a garden. The scene with the little boy imploring her not to become an angel yet is cruel. The very anguish of the boy informs her of her imminent death and she breaks out into violent sobbing.

> ... but it was not long before she looked upon him with a smile, and promised him in a very gentle, quiet voice, that she would stay, and be his friend, as long as Heaven would let her. (510)

The scene is poignant because the boy implores Nell to stay as if it lay in her power to do so, whereas the reader knows that she is going to die. However, Nell's concern for the boy is natural. After all, he is still a small child, asking for Nell's sympathy and her understanding. But, as we have seen, her grandfather does not differ much from this boy. The parental figure who seems so powerful in imposing his needs upon those of Nell, is seen as a weak old man, wholly dependent on her care. He tyrannizes her with his clinging. They always walk like lovers, hand in hand, and Nell must on no account grow up and become a woman. Her literal death is a symbolic death, too. A child who has never been given the opportunity to feel her own emotions, who has

---

19 Kit, too, is repeatedly praised by the author for "determining to be in a good humour" (393). See also pp. 131, 215 and 561.

had to suppress them and to distort them, is not more alive than Dickens's "living dead in many shapes and forms ... [who] see the closing of that early grave" (658).

Gabriel Pearson appropriately calls her a "monster of goodness".[20] Her grandfather, sneaking into her room to steal every penny she owns, can be seen as robbing her of her sexual innocence. Thus, Steven Marcus connects the grandfather's wishes with Quilp's desire to defile purity[21] and with Dickens's life story and his suppressed sexual wishes with regard to Mary Hogarth. Moreover, Mark Spilka refers to Freud's interpretation of gambling as a substitution for masturbation.[22] In my opinion, however, the violation goes deeper than that: Nell has been robbed of her own natural emotions, being allowed only to experience "suitable" feelings. This is the most subtle and the most sinister form of exploitation. Nell is never allowed to relax, sleep does not come easily to her. Only when her grandfather is taken care of by other people (the driver of the cart, the Punch and Judy show, the schoolmaster, the furnace man, Mrs. Jarley), can she give up her parental role and enjoy a refreshing sleep.

Her repression of, and flight from, her Quilpish nature is hinted at by Dickens several times. We hear at the beginning of the novel of her lonely evenings when her grandfather is out gambling, and of her seeing a coffin

> which made her shudder and think of such things [i.e. scenes of death] until they suggested afresh the old man's altered face and manner ... If he were to die – if sudden illness had happened to him, and he were never to come home again, alive – if, one night, he should come home, and kiss and bless her as usual, and after she had gone to bed, and had fallen asleep and was perhaps dreaming pleasantly, and smiling in her sleep, he should kill himself and his blood come creeping, creeping, on the ground to her own bedroom door ... (120-21)

Even in the purged text the connection between aggression, death and her grandfather seems clear enough.[23]

Later, when her grandfather breaks down under the burden of his defeat, Nell, the good, compassionate Nell, begs:

> If you are sorrowful, let me know why and be sorrowful too; if you waste away and are paler and weaker every day, let me be your nurse and try to comfort you. (122)

But her other half, the rebellious child, is participating in the scene. Mr. Quilp has entered unseen and has overheard their conversation (125). The symbolism of Quilp's usurpation of Nell's bed has been pointed out by various critics. When she and her grandfather flee, Nell has to get the door-key from her room in which Quilp is sleeping and comes across the following sight:

> Mr Quilp ... was hanging so far out of bed that he almost seemed to be standing on his head, and ... either from the uneasiness of this posture or in one of his agreeable habits,

20 Gabriel Pearson, "The Old Curiosity Shop", *Dickens and the Twentieth Century*, p. 84.
21 Steven Marcus, *Dickens: From Pickwick to Dombey*, p. 154. See also Mark Spilka, "Little Nell Revisited", p. 430 and Michael Steig, "The Central Action of *The Old Curiosity Shop* or Little Nell Revisited Again", *Literature and Psychology*, vol. 15 (1965), p. 163.
22 Mark Spilka, "Little Nell Revisited", p. 430.
23 *which made her shudder.* The manuscript adds: "and think of such things until she was obliged to go close up to an old oaken table that stood in the middle of the room and turn its cover up to convince herself that there was no corpse or coffin there. After glancing about the room, she would resume her station at the window, and ... wonder where her grandfather was ... This suggested afresh, his altered face and manner ..." (Notes, p. 686).

was gasping and growling with his mouth wide open, and the whites (or rather the dirty yellows) of his eyes distinctly visible. (150)[24]

The pure, clean, beautiful Nell who has no body at all is suddenly confronted with a growling and gasping being – a creature who emits noises and smells (Quilp's smoking!) and performs grotesque movements.

Later, when Nell is engaged by Mrs. Jarley and has just accompanied the old man to his sleeping place, she watches the old gateway of the town:

> There was an empty niche from which some old statue had fallen ... and she was thinking what strange people it must have looked down upon when it stood there, and how many hard struggles might have taken place, and how many murders might have been done, upon that silent spot, when there suddenly emerged from the black shade of the arch, a man. The instant he appeared, she recognised him – ... the ugly mis-shapen Quilp. (276)

Once more the Quilpish aggression seems to be a threat to the old man's life. Nell hurries back "to where she had left her grandfather, feeling as if the very passing of the dwarf so near him must have filled him with alarm and terror. But he was sleeping soundly, and she softly withdrew." (278) Nell "felt as if she were hemmed in by a legion of Quilps" (278) and "Quilp indeed was a perpetual nightmare to the child, who was constantly haunted by a vision of his ugly face and stunted figure." (288) Indeed, the return of the repressed is always imminent. The wanderers, who wanted to leave their Quilpish nature behind in London and to return to a preambivalent paradise in the country, are reminded of it at every stage of their journey. When they meet Codlin and Short in the churchyard, mending their puppets' clothes, the old man is delighted. He touches the puppets "drawing away his hand with a shrill laugh" (183) and he "would have remained in the churchyard all night, if his new acquaintance had stayed there too" (184). He is delighted at the thought that they will all put up for the night at the same inn, and when they all walk there together, he keeps "close to the box of puppets in which he was quite absorbed" (184). Whatever the variations of the Punch and Judy show that they afterwards enjoy, the central theme is always that Punch can commit a series of crimes with impunity: he throws his crying baby out of the window and kills him, he kills his wife, his dog, the doctor and the hangman,[25] and finally even triumphs over the devil.[26] They next arrive at the poor schoolmaster's house. While they are staying there, "the little scholar", a particularly bright pupil who is the schoolmaster's best friend, dies. The boy's grandmother then accuses the schoolmaster

> It's all along of you ... This is what his learning has brought him to ... If he hadn't been poring over his books out of fear of you, he would have been well and merry now, I know he would. (259)

Although Dickens sides with the schoolmaster, implying that it is only the old woman's grief that makes her speak thus, the scene is a disturbing one: a child has been overtaxed and has died. We can understand, then, why Nell conceals her sadness about the boy's death from her grandfather, "for the dead boy had been a

---

24 There are two other scenes in which Quilp employs an upside-down position: when forcing his wife to look at him (p. 81) and when performing his gymnastic feats on the roof of the coach (p. 454).

25 See also Dickens's description of the hanging of Dennis, the hangman, in *Barnaby Rudge*.

26 Cp. Rachel Bennet, "Punch Versus Christian in *The Old Curiosity Shop*", *The Review of English Studies*, vol. 22 (1971), pp. 423-434.

grandchild, and left but one aged relative to mourn his premature decay" (261) and –
only dimly perceived by her – both children have to bear more than they are able to.

When the two wanderers are given shelter at the wax-works, Nell has to explain the
figures to the visitors to the exhibition. Among such curiosities as "the fat man ..., the
thin man, the tall man, the short man," there is also the woman "who poisoned
fourteen families with pickled walnuts" and there is a sort of blue-beard, too,

> Jasper Packlemerton of atrocious memory, who courted and married fourteen wives, and
> destroyed them all by tickling the soles of their feet when they was sleeping in the
> consciousness of innocence and virtue. On being brought to the scaffold and asked if he
> was sorry for what he had done, he replied, yes, he was sorry for having let 'em off so
> easy ... (283-85)

Once more their suppressed aggression accompanies them and is shown in what
happens in their surroundings. The particular means of killing others (by giving them
poisoned food and by making them laugh) are not chosen at random. We have
already talked about the release of aggression in wit and shall come back to the
question of food in 2.3.

Finally, when they reach their place of destination and Nell first enters the church
whose warden she is to become, she finds

> effigies of warriors stretched upon their beds of stone with folded hands, cross-legged –
> those who had fought in the Holy Wars – girded with their swords, and cased in armour
> as they had lived. Some of these knights had their own weapons, helmets, coats of mail,
> hanging upon the walls hard by, and dangling from rusty hooks. Broken and dilapidated
> as they were, they yet retained their ancient form, and something of their ancient aspect.
> Thus violent deeds live after men upon the earth, and traces of war and bloodshed will
> survive in mournful shapes, long after those who worked the desolation are but atoms of
> earth themselves. (494)

Not unlike Nell, the bachelor, who explains the various sights of the church to her
and attempts to correct history, denies the existence of rebellion and discontent.

> As he was not one of those rough spirits who would strip fair Truth of every little
> shadowy vestment in which time and teeming fancies love to array her – and some of
> which become her pleasantly enough, ... he trod with a light step and bore with a light
> hand upon the dust of centuries, unwilling to demolish any of the airy shrines that had
> been raised above it, if one good feeling or affection of the human heart were hiding
> thereabouts. Thus in the case of an ancient coffin of rough stone, supposed for many
> generations to contain the bones of a certain baron, who, after ravaging, with cut, and
> thrust, and plunder, in foreign lands, came back with a penitent and sorrowing heart to
> die at home, but which had been lately shown by learned antiquaries to be no such thing,
> as the baron in question (so they contended) had died in battle, gnashing his teeth and
> cursing with his latest breath, – the bachelor stoutly maintained that the old tale was the
> true one ... and that if ever baron went to heaven, that baron was then at peace. (...)
> In a word, he would have had every stone and plate of brass, the monument only of deeds
> whose memory should survive. All others he was willing to forget. They might be buried
> in consecrated ground, but he would have them buried deep, and never brought to light
> again. (496-98)

Nell and her grandfather attempt to suppress any kind of violence. With the
grandfather, though, it breaks out in his wild gambling and his impetuous demands
for money. When it cannot be denied altogether any longer it is called "a dream".
When Nell fears that her grandfather will rob and possibly murder Mrs. Jarley, she
says to him:

'I have had a dreadful dream ... A dreadful, horrible dream. I have had it once before. It is a dream of grey-haired men like you, in darkened rooms by night, robbing the sleepers of their gold.' (405)

The "once before" refers to the scene in which her grandfather robbed her at the inn. However, the reality of this event is denied, too. It was only an uneasy dream.[27] The violence which is confined to the world of dreams is less frightening and less shameful. When Nell and the old man live at the peaceful village together with the schoolmaster, they try to forget their former hardships. This time, Nell says, "shall be only as some uneasy dream that has passed away." Her grandfather's answer is revealing: "Hush! ... no more talk of the dream, and all the miseries it brought. There are no dreams here" (504).

Thus Dickens suggests that dreams are inflicted on the innocent sufferer by the outside world (on Kit in prison, on Dick in his illness, on Nell in her wanderings), that, in other words, they have nothing to do with the dreamer. When one Dr. Stone wants to contribute to Dickens's periodical *Household Words* with a paper on dreams, Dickens refutes his statement, that virtuous people have innocent dreams. Dickens is convinced that there are a number of dreams which are "common to us all". According to him they are the dreams of falling from towers or high places, the dreams of going into society in night dresses, the dreams of "being able to skim along with airy strides a little above the ground" and he adds that "it is probable that we have all committed murders and hidden bodies".[28] The common experience does not, however, point to the fact that all the feelings which find expression in dreams are part of human nature, that, in other words, there is such a thing as violence and murderous aggression in every one of us. To Dickens these dreams, which may be dreamt – as he points out – even by the Queen, prove that the dreamer has nothing to do with them. Although his enumeration shows surprising insight, he cannot, in this pre-Freudian age, see in the dreams a meaningful psychic expression of the dreamer. But Dickens's unconscious knew better: When Nell stops dreaming she is dead.[29] Nell, it seems, has either to live with her "dismounted nightmare" (462) or to die. Dickens has poignantly described the tragic end of a child who has had to split her self-image into two entirely contradictory parts and could not reconcile them. Both children, i.e. both of these parts have to die.

Let us, then, look more closely at what Dickens describes as Quilpish nature. Quilp, who has been called "the devil" by so many critics,[30] can be understood in

27 After the theft Nell at first tries to suggest that the money "was taken by somebody in jest" (305).

28 Charles Dickens, "Lying Awake", *UT & RP, OID,* 433. See also his letter to Dr. Stone, *Letters,* II, pp. 267-270 and the interesting paper by W. Winters, "Dickens and the Psychology of Dreams", *PMLA,* vol. 63 (1948), pp. 984-1006. John W. Noffsinger pursues in his paper "Dream in *The Old Curiosity Shop*", *South Atlantic Bulletin,* vol. 42 (1977), pp. 23-34) different aims, namely to trace out the " 'fleshing of allegory' ... through the motif of dream in the novel" (p. 24).

29 See also Noffsinger, p. 29. Dickens speaks of the dead as of "those dreamless sleepers" (484).

30 For some views on Quilp see for instance Robert Simpson McLean, "Putting Quilp to Rest", *Victorian Newsletter,* vol. 34 (1968), pp. 29-33; Toby A. Olshin, "The Yellow Dwarf and *The Old Curiosity Shop*", *Nineteenth Century Fiction,* vol. 25 (1970), pp. 96-99; Robert Simpson McLean, "Another Source for Quilp", *Nineteenth Century Fiction,* vol. 26 (1971), pp. 337-339; Branwen Pratt, "Sympathy for the Devil: A Dissenting View of Quilp", *Hartford Studies in Literature,* vol. 6 (1974), pp. 129-146.

human terms, too. He is the dirty child of the anal period. Unlike Nell, who is clean and pure, he is always dirty. His hands, his fingernails, his linen are dirty. He washes in the following manner:

> [he] proceeded to smear his countenance with a damp towel of very unwholesome appearance, which made his complexion rather more cloudy than it was before. (85)

Nell's beauty is admired everywhere, whereas Quilp is disparaged (the author calls him "this unknown piece of ugliness", 223) and reacts to the slights as follows:

> 'Monster!' said Quilp inwardly, with a smile. 'Ugliest dwarf that could be seen anywhere for a penny – monster – ah!' (455)

and plots his insulter's downfall. Wherever Nell goes she commences tidying up, mending and cleaning. She mends the clothes of the Punch and Judy puppets, puts the brambles into place at the first churchyard and makes gardens of the graves of the second, tidies up the schoolmaster's cottage, helps to put everything in order at Mrs. Jarley's and finally improves the condition of the curtains and carpets at their last habitation. Quilp, on the other hand, enjoys spreading disorder. Instead of making life comfortable – as Nell endeavours to do – he makes it unbearable to his visitors by his incessant smoking:[31]

> Quilp looked at his legal adviser, and seeing that he was winking very much in the anguish of his pipe, that he sometimes shuddered when he happened to inhale its full flavour, and that he constantly fanned the smoke from him, was quite overjoyed and rubbed his hands with glee. 'Smoke away, you dog,' said Quilp, turning to the boy ... (139)

Quilp is often described as having a "dog-like smile", and he constantly calls his boy (a sort of double) by that name as well as Kit and Sampson Brass or an anonymous boy carrying his luggage. He treats the others in the same way he has been treated himself.[32] His love of disorder is also shown in Dickens's description of the counting-house, Quilp's wharf and Quilp's summer-house. The counting-house is described as

> a dirty little box ... with nothing in it but an old ricketty desk and two stools, a hat-peg, an ancient almanack, an inkstand with no ink and the stump of one pen, and an eight-day clock which hadn't gone for eighteen years at least and of which the minute-hand had been twisted off for a tooth-pick (88)

and·Quilp sleeps there "amidst the congenial accompaniments of rain, mud, dirt, damp, fog, and rats" (472). The summer-house

> was a rugged wooden box, rotten and bare to see, which overhung the river's mud, and threatened to slide down into it. The tavern to which it belonged was a crazy building, sapped and undermined by the rats, and only upheld by great bars of wood which were reared against its walls, and had propped it up so long that even they were decaying and

---

31 The smoking can be regarded as a combination of oral and anal gratifications. Not only does Quilp often smoke and drink at the same time, but he also swallows the smoke. The aggressiveness of the odours he emits has been mentioned. However, Quilp not only hurts the others, but also himself, as his violent coughing and his highly inflamed red eyes tell us. Cp. pp. 82-3, 137, 139, 226, 470.

32 The editor of the Penguin edition of *The Old Curiosity Shop* points out Quilp's relatedness to Shakespeare's Richard III – who also was a physical and therefore a psychic monster – in various footnotes. See pp. 684, 716f., 708.

yielding with their load, and of a windy night might be heard to creak and crack as if the whole fabric were about to come toppling down. The house stood ... on a piece of waste ground, blighted with the unwholesome smoke of factory chimneys, and echoing the clank of iron wheels and rush of troubled water. Its internal accomodations amply fulfilled the promise of the outside. The rooms were low and damp, the clammy walls were pierced with chinks and holes, the rotten floors had sunk from their level, the very beams started from their places and warned the timid stranger from their neighbourhood. (225)

Dickens clearly wants to characterize Quilp by his surroundings, which are as dirty and as threatening as he – always ready to drop down upon the visitor.[33] Dickens usually showed his disgust by introducing rats into the scene – the blacking ware-house, too, had been a rat-infested building.[34] In our context it is essential to remember that Nell herself does not live in entirely different surroundings. Only through Nell's busily cleaning and tidying up do they come to differ from Quilp's dwellings. The old curiosity shop and the old house in which they live at the end of the book are as old and dilapidated as Quilp's houses. Whereas, however, Dickens meant to show the basic similarity between Quilp himself and his environment, he was at pains to point out that Nell exists in "a kind of allegory" in

the old dark murky rooms – [with] the gaunt suits of mail with their ghostly silent air – the faces all awry, grinning from wood and stone – the dust and rust, and worm that lives in wood – and alone in the midst of all this lumber and decay, and ugly age, the beautiful child in her gentle slumber, smiling through her light and sunny dreams (56).

Quilp has the bodily proportions of a child: a big head and a proportionately small body with short and crooked legs. Nell is nearly fourteen years old, but her smallness is continually emphasized. Dickens only rarely calls her "Nell", most often she is introduced as "the child" or perhaps as "Little Nell". But while her helplessness and timid bearing are meant to arouse the reader's sympathy, Quilp's child-like figure is only seen as some sort of distortion. Nell is self-sacrificing, Quilp is greedy and demanding. He selects for himself the most comfortable chair and assigns "an especially hideous and uncomfortable one" (137) to Brass – Nell always gives the best food to her grandfather and when they suffer from hunger, she gives him all the bread

33 In *Little Dorrit* there is the description of the house of Mrs. Clennam – another dilapidated and bleak building, full of mysterious cracking noises which announce its future collapse. Mr. Flintwinch reproaches Mrs. Clennam for having "dropped down upon me" (223) and when she tries to correct him "I remonstrated with you", he replies: "I won't have it! ... You dropped down upon me" (223). In *Little Dorrit*, then, the similarity between the house and its owner is spelt out even more clearly.

34 The most striking example is of course the story of the shipwright called Chips in *Nurse's Story, UT & RP, OID*, 153-57. Chips, who has sold his soul to the devil for "an iron pot and a bushel of tenpenny nails and half a ton of copper and a rat that could speak", hates the animal that spoils everything for him, even his love-affair with a young girl, and attempts to kill it. However, he cannot get rid of it and is addressed by it thus:
"A Lemon has pips,
And a Yard has ships,
An I'll have Chips!" and these are the very words that the devil used to speak. I wonder whether the name of the autobiographical hero Pip in *Great Expectations* has some hidden connection with this story. The children in Dickens's novels are often threatened with a bad end. Oliver, for instance, is repeatedly awed with "That boy will be hung!" 'Quilp's Wharf', too, is "rat-infested" (73).

they have. Either we eat, or we are eaten – this seems to be the conflict Dickens is expressing. The child either greedily destroys the adult in a Quilpish manner (Quilp destroys Nell's grandfather and harms Mrs. Quilp, Fred takes part in the destruction by his connection with the gamblers) or the child is exploited himself by a hungry adult (both Nell and the Marchioness are starved). Either the child is not allowed to feel his emotions or he is compelled to act them out:

'How could I be so cruel! cruel!' cried the dwarf. 'Because I was in the humour. I'm in the humour now. I shall be cruel when I like'. (463)

There is no envy or jealousy in Nell, while Quilp is permeated by these feelings. When Nell follows the two sisters in order to share their company Dickens adds:

Let us not believe that any selfish reference – unconscious though it might have been – to her own trials awoke this sympathy [for the sisters], but thank God that the innocent joys of others can strongly move us, and that we, even in our fallen nature, have one source of pure emotion which must be prized in Heaven! (316, emphasis added.)

Quilp's enormous hatred of Kit is aggravated by the fact that Kit is loved by many people, whereas he, Quilp, is feared and hated. He is truly an outcast who can only be happy at his "bachelor's wharf". It should not surprise us that the child who feels dirty and repulsive, an "ugly plaything" (620) of the waters that drown him, reacts with frustrated and distorted aggression and also with fantasies of magical power. As long as Quilp seems to us no more than blunt, as compared with the too sweet Nell, he makes us laugh, for instance when he comments on Fred's visit at his grandfather's: "so much for dear relations. Thank God I acknowledge none!" (68), or when he teases his mother-in-law who praises her dead husband:

'Her [Mrs. Quilp's] father was a blessed creetur, Quilp, and worth twenty thousand of some people,' said Mrs. Jiniwin; 'twenty hundred million thousand.'
'I should like to have known him,' remarked the dwarf. 'I dare say he was a blessed creature then; but I'm sure he is now. It was a happy release. I believe he had suffered a long time?' (80)

Later, when Mrs. Quilp carries Sally's important letter to Quilp's "lair", he greets her with the words "Is it good news, pleasant news; news to make a man skip and snap his fingers? ... Is the dear old lady dead?" (614) These seem prime examples of Freud's theory that when we no longer need our psychic energy to repress a hostile impulse because the hostility itself is expressed in the form of humour, the sudden release of this energy makes us laugh.[35] Our own aggression against relatives in general, against babies ("Don't be frightened, mistress, ... I don't eat babies; I don't like 'em", 223) and against maternal figures is so blatantly expressed by Quilp that we can momentarily give up our own repression of it. Once more Nell is shown as Quilp's opposite. She admonishes her brother Fred in these words:

'I love you dearly, Fred ... I do indeed, and always will ... but oh! if you would leave off vexing him and making him unhappy, then I could love you more. (66-67)

Nell's protestations sound false and we can understand Fred's reply:

'There – get you away now you have said your lesson.' (67)

---

35 See Sigmund Freud, Der Witz und seine Beziehung zum Unbewussten, Studienausgabe, vol. IV, pp. 13-219.

There are, however, some scenes in which Quilp's destructiveness assumes truly frightening colours. This is how Quilp addresses the two fighting boys Tom Scott and Kit:

> 'I'll beat you to a pulp, you dogs ... I'll bruise you till you are copper-coloured, I'll break your faces till you haven't a profile between you, I will.' (94)

Another example of his aggression gone wild is the scene at his wharf in which he batters the figure-head. As he tells his "legal adviser" he has "been screwing gimlets into him, and sticking forks in his eyes, and cutting my name on him. I mean to burn him at last" (566). The enemy seems to be a giant who fills the dwarf with such an unbearable fear that he must be rendered impotent. The smaller the dwarf feels the bigger the giant becomes.[36]

Moreover, the image of the enemy is immovable, does not hit back and can be turned into something owned by the inscription of Quilp's name on it. As Spitz has shown, it is an important stage in the child's development when he learns to distinguish between the animate and the inanimate. The inanimate object, Spitz contends, is useful to the child for the discharge of aggression. But sooner or later he will find out that there is no response from it or, in Spitz's words, there is no evolution of a dialogue:

> The dialogue, the circular exchange of action and response, serves the child to test whether something he sees is animate.[37]

However, in his rage, Quilp seems to have lost this capacity – the image of his enemy and the enemy himself become one and the same thing. The boundaries between the animate and the inanimate are blurred. Nell, too, can sometimes no longer distinguish between the living and the inanimate. Her task of explaining the wax-works is symbolic. As Mrs. Jarley has it, wax-work is

> 'always the same, with a constantly unchanging air of coldness and gentility; and so like life, that if wax-work only spoke and walked about, you'd hardly know the difference. I won't go so far as to say, that, as it is, I've seen wax-work quite like life, but I've certainly seen some life that was exactly like wax-work.' (272)

The children at the fair believe Nell's grandfather to be a "cunning device in wax" (280) – the person who has brought up the girl is about as capable of beginning a dialogue with her as the dead figures.

In their wanderings Nell and her grandfather meet a rough-looking and blackened man whose work consists in feeding a huge furnace. He takes the old man and the girl to the roaring furnaces and prepares a dry and warm sleeping-place for them. Later he

---

36 Nell meets the children of Mr. Grinder, a boy and a girl on stilts, who seem like "two monstrous shadows ... stalking towards them ... The child was at first quite terrified by the sight of these gaunt giants – for such they looked as they advanced with lofty strides beneath the shadow of the trees" (192). Another hint of Nell's similarity to Quilp.

37 See René A. Spitz, "The Evolution of Dialogue", in *Drives, Affects, Behavior* (ed. by Max Schur), New York 1965, pp. 170-190.
These objects are of course not to be equated with Winnicott's transitional object (i.e. the child's first 'not-me' possession, for instance a teddy, a cushion or a blanket which he uses to go to sleep or to soothe him in anxiety and which "stands for the breast, or the object of the first relationship"). See D. W. Winnicott, *Playing and Reality*, Pelican Books, Harmondsworth 1974 (first published in 1971), pp. 1-30.

tells Nell his story: his mother died when he was a baby. His father had to work but brought him up

> 'Secretly at first, but when they found it out, they let him keep me here. So the fire nursed me – the same fire. It has never gone out.' (420)

The man remembers how his father died and how lonely he felt and recognizes a similar basic mood in Nell:

> 'You may guess from looking at me what kind of child I was, but for all the difference between us I was a child, and when I saw you in the street to-night, you put me in mind of myself as I was after he died, and made me wish to bring you to the old fire.' (420)

Thus the fire becomes a symbol for human warmth and affection:

> 'It's like a book to me,' he said, 'the only book I ever learned to read; and many an old story it tells me. It's music, for I should know its voice among a thousand ... It has pictures too. ... It's my memory, that fire, and shows me all my life.' (419-20)

We may well guess how starved a child must be to seek tenderness from such sources. We shall come back to this "comforting" in 2.3. Once more an apparent difference between Nell and Quilp disappears on closer scrutiny. By conducting Nell in her wanderings first to the wax-works and afterwards to the man who was brought up not by human beings but by the fire, Dickens shows us that she, too, has experienced the same lack of dialogue that Quilp has. Such a situation must arouse both despair and rage in a child. The despair is expressed by Nell, the rage by Quilp.

There are other features in Quilp which remind us of a small child. Quilp's display of his grotesque muscular prowess makes me think of the pride of the child who has learned to walk, to keep his balance and to control his movements.[38] Quilp can skip on to the back of a chair with the agility of a Grock; he terrifies Mrs. Nubbles and Nell with his hanging upside down; his ability to grimace and to throw children into fits is unparalleled.[39]. His boy – a sort of younger version of himself – is most often seen walking about standing on his hands or jumping somersaults. After Quilp's death Tom

> determined to go through it [the world] upon his head and hands, and accordingly began to tumble for his bread. (666)

Quilp's envy of Tom's skill and his fascination with it – he tells him for instance to stop standing on his head: "stand upon your head again and I'll cut one of your feet off" (88) – point to his relatedness to the child of the anal period – the child whose greatest accomplishment is the control of his bowel movements.

Furthermore, Quilp's magic powers relate him to the same period of development. He can drink "fire", i.e. either burning hot tea (86) or boiling raw liquor (226, 567/8) and he can smoke until everyone in his vicinity chokes. He seems to tell us that he cannot be harmed by boiling beverages, that, in fact, he is invulnerable. Significantly enough, the most detailed description of Quilp's invulnerability is given in the context

---

38 As Grotjahn has shown, the circus performance gives particular pleasure to the person (child or adult) who has learned to keep his balance but who remembers the time when it could easily be disturbed and who either enjoys his present superiority over the clumsy clowns or gains security by identifying with the artiste's performances. See M. Grotjahn, *Beyond Laughter*, p. 117.

39 See pp. 124, 141, 223, 226, 244, 463.

of the figure-head, i.e. when Quilp assumes power over his enemy in the manner of a small child.

This is the description of his drinking:

> Quilp ... [was] heating some rum in a little saucepan, and watching it to prevent its boiling over. ... 'Why sir,' returned Brass, 'he – dear me, Mr Quilp, sir – '
> 'What's the matter?' said the dwarf, stopping his hand in the act of carrying the saucepan to his mouth.
> 'You have forgotten the water, sir', said Brass. 'And – excuse me, sir – but it's burning hot.'
> Deigning no other than a practical answer to this remonstrance, Mr Quilp raised the hot saucepan to his lips, and deliberately drank off all the spirit it contained; which might have been in quantity about half a pint, and had been but a moment before, when he took it off the fire, bubbling and hissing fiercely. Having swallowed this gentle stimulant and shaken his fist at the admiral, he bade Mr Brass proceed. (567/8)

His power over the enemy and his entire control of his own body are linked together. Both of them are to a certain extent imaginary, since Quilp cannot bring about Kit's transportation after all and he can only endure the pains he inflicts upon himself – as has already been mentioned in note 31 – but cannot eliminate them. When Dick exclaims at the dwarf's summer-house, "Why, man, you don't mean to tell me that you drink such fire as this?" Mr. Quilp rejoins:

> 'No! ... Not drink it! Look here. And here. And here again. Not drink it!'
> As he spoke, Daniel Quilp drew off and drank three small glasses of the raw spirit, and then with a horrible grimace took a great many pulls at his pipe, and swallowing the smoke, discharged it in a heavy cloud from his mouth. This feat accomplished he drew himself together in his former position, and laughed excessively. (226)

He laughs triumphantly, enjoying his own power. But his laughter is excessive, which makes us guess that Quilp still feels insecure and full of anguish underneath.

Very often Quilp laughs at the expense of others. Whereas it is Kit's and Nell's obligation and duty to be cheerful themselves and to cheer others up, Quilp's joy at his enemy's downfall is exactly the opposite attitude. There is no tender loving concern, but there is spite and malice, which is openly expressed. Instead of the obligation to bring joy to one's relatives, we have its antithesis: a malicious gloating over the misfortune of others. Quilp's silent laughter, the laughter of a person who "laughs heartily but at the same time slyly and by stealth" (83) is often somewhat uncanny. He laughs in this way when he finds out that the Marchioness is his own daughter who is tormented by the "gentle Sally", he laughs until he nearly bursts when Kit is taken to prison, he laughs when he realizes how his wife, whom he is keeping up for the whole night, is weary. He enjoys his superiority but at the same time he tries to hide this feeling. Thus he cannot laugh aloud but has to suppress laughter. Instead of being a social gesture, as Bergson describes it, it increases his isolation. It is not shared by others but must be hidden from them.

We find, in other words, variations on the same theme of sadomasochistic relationships in this novel. The two modes of being are expressed most clearly by the characters Nell and Quilp. Mrs. Quilp is a sort of second Nell, whereas Nell's grandfather can in many ways be compared to Quilp. In the above-mentioned scene at Quilp's wharf, in which he drinks boiling liquor, the sado-masochistic elements are spelt out. Brass, who wishes to get some water, is answered thus by Quilp:

'There's no such thing to be had here,' cried the dwarf. 'Water for lawyers! Melted lead and brimstone, you mean, nice hot blistering pitch and tar – that's the thing for them – eh, Brass, eh?'
'Ha, ha, ha!' laughs Brass. 'Oh very biting! and yet it's like being tickled – there's a pleasure in it too, sir!'
'Drink that,' said the dwarf, who had by this time heated some more.'Toss it off ... scorch your throat and be happy.'
The wretched Sampson took a few short sips of the liquor, which immediately distilled itself into burning tears, and in that form came rolling down his cheeks ... turning the colour of his face and eyelids to a deep red, and giving rise to a violent fit of coughing, in the midst of which he was still heard to declare with the constancy of a martyr, that it was 'beautiful indeed!' (568)

Brass attempting to be cheerful at Quilp's summer-house "with the rain plashing down into his teacup" (477) can be read as Dickens's unconscious caricature of Little Nell, particularly when he answers Quilp's question as to whether it is damp and aguish with "Just damp enough to be cheerful, sir" (475) or when he moralizes that "we should be gay as larks" and "A contented spirit ... is the sweetness of existence" (519). With Quilp, as with the lodger, Brass "deemed it prudent to pocket his ... affront along with his cash" (354). The difference between Brass and Nell (just as we have seen with Ruth Pinch and Charity Pecksniff) seems to be that the one is mercenary whereas the other is not. But Nell, too, is gaining something by her submissiveness, namely the "love" of her grandfather as well as of the schoolmaster, Mrs. Jarley, the bachelor and everybody at the country village.[40]

Quilp, who is forcing people to drink boiling hot liquor, is not very different from the single genleman, who is constantly convinced that Kit's mother stands in need of "a glass of hot brandy and water" (442):

It was in vain for Kit's mother to protest that she stood in need of nothing of the kind. The single gentleman was inexorable; and whenever he had exhausted all other modes and fashions of restlessness, it invariably occurred to him that Kit's mother wanted brandy and water. (442)

A little later he insists on her eating a large meal, although she is not hungry and

calling for mulled wine as impetuously as if it had been wanted for instant use in the recovery of some person apparently drowned, the single gentleman made Kit's mother swallow a bumper of it at such a high temperature that the tears ran down her face. (442)

The link between Quilp and Nell's grandfather via the latter's brother is evident.
The good child, then (Nell, Kit, Abel Garland, the Marchioness) is masochistically submissive to an exploiting parent[41] (Nell's grandfather, the Garlands, Miss Brass,

---

40 Cp. Freud's thoughts on moral masochism in Sigmund Freud, "Das ökonomische Problem des Masochismus", *Studienausgabe,* vol. III, pp. 349-54. Nell is also parodied in the "Little Busy Bee" of the Monflathers establishment.
41 According to Goldfarb, Dickens only knows two kinds of parent-child relationships, either an incestuous bondage between parent and child (which I would include in my term 'exploitation') or a child with no parents at all. Orphanhood is in Dickens often preferable to incestuous relationships since "the orphan is free to extend himself by embracing the world and loving outwardly. This ability to love outwardly contrasts diametrically in Dickens with the ability for love consequent upon the constrictions of incest." (See Russell Goldfarb, "Charles Dickens; Orphans, Incest, and Repression" in: *Sexual Repression and Victorian Literature,* Lewisburg 1970, pp. 114-138; quotation taken from p. 133.)

Quilp). The bad child (Quilp, Fred, the pony) enslaves the parental figure (Mrs. Quilp, Nell's grandfather, the Garlands). The same person can be victimizer as well as victim. Nell's grandfather, for instance, is victimized by Quilp and by Fred but exploits Nell; the Garlands keep their son infantile but are in turn unable to tame the rebellious pony. Between two persons, however, the pattern is always the same. There is a powerful adult versus a weak child or a powerful child versus a weak adult. In Dickens's view the child who has to peep through keyholes in order to participate in the primal scene – and I understand this in a larger sense, namely to take a share in the parental love – can only be either a victim or a victimizer.[42] Both roles, however, bring doom upon him. Quilp as well as Nell have to die. It is psychologically sound that Quilp's death happens first. If a person has to kill in himself all the vitality that Quilp embodies (although, admittedly, sometimes in a distorted form), he may be virtuous and kind just as Nell is, but he is dead, too.

It is in keeping with the "anal" mood of the novel[43] that most of its characters are obsessed with money. Nell's grandfather thirsts for it and is at once ready to rob Mrs. Jarley when Isaac List talks of

> the pleasures of winning! The delight of picking up the money – the bright, shining yellow-boys – and sweeping 'em into one's pocket! The deliciousness of having a triumph at last, and thinking that one didn't stop short and turn back, but went half-way to meet it. (402)

Nell herself is introduced to the reader in the original manuscript as "selling diamonds" and is called by Quilp "my duck of diamonds" (140). Fred wants to get his share in the supposed riches and joins the gamblers to achieve this end and Quilp, who is sometimes nearly as invisible as Alberich with his magic coat, is a very Nibelung – hoarding his gold. As Kincaid puts it "Quilp is chasing the old man for the gold the old man is also chasing; the dog is, indeed, chasing its tail and driving itself mad."[44]

It is not clear to Mr. Chuckster whether Kit, who is given a shilling for holding the pony because Mr. Garland has no change and who returns the following week "to work it out", although nobody expects it of him, is "precious raw" or "precious deep". It is psychologically convincing that he is later accused of having stolen the five pound note. As Mr. Chuckster rightly feels, the display of so much virtue is unnatural and gives rise to suspicions.[45]

42 The fact that Fagin and Nell (i.e. devil and angel) leave no footprints points to their basic affinity.

43 Michael Steig deals in his essay "Dickens' Excremental Vision", *Victorian Studies* 13 (1970), pp. 339-54, with Dickens's "anality" in the *Christms Carol* and *Bleak House.*

44 James R. Kincaid, "Laughter and Pathos: *The Old Curiosity Shop*" in: R. L. Partlow (ed.), *Dickens the Craftsman,* pp. 77-78.

45 Kit's full name is Christopher Nubbles; his surname sounds similar to the verb *to nobble,* i.e. to obtain dishonestly.

When Dickens spoke for the International Copyright in America and was attacked by his opponents for having mercenary motives, he defended himself fiercely in a revealing language. Consider for instance his Hartford speech: "Gentlemen, ... I came here in an open, honest, and confiding spirit, if ever man did, and because I heartily inclined toward you; had I felt otherwise I should have kept away. As I came here, and *am* here, *without the least admixture of the hundredth portion of a grain of base alloy, without the faintest unworthy reference to self in any word I have ever addressed to you,* ... I assert my right tonight, in regard to the past for the last time, ... to appeal to you, as I have done on two former occasions, on a question of universal literary interest in both countries." (Emphasis mine except for "am" which was stressed by Dickens; quoted in *PE,* vol. III, p. 83.)

The Brasses are "sharks" and when they are in high spirits, Dick concludes "that they had just been cheating somebody and receiving the bill" (520).

Codlin is ready to sell Nell while at the same time protesting his friendship and Miss Edwards is treated with cruelty at the Monflathers establishment because of her poverty.

Even the delightful Dick thinks of marrying Nell's money or muses in the following way:

> 'These old people – there's no trusting 'em, Fred. There's an aunt of mine down in Dorsetshire that was going to die when I was eight years old, and hasn't kept her word yet. They're so aggravating, so unprincipled, so spiteful – unless there's apoplexy in the family, Fred, you can't calculate upon 'em, and even then they deceive you just as often as not' (105)

and is trying to get some money from this same aunt by sprinkling his begging letter with some water "to make it look penitent" (110). The streets in which there are shops where he owes money are no thoroughfares to him. He enters them in his notebook in order to avoid them in future. The reader feels sympathy for him, however, because he bears his burden with such good grace and is truly witty. When the single gentleman, for instance, disturbs the Brasses by sleeping twenty-six hours at a stretch, Dick remonstrates with him thus:

> 'The short and the long of it is, that we cannot allow single gentlemen to come into this establishment and sleep like double gentlemen without paying extra for it.'
> 'Indeed!' cried the lodger.
> 'Yes, sir, indeed,' returned Dick, yielding to his destiny and saying whatever came uppermost; 'an equal quantity of slumber was never got out of one bedstead, and if you're going to sleep in that way, you must pay for a double-bedded room.' (343)

Dick, then, is a vehicle for the author to make fun of the money-mindedness of the other characters. Although he is poor himself, he is not crushed by poverty but displays an extraordinary resourcefulness. We shall have to talk more about him in the next few pages. As we shall see, he cannot counterbalance the deadly weight of the Nell/Quilp dichotomy – although he surely is the most positive character in the book.


## 2.3 A "Modest Quencher" and a "Little Thin Sandwich of Fire"

E. M. Forster's statement that

> Food in fiction is mainly social. It draws characters together, but they seldom require it physiologically, seldom enjoy it and never digest it unless specially asked to do so. They hunger for each other, as we do in life, but our equally constant longing for breakfast and lunch does not get reflected[46]

is, on the whole, not true with regard to Dickens's novels. Though his characters are drawn together by shared breakfasts, lunches, teas, and suppers, they also require it

---

46 E. M. Forster, *Aspects of the Novel* (1927), Penguin Edition, Harmondsworth 1971, pp. 60-61.

physiologically and do not only hunger for each other's company, but for food itself. Furthermore, there is often a very sensuous enjoyment of food, too. In all Dickens's fiction food and drink play a rather prominent part; among his books *The Old Curiosity Shop* is particularly rich in eating and drinking scenes and images. It is easy to recall at once a number of these highly cathected scenes. We may remember Quilp's performances at the breakfast table (86), the tea-party at Tower Hill (74-78), the supper at the Jolly Sandboys (195-203), Mrs. Jarley taking her tea in front of the caravan (263-65), the Brasses and Mr. Quilp having tea and a "cold collation" at the summer-house (474-79), Kit's party, enjoying their oysters and their beer (378-9), the comfortable assembly, drawing up a description of Quilp's body and happily drinking his punch (458-62), or Kit eating away in prison to comfort his mother (561).

Nell, Tom Scott, Mrs. Quilp and her mother, the single gentleman, and the Marchioness are all shown to the reader while preparing breakfast. Quilp performs his magic feats at the breakfast table; Codlin cheats Nell and her grandfather by drinking all the ale and then dividing the bill for breakfast into two equal halves. When Kit is in prison he gets his breakfast in a "tin porringer" and when he and the single gentleman are ready to set out in search of Nell, "there was nothing but breakfast to fill up the intervening blank of one hour and a half" (630).

Other meals are frequently referred to as well. There are various tea-parties, some of which have already been mentioned, there are lunches (Dick takes a "rather strong lunch with a friend" and Mr. Chuckster is invited to lunch at Abel Cottage), there are dinners (for instance the dinner Dick offers to Fred), and there are a number of suppers (the scanty but cheerful meals of Kit's family as well as those of Nell and the old man and the meals Nell and her grandfather get at various stages of their journey). Indeed, to do justice to all the references to food and drink would require a paper devoted solely to this subject.

The references to various kinds of drinks are even more numerous. Mrs. Quilp and her neighbours, Mrs. Jarley, Mrs. Nubbles and her neighbour, Mrs. Nubbles and Barbara's mother, the Marchioness and the ailing Dick, Quilp at breakfast and Quilp and the Brasses at the summer-house all drink tea. On their pilgrimage Nell once asks for a draught of milk; the ridiculous Mr. Cheggs is seen "quaffing lemonade" (118), and the single gentleman as well as Quilp are once said to have coffee for breakfast.

Most often, however, the characters are provided with alcoholic beverages be it with Jamaica rum or the renowned Schiedam (a Dutch brand of rum), gin and water, grog, brandy, "strong waters", "a glass of something warm and spicy", "a glass of something hot", punch, wine, mulled wine and – above all – beer. Often simply called "beer" it also crops up as "double stout", "(small) ale", "mild porter" and "choice purl". More often than not it is served warm or even hot.

That the alcoholic drinks fulfil the function of a comforter is seen in Richard, who "can be merry under any circumstances" (102) but only, we suspect, because he has habitually had "the sun very strong in his eyes" (60), i.e. because he is always a little or very drunk. His "spirit is expanded by means of the rosy wine" (60) and he is given to "assuaging the pangs of thirst" by his "modest quenchers" (344). Thus by means of spirits discomfort is warded off and comfort is increased or regained. When Richard is dejected on the receipt of his former love's wedding cake

> Daniel Quilp adopted the surest means of soothing him, by ringing the bell, and ordering in a supply of rosy wine. (467)

When he wants to comfort Kit in prison by sending him a jug of beer, Dick speaks, in one of his many quotations, of beer as possessing "a spell in its every drop 'gainst the ills of mortality" (562). Mrs. Jarley, too, is in the habit of raising her spirits with "a bottle of rather suspicious character" (263) and after the deadly affront she has endured from Miss Monflathers the bottle helps her to become "increasing in smiles and decreasing in tears" (313). Even the surly Mr. Codlin is cheered by warm ale, he is said to be "greatly softened by this soothing beverage" (198). The card-players who deceive the old man pour themselves some brandy or, as they call it, "a drop of comfort" (403) and Quilp, too, resorts to brandy in his lonely mood of resentment (453-54) or is seen "solacing himself all the time with the pipe and the case-bottle" (470). Indeed, Quilp's case-bottle and Mrs. Jarley's "suspicious bottle" are reminiscent of the infant's bottle – drink as comforter is the comforter of the nursery. Both Quilp and Mrs. Jarley are particularly attached to their respective bottles; even Mrs. Jarley, who is otherwise so generous, grudges others the use of it. Quilp only presides "over the case-bottle of rum with extraordinary open-heartedness" when he wants to entrap his wife whom he suspects of being in love with Fred. His "generosity" enables him to torture Mrs. Jiniwin simultaneously by excluding her from her beloved card-game as well as from the liquor and

> if she so much as stealthily advanced a tea-spoon towards a neighbouring glass (which she often did), for the purpose of abstracting but one sup of its sweet contents, Quilp's hand would overthrow it in the very moment of her triumph, and Quilp's mocking voice implore her to regard her precious health. (244)

When he has to watch the others share in the contents of his case-bottle he, again like a child, embraces the bottle and hugs it as soon as he can get hold of it and does not let it go any more. He is dependent on and in need of the bottle and might have expressed this state in Mrs. Gamp's famous words:

> leave the bottle on the chimley-piece, and don't ask me to take none, but let me put my lips to it when I am so dispoged (*MC*, 379)

This indeed is almost like being breast-fed on demand!

Dick does not only combat his bodily discomfort when he seeks relief from his "pangs of thirst" by drinking spirits. After the news of his former love's marriage, Dick puts a black hatband on his hat and spends the evening drinking purl and playing cards with the Marchioness. When he returns to his lodging, he suddenly remembers that he has lost Sophy and Dickens comments on this:

> Some men in his blighted position would have taken to drinking; but as Mr Swiveller had taken to that before, he only took ... to playing the flute (533),

and he plays it so miserably that he is given notice to quit on the following morning. It is natural for him and the other characters to resort to drink first when they are in low spirits.

The warmth of a cheerful fire seems to serve as a comforter, too. Very often it is contrasted with the cold outside, for instance when Master Humphrey returns from his visit at the Shop:

> A cheerful fire was blazing on the hearth, the lamp burnt brightly, ... everything was quiet, warm, and cheering, and in happy contrast to the gloom and darkness I had quitted. (55)

When Kit passes by the abandoned Curiosity Shop

> the house looked a picture of cold desolation; and Kit, who remembered the cheerful fire that used to burn there on a winter's night and the no less cheerful laugh that made the small room ring, turned quite mournfully away. (163)

Codlin, Short, Nell and the old man are wet through when they arrive at the inn *The Jolly Sandboys*. However,

> A mighty fire was blazing on the hearth and roaring up the wider chimney with a cheerful sound (196),

and, as Dickens adds,

> It is not difficult to forget rain and mud by the side of a cheerful fire. (198)

At the end of their laborious journey Nell and her grandfather live in a house close to that of the poor schoolmaster and

> In a short time each had its cheerful fire glowing and crackling on the hearth, and reddening the pale old wall with a hale of healthy blush. (483)

Enough food, warm drinks, preferably shared with others, and a cheerful fire make for what Dickens calls *comfort. Comfort* is indeed a key-word in the novel. It is used in the sense of 'physical well-being' on the one hand (as in the adjective *comfortable*) and in the sense of 'consolation' on the other, and it is implied that by being comfortable in the first sense of the word one will gain comfort in the second sense, too.

It has been mentioned that Nell is often seen busily tidying up or – as Dickens calls it – making everything "neat and comfortable" (252). It seems that the characters take pains to brighten up their houses while at the same time being unable to give them a firm foundation. Like Dickens himself, who to his very end was constantly improving his home at Gad's Hill,[47] they try to ward off their inner loneliness by making their environments comfortable.

In the second half of the novel we find the protagonists Quilp and Nell both on the look-out for some nice and warm, comfortable corner for themselves. After having witnessed the mock funeral scene at Tower Hill, Quilp feels driven away and quits his home, just as Nell and her grandfather had to leave theirs. It has been mentioned that both Quilp and Nell live in decaying old houses and both try to make them habitable. Quilp has a large breakfast to begin with, buys a hammock for himself and an old stove and

> shut himself up in his Bachelor's Hall, which, by reason of its newly-erected chimney deposing the smoke inside the room and carrying none of it off, was not quite so agreeable as more fastidious people might have desired. Such inconveniences, however, instead of disgusting the dwarf with his new abode, rather suited his humour; so, after dining luxuriously from the public-house, he lighted his pipe, and smoked against the chimney until nothing of him was visible through the mist but a pair of red and highly-inflamed eyes, with sometimes a dim vision of his head and face, as, in a fit of violent coughing, he slightly stirred the smoke and scattered the heavy wreaths by which they were obscured. In the midst of this atmosphere, which must infallibly have smothered any other man, Mr Quilp passed the evening with great cheerfulness; solacing himself all

---

47 Sir Henry Dickens writes about his father: "To him Gad's Hill was everything. He was always making some new improvement, increasing its comforts and adding to its attractions." (*The Recollections of Sir Henry Dickens,* p. 15.)

the time with the pipe and the case-bottle and occasionally entertaining himself with a melodious howl, intended for a song, but bearing not the faintest resemblance to any scrap of any piece of music, vocal or instrumental, ever invented by man. Thus he amused himself until nearly midnight, when he turned into his hammock with the utmost satisfaction. (469-70)

Just as we have talked of the suppressed Quilpish nature in Nell we can also mention the suppressed Nellish part in Quilp. His desolation, his suffering and his insecurity are denied in the above passage. Only the admission that he is "solacing himself all the time with the pipe and the case-bottle" and the ensuing howl prepare us for the next paragraph:

The first sound that met his ears in the morning – as he half opened his eyes, and, finding himself unusually near the ceiling, entertained a drowsy idea that he must have been transformed into a fly or blue-bottle in the course of the night, – was that of a stifled sobbing and weeping in the room. Peeping cautiously over the side of his hammock, he descried Mrs Quilp ... (470)

We know that during the night our unconscious is at work, that the censor in us is less watchful than during the day and that suppressed emotions may come to the surface. This is what happens to Quilp. His suppressed conviction of his own worthlessness emerges and he feels "transformed into a fly or a blue-bottle".[48] And his grief – which Dickens never allows him to feel directly – is expressed by Mrs. Quilp, i.e. by Nell's double or, as we have seen before, by Quilp's split-off other half.

His search for comfort, then, is not much different from that of Nell, who, together with her grandfather and the schoolmaster, attempts to "make these dwellings as habitable and full of comfort" (483) as she could. When the others have gone to bed, Nell remains behind, looking at the stars and the churchyard. She becomes aware of the "dreamless sleepers" that lie "close within the shadow of the church – touching the wall, as if they clung to it for comfort and protection" (484). Even the dead try to obtain security from a building.

It is characteristic of Dickens to give us a pair of nouns that are semantically related, "comfort and protection", just as Nell feels "the tranquil air of comfort and content" at the cottage where she buys her milk and is full of "comfort and content" when she follows the two sisters from afar. In the much used expression "to comfort and console" the two elements become tautological. The bachelor has come to the clergyman's house in order to "comfort and console him" after the death of his wife (486). The two sextons who are frightened of death are "greatly consoled and comforted by the little fiction they had agreed upon" (502), namely that the woman they have just buried was not of their own age but at least ten years older than they themselves. When Quilp watches Kit being taken to prison he exultingly exclaims: "Let him have the Bethel minister to comfort and console him" (550) and the single gentleman tries in vain to make his brother comprehend who he is by declaring that he has returned to England in order "to comfort and console" him (651). It has been mentioned that Kit, Abel Garland and Nell are praised for being comforts to their parental figures. If we replace *comfort* by *consolation* the role these children have to play becomes even more evident.[49]

---

48 This image may remind the reader of Kafka's *Die Verwandlung* – the most moving account of a disturbed narcissistic development that I know.
49 Children as comforters of adults are mentioned on pp. 166, 249, 363, 488, 560, 718.

We can modify our earlier statement that in Dickens's world people either eat or are being eaten themselves. It seems that a child who does not take on the role of being a comforter does not become neutral or indifferent but appears greedy and cannibalistic; in other words, the child can only prove that he does not devour his parent by becoming his comforter. In Dickens's world it is only being "a comfort" that protects a child from being "a shark". Dickens calls the Brasses "sharks", which does not surprise us. However, at first sight it is rather strange that he calls his son Alfred "Sampson Brass", nicknaming him after a most unlikeable character. Sidney, one year older than Alfred, is called "Chickenstalker" after Mrs. Chickenstalker in *The Chimes*.[50] Mrs. Chickenstalker is a shopkeeper. The protagonist of the tale, Trotty Veck, is sometimes given food by Mrs. Chickenstalker without having to pay cash for it at once. At the end of the story Trotty's daughter Meg gets married and Mrs. Chickenstalker provides the party with a big pitcher full of a delicious drink made of ale, beaten eggs and spirits and served warm. Thus, it seems that Dickens assigns the roles of the supporting and the greedy child to Sidney and Alfred respectively. However, in Trotty's dream Mrs. Chickstalker's shop is seen thus:

> A little shop, quite crammed and choked with the abundance of its stock; a perfectly voracious little shop, with a maw as accommodating and as full as any shark's. Cheese, butter, firewood, soap, pickles, matches, bacon, table-beer, peg-tops, sweetmeats, boys' kites, birdseed, cold ham, birch brooms, hearthstones, salt, vinegar, blacking, red herrings, stationery, lard, mushroom-ketchup, staylaces, loaves of bread, shuttlecocks, eggs, and slate pencil: everything was fish that came to the net of this greedy little shop, and all the articles were in its net. (*The Chimes, CB,* I, 225)

Mrs. Chickenstalker's generosity, her capacity and willingness to feed others becomes threatening for it is based on a voracious and greedy little shop that is compared to a shark's maw. Blacking is one of the fish that come into its net – small wonder that the man who imagined it tries to keep away from it. We become aware of an underlying fear of coming too close to this feeding woman. Symbiosis is at once wished for and dreaded. As Laing so aptly put it

> instead of the polarities of separateness and relatedness based on individual autonomy, there is the antithesis between complete loss of being by absorption into the other person (engulfment), and complete aloneness (isolation).[51]

The conflict between the longing for and the dread of symbiosis is illustrated in the suggestive scene at the Jolly Sandboys'. Codlin and Short travel together with Nell and her grandfather and arrive in the evening at an inn called "The Jolly Sandboys". Codlin gets there first; in the kitchen

> A mighty fire was blazing on the hearth and roaring up the wide chimney with a cheerful sound (196)

and there is a delicious "savoury smell" in the air. The landlord proudly tells Codlin that he is preparing

> 'a stew of tripe,' smacking his lips, 'and cow-heel,' smacking them again, 'and bacon,' smacking them once more, 'and steak,' smacking them for the fourth time, 'and peas,

---

50 See *The Recollections of Sir Henry Dickens,* p. 39, and Dickens's letter to Forster of November 10, 1844, *PE,* vol. IV, p. 216.

51 R. D. Laing, *The Divided Self,* first published 1960, Penguin Books, Harmondsworth 1976, p. 44.

cauliflowers, new potatoes, and sparrow-grass, all working up together in one delicious gravy.' (196)

Codlin gets his warm beer and shortly afterwards Short, Nell and the old man arrive. They are wet to the skin from the heavy rain. When the landlord sees them coming, he rushes into the kitchen to take the lid off the iron cooking pot:

> The effect was electrical. They all came in with smiling faces, though the wet was dripping from their clothes upon the floor, and Short's first remark was, 'What a delicious smell!' (198)

They are all given dry clothes, and Nell and her grandfather soon fall asleep "overpowered by the warmth and the comfort and the fatigue they had undergone" (198). But as soon as they have given way to the warmth and comfort, as soon as they have given up their vigilance and have comfortably fallen asleep, Codlin and Short start talking about them and plan to "take measures for detaining of 'em and restoring 'em to their friends" (199) in order to earn some money. Suddenly even Codlin becomes solicitous and while he means to betray little Nell and the old man protests his friendship. While doing so, he also wants to exclude Short from the prospective reward. Thus Codlin admonishes Nell

> 'God bless you. Recollect the friend. Codlin's the friend, not Short. Short's very well as far as he goes, but the real friend is Codlin – not Short.' (207)

In other words, it is dangerous in Dickens's world to trust the comfort of the warm fire, it is dangerous to follow one's longing to be taken care of. The fire seems to be a trap; it has promised the two something it cannot keep, just as the fire of the furnace man cannot fulfil his expectations.

Supper is being served at the inn:

> When everything was ready, the landlord took off the cover for the last time, and then indeed there burst forth such a goodly promise of supper, that if he had offered to put it on again or had hinted at a postponement, he would certainly have been sacrificed on his own hearth. (202)

However, by this supper Dickens shows us that the very means of cheering people up can be perverted in its use. A travelling showman called Jerry is among the guests, together with his troup of performing dogs. One of the dogs has lost a halfpenny and is punished for that: "*He* goes without his supper" (202). This is how Jerry feeds his dogs who

> formed in a row, standing upright as a file of soldiers.
> 'Now, gentlemen,' said Jerry, looking at them attentively. 'The dog whose name's called, eats. The dogs whose names aren't called, keep quiet. Carlo!'
> The lucky individual whose name was called, snapped up the morsel thrown towards him, but none of the others moved a muscle. In this manner they were fed at the discretion of their master. Meanwhile the dog in disgrace ground hard at the organ, sometimes in quick time, sometimes in slow, but never leaving off for an instant. When the knives and forks rattled very much, or any of his fellows got an unusually large piece of fat, he accompanied the music with a short howl, but he immediately checked it on his master looking round, and applied himself with increasing diligence to the Old Hundredth. (203)

Surely Jerry's cruelty could not be better expressed than by his making the poor hungry dog produce the music for the Old Hundreth in which we sing "The Lord, ye know, is God indeed ... We are His folk, He doth us feed." The dog, who only dares to express his hunger in short howls, has to grind the music to this thanks-giving song!

In its cruelty the scene can be parallelled to the feeding of the Marchioness by Sally Brass. The dependent and helpless dog, who does all he can to satisfy his master, is punished for having missed a halfpenny he probably could not have been expected to get anyway. While everybody is eating and while the air itself is steeped in the smell of the dinner, while the adult human beings threaten to murder the landlord for a delay of it, the dog, who, like a child, is more governed by the demands of his instincts, is not given anything at all and has to thank the Lord for feeding him. The Holy Communion, which on one level can be interpreted as a merger between Christ and his disciples (the wine and bread standing for his blood and body), between father and sons, between parents and children, is here travestied into a very unholy affair indeed.

It seems better to rely on oneself than feeling one's symbiotic needs and then being forsaken. Thus Goldfarb's statement (see footnote 41, p. 81) can be modified. Dickens not only lets his children be orphans because of the deleterious incestuous attachment that seems the only alternative, but he also keeps them in loneliness, cold, hunger and desolation to protect them from being devoured by sharks. The "little thin sandwich of fire" (350) that is granted to the Marchioness – an image in which the two basic symbols of warmth and food are combined – may be better than the plentiful board and cheerful fireside of Abel Garland, who cannot even spend a weekend apart from his parents without feeling great distress.

And yet, even the Marchioness is constantly frightened of being burnt alive. She tells Dick that Sally used to keep her locked in the kitchen at night and adds:

> I was terribly afraid of being kept like this, because if there was a fire, I thought they might forget me and only take care of themselves you know. (587)

And when Dick hears that the Marchioness has pawned all his clothes in order to be able to buy food for him, he exclaims:

> 'It's embarrassing ... in case of fire – even an umbrella would be something – but you did quite right, dear Marchioness. (589)

The symbol of the fire is, of course, overdetermined. We know that there were more fires in the Victorian age than today but – taking into account the novel as a whole – we can say that Dickens uses the familiar dread of the fire to express the fear of too close a contact as well. Similarly, as we have seen, the nice warm beverages that make for good company become burning hot liquids with which people are tormented. Warm and tender affection is replaced by a burning possessiveness, by an inability to distinguish between the self and the other, by a need to govern the other like the limbs of one's own body.[52] To withstand such possessiveness, such "fire" one must become a Quilp. Quilp is once called "a salamander" (249), and the salamander proverbially lives in the fire which it quenches with the coldness of its body. Treating

---

52 There is an interesting unpublished seminar paper by Hans ten Doornkaat on the function of food and drink in Dickens's *Dombey and Son* where he comes to the conclusion that "food is only meant to be enjoyed where it is served hot and for company or somebody willing to share" (p. 20). This contrasts with the function of food and drink in *The Old Curiosity Shop.* As we have seen, it can be too hot and in that case can only be endured but not enjoyed. It has a social function, too, but this can be perverted. A last example of the perverted use may be Quilp's fantasy, looking round the wharf in a dark night, "If I took it in my head to be a widower, now, I only need invite Mrs. Quilp to take tea here one foggy night", a deleted passage from the original manuscript. (See *The Old Curiosity Shop,* footnotes, pp. 713-14.)

others cruelly, attacking them, provoking their anger seems the best way of keeping them at the needed distance.

This pattern, too, is only broken by Dick, the character who is defined by his generosity. His constant saying is "may we never want a friend nor a bottle to give him" and he not only provides the starved Marchioness with food and drink, but he also sends a pot of porter to Kit in prison every day and shares "the rosy" with Fred and Mr. Chuckster, drinks in the company of Quilp and even of Sally Brass, and introduces her as well as the single gentleman into the mystery of where to get "exceedingly mild porter in the neighbourhood". The critics are rightly charmed with Mr. Swiveller. Like his creator, Dick can bear his situation through his power of imagination. Gin and water, a cheap drink that is unbecoming to a gentleman,[53] is passed off as "the rosy", his single bedroom becomes "his rooms, his lodgings, or his chambers", his bedstead changes into a bookcase when Dick needs the support of this little fiction:

> There is no doubt that by day Mr Swiveller firmly believed this secret convenience to be a bookcase and nothing more; that he closed his eyes to the bed, resolutely denied the existence of the blankets, and spurned the bolster from his thoughts ... Implicit faith in the deception was the first article of his creed. To be the friend of Swiveller you must reject all circumstantial evidence, all reason, observation, and experience, and repose a blind belief in the bookcase. It was his pet weakness and he cherished it. (101)

It seems that the longing to be cared for − be it by the warmth of the blankets and the support of the bolster − has to be suppressed by Dick as well. Often, however, he can enlarge his cramped living quarters. The above example is an instance of that tendency as well. By denying the bedroom Dick also makes believe that he lives in two rooms, a living-room and a bed-room. When Dick regains consciousness after his long illness, he falls to

> staring at some green stripes upon the bed-furniture, and associating them strangely with patches of fresh turf, while the yellow ground between them made gravel-walks, and so helped out a long perspective of trim gardens. (579-80)

His inventive mind creates new words. His destiny is "a crusher", the blows of destiny are "staggerers", the comforting drink is "a modest quencher", Nell's and her grandfather's flight is "a baffler" to him, the rejection of his affection by Sophy is "a stifler", peaceful sleep is "the balmy". Dick and Mrs. Jarley both have "an inventive genius" and share their food with others. The Marchioness belongs to this group as well. When Dick is ill, she nurses him and provides him almost miraculously with everything he needs. She also shares in his linguistic ability. Mr. Brass is in her words "such a wunner" and, as we have seen, Dick is called "Mr. Liverer" by her. She can, furthermore, not only transform gin and water into the rosy but orange peel and water becomes quite a nice drink "if you make believe very much" (537). However, delightful as the relationship between Dick and the Marchioness is, it belongs to the fairy-tale elements in the world of this novel. The story of Quilp and Nell is foreign to the fairy-tale in its pessimism and it sets the scene of the novel as well as its atmosphere. Within this Quilp-Nell world the Dick-Marchioness story seems like an escape into fantasy. Only people who are slightly drunk can manage this escape, an

---

53 See Trollope's *Ayala's Angel,* where Mr. Dosett is despised by his niece for drinking such a vulgar drink as gin and water, because she does not realise that he cannot afford wine.

escape into the rosy, the balmy, the mazy and innumerable quotations.[54] Even the single gentleman, who wants to become the provider for his brother, is connected with the fairy-tale, for his trunk is described by Dick as containing

> a specimen of every kind of food and wine known in these times, and in particular that it was of a self-acting kind and served up whatever was required ... and ... that he had distinctly seen water boil and bubble up when the single gentleman winked ... (346)

What else is it but a magic table and what else is Mrs. Garland's basket but the creation of a land of milk and honey? Consider this description of her basket. It

> disgorged such treasures of tea, and coffee, and wine, and rusks, and oranges, and grapes, and fowls ready trussed for boiling, and calves'-foot jelly, and arrow-root, and sago, and other delicate restoratives, that the small servant ... stood rooted on the spot ... (601)

Food, then, is a comforter to the people living in the world of *The Old Curiosity Shop*. It draws people together and – similar to warmth – it ought to make people feel at home. However, this function if often no longer valid and is replaced by its opposite. Giving or withholding food and drink and warmth to others becomes a means of torturing or manipulating them. Where food and drink are freely and generously given, a fairy-tale atmosphere begins to prevail. Food, drink and warmth can be seen as the necessary elements that have to be freely given in the symbiotic situation. Symbiosis is indeed wished for, but its concomitant helplessness and dependency are dreaded. It is torture to drink the boiling hot liquor and there is a constant fear of fire among the characters. Therefore, the "little thin sandwich of fire", i.e. the bare minimum of food and warmth may be preferable to "comfort", for it at least allows the character to move in his own sphere.

The longing for, and the simultaneous fright of, symbiosis is expressed in the story of Nell's death, as well. Though Dickens seems to covet death, and has been accused of "spiritual necrophilia",[55] there is a large amount of ambivalence with regard to it. This ambivalence is in my view the reason for Dickens's lack of decision as to whether Nell ought to die or not.

Forster says in his biography of Dickens:

> He had not thought of killing her, when, about half-way through, I asked him to consider whether it did not necessarily belong even to his own conception, after taking so mere a child through such a tragedy of sorrow, to lift her also out of the commonplace of ordinary happy endings, so that the gentle pure little figure and form should never change to the fancy. All that I meant he seized at once, and never turned aside from it again.[56]

---

54 It has been suggested by Pearson ("*The Old Curiosity Shop*" in: *Dickens and the Twentieth Century,* ed. by John Gross and Gabriel Pearson, London 1962, p. 90) and by Dyson ("*The Old Curiosity Shop*. Innocence and the Grotesque" in: *Dickens. Modern Judgements,* ed. by A. E. Dyson, London 1968, p. 73) that Dick is a partial self-portrait of the author. It is interesting, then, that the other "inventive genius", Mrs. Jarley, is also connected with Dickens's personal fate. Mrs. Jarley employs one Mr. Slum for advertising whose poetry has helped "the perfumers, ... the blacking-makers ..., the hatters" (282) in their business and he suggests an acrostic: "the name at the moment is Warren, but the idea's a convertible one" (282).

55 Steven Marcus, *Dickens: From Pickwick to Dombey,* p. 146.

56 John Forster, *The Life of Charles Dickens,* vol. I, p. 123.

In his essay, "The Decline and Fall of Little Nell: Some Evidence from the Manuscripts", Stanley Tick shows that Forster's responsibility is not as great as he had assumed.[57] According to Tick, Dickens "had contemplated such an ending before anyone suggested it to him" (p. 65) on the one hand, and "Dickens's continual, deliberate equivocation about Nell's fate (long after he apparently decided it) would have permitted the heroine to survive" (68) on the other. Thus Dickens keeps his options open as long as possible or, we might say, his ambivalence does not let him make up his mind. Consciously, as I have pointed out, Dickens praises the peace and beauty of death. Before Nell dies, she hears celestial music and in Cattermole's tailpiece she is surrounded by angels who carry her to heaven. This is Dickens's description of her body:

> No sleep so beautiful and calm, so free from trace of pain, so fair to look upon. She seemed a creature fresh from the hand of God, and waiting for the breath of life; not one who had lived and suffered death (652)

and

> Sorrow was dead indeed in her, but peace and perfect happiness were born; imaged in her tranquil beauty and profound repose. (654)

Dickens, who pictures to himself a preambivalent, even a prenatal paradisiac homoeostasis, seems to have forgotten what he has written only a few hundred pages earlier, commenting upon the old man's senility:

> We call this a state of childishness, but it is the same poor hollow mockery of it, that death is of sleep. ... Where, in the sharp lineaments of rigid and unsightly death, is the calm beauty of slumber, telling of rest for the waking hours that are past, and the gentle hopes and loves for those which are to come? Lay death and sleep down, side by side, and say who shall find the two akin. (146)

The theme of death or death imagery crops up so frequently in the novel that only a few of the allusions can be studied in detail. However, in the symbol of the old church in which Nell is going to be buried, Dickens's conflicts are clearly expressed. On the one hand, as we have seen, Nell does not die but is passing from death to life. Her grave will be caressed by the sunshine, by the murmuring wind, and by the shadows of the leaves that flutter in the wind and will fall upon her tomb; the songs of birds and the shouting of schoolboys will be heard in the church and greet her. When Nell thinks of her death in the decaying church and consoles herself with these thoughts, she concludes

> Die who would, it [i.e. the church] would still remain the same; these sights and sounds would still go on as happily as ever. It would be no pain to sleep amidst them. (494)

Once more the reality of death is denied. Although the church is almost collapsing, we are meant to believe that there will be some sort of eternity there.

Nell climbs the church tower and enjoys the view:

> Oh! the glory of the sudden burst of light; the freshness of the fields and woods, stretching away on every side and meeting the bright blue sky; the cattle grazing in the pasturage; the smoke, that, coming from among the trees, seemed to rise upward from the green earth; the children yet at their gambols down below – all, everything, so beautiful and happy. It was like passing from death to life; it was drawing nearer to Heaven. (494-96)

---

57 Stanley Tick, "The Decline and Fall of Little Nell: Some Evidence from the Manuscripts", *Pacific Coast Philology,* 9 (1976), pp. 62-72.

In other words, her death, her going to Heaven is "like passing from death to life". This is, of course, a Christian conception. However, Dickens does not praise an eternal life in heaven, but an eternal continuation of a happy life on earth. Everything that Nell perceives from her tower is earthly beauty. This tendency was criticized in a review of the *Christian Remembrancer* in December 1842. It says:

> not a single christian feature is introduced. ... The whole matter is one tissue of fantastic sentiment, as though the growth of flowers by one's grave, and the fresh country air passing over it, and the games of the children near it, could abate by one particle the venom of death's sting, or cheat the grave of any the smallest element of his victory. ... to work up an elaborate picture of dying and death, without the only ingredient that can make the undisguised reality other than an 'uncouth hideous thing' ... is not dealing fairly by us.[58]

The same church that is described as providing her with eternal life is introduced to Nell by the sexton in these words:

> 'You have been into the church?'
> 'I'm going there now,' the child replied.
> 'There's an old well there,' said the sexton, 'right underneath the belfry; a deep dark echoing well. Forty years ago, you had only to let down the bucket till the first knot in the rope was free of the windlass, and you heard it splashing in the cold dull water. By little and little the water fell away ... and now, if you lower the bucket till your arms are tired and let out nearly all the cord, you'll hear it of a sudden clanking and rattling on the ground below, with a sound of being so deep and so far down, that your heart leaps into your mouth, and you start away as if you were falling in.'
> 'A dreadful place to come on in the dark!' exclaimed the child, who had followed the old man's looks and words until she seemed to stand upon its brink.
> 'What is it but a grave!' said the sexton. (492)

When she arrives at the church she is frightened of the "hollow sound" that the turning of the key awakes in the church. This is Dickens's description of the building:

> ... the very light, coming through sunken windows, seemed old and grey; and the air, redolent of earth and mould, seemed laden with decay. ... Here were the rotten beam, the sinking arch, the sapped and mouldering wall, the lowly trench of earth, the stately tomb on which no epitaph remained – all, marble, stone, iron, wood, and dust, one common element of ruin. (493)

It seems to me that Dickens tries hard to paint a peaceful slumber, to evoke a picture of sunshine and music, of green trees and blossoms, of the song of birds, while at the same time he cannot help expressing his fear of death in the pictures of the various old decaying houses, the dilapidated church, the well, and the conception of death as "a hollow mockery of sleep".

In *The Old Curiosity Shop* Dickens, in a long-drawn process, slaughters Nell. She never protests or revolts, she masochistically submits to her fate. I wonder whether Dickens's next novel, *Barnaby Rudge,* which depicts with much sympathy and understanding the most violent riots, owes something of its violence to the suppres-

---

58 Quoted in the introduction to *PE,* vol. II, p. xi.

sion of this very feeling in the preceding novel. As we know, the suppressed is liable to return.[59]

The first number of *The Old Curiosity Shop* was published in April 1840, the first number of *Little Dorrit* in December 1855, more than fifteen years lie between. *Little Dorrit* takes us into another world, similar and yet different.

59 It is interesting to note that fire is the destructive element in *Barnaby Rudge*. When the rioters burn the Warren (!) down
"Men ... rushed to and fro, stark mad, setting fire to all they saw – often to the dresses of their own friends – and kindling the building in so many parts that some had no time for escape, and were seen, with drooping hands and blackened faces, hanging senseless on the window-sills to which they had crawled, *until they were sucked and drawn into the burning gulf.*"
"There were men who cast their lighted torches in the air, and suffered them to fall upon their heads and faces, blistering the skin with deep unseemly burns. There were men who rushed up to the fire, and paddled in it with their hands as if in water; and others who were restrained by force from plunging in, *to gratify their deadly longing.*"
(*BR,* pp. 506 and 508 respectively; emphasis mine.)

# 3. Little Dorrit

There are many parallels between *Little Dorrit* and *The Old Curiosity Shop:* A self-sacrificing young girl is tied with strong bonds to an old man who exploits her love ruthlessly. The parental figures (father and grandfather respectively) become the children and are looked after by their young charges, who are overburdened. Maternal figures are characteristically absent. The two innocent and loving girls are not aware of the exploitative manner of their relations' love for them; neither do they seem to feel any disappointment, anger, rage or shame. Little Nell's unconscious hostility has already been pointed out. There are only few instances in *Little Dorrit* where the author comes near to hinting at something similar in Amy, e.g. the episode when she nearly addresses her father "as poultry, if not prunes and prism too, in her desire to submit to Mrs General and please him" (529). But even the quotation shows Dickens's attempt to give this slip another, albeit unconvincing, interpretation: Little Dorrit's dutiful obedience, and by no means her rebellion, is responsible for the parapraxis. In both novels the oedipal nature of the attachment between the paternal and the child figure is evident. But whereas both girls are slightly built, timid, always working and toiling for others, always cheerful and full of loving kindness, never seeking their own satisfaction, Little Nell, though prettier than Little Dorrit, is completely asexual, whereas Little Dorrit may at least dream of her elderly love. Although Nellie is beautiful and Amy is plain, it is the latter who is allowed to find a limited kind of happiness with Arthur. The most important difference in their fate is the fact that Nellie has to die young, while Amy is granted "a modest life of usefulness and happiness" (895).

The search for the culprit, however, goes on. As has been mentioned, the original title *Nobody's Fault* points to Dickens's most persistent conflict about the nature of guilt which is to be found in parents and children. This remains true in spite of the fact that – as Dickensian critics have pointed out time and again – the later Dickens becomes a critic of society. His earlier novels essentially move within the domestic sphere, but the post-Copperfieldian works are concerned with society as a whole. This society, as embodied in the Circumlocution Office, bears a large part of the guilt in *Little Dorrit.* Incidentally, it is interesting to note that Dickens's move from individual psychology to social psychology is a step that has been taken by modern science as well. However, the old conflicts between the characters themselves, with which we are mainly concerned, remain there all the same.

## 3.1 "The History of a Self-Tormentor"

There is an interpolated story in *Little Dorrit,* Miss Wade's account of her life, which is called "The History of a Self-Tormentor". As Dickens himself wrote to Forster that

> In Miss Wade I had an idea, which I thought a new one, of making the introduced story so fit into surroundings impossible of separation from the main story, as to make the blood of the book circulate through both (*F,* II, 184-5),

we may take this chapter as a starting point for our reflections. The story does indeed contain in a nutshell all that Dickens was to expose in the novel. It is concerned with the fate of a human being who has never been loved and with the by now familiar question of who is responsible for this lack of love.

Furthermore, it clearly shows how the emotional void is covered up with a false parade of concern and affection. Whenever Dickens ridicules condescension – and, as we shall see, there is plenty of it in the novel – he points out that there is no genuine love between the people concerned.

Miss Wade tells us how she was brought up. Although she talks of her childhood, we never learn her Christian name. This may be an indication of how unimportant she might have felt – being brought up in the company of nine other girls by a lady who calls herself her grandmother but who is not related to her at all. Miss Wade is told after some time that she is an orphan. She does not miss her dead parents so much as she suffers from the other girls' condescension:

> There was not other orphan among us; and I perceived ... that they conciliated me in an insolent pity, and in a sense of superiority. (726)

She passionately loves Charlotte, one of the girls, who, however, does not single her out but distributes "pretty looks and smiles to every one of them" (726).

When Miss Wade is invited to Charlotte's house she suffers tortures since Charlotte

> had a crowd of cousins and acquaintances, and we had dances at her house, and went out to dances at other houses, and, both at home and out, she tormented my love beyond endurance. Her plan was to make them all fond of her – and to drive me wild with jealousy. To be familiar and endearing with them all – and to make me mad with envying them. When we were left alone in our bedroom at night, I would reproach her with my perfect knowledge of her baseness; and then she would cry and cry and say I was cruel, and then I would hold her in my arms till morning: loving her as much as ever, and often feeling as if, rather than suffer so, I could so hold her in my arms and plunge to the bottom of a river – where I would still hold her after we were both dead. (726-7)

An aunt of Charlotte's gently reproaches her with caring too much for Miss Wade and with wearing herself to death and the girl answers:

> 'Dear aunt, she has an unhappy temper; other girls at school, besides I, try hard to make it better; we all try hard.' (727)

Miss Wade, who overhears this conversation and their calling her "a poor miserable girl", insists on being sent home at once.

She is then brought up with other young women and is later hired as a governess. At her first place of employment there are two children whom she likes, but the children prefer their rosy-faced nurse to Miss Wade, "their arms twining round her neck, instead of mine" (729), and she feels that this nurse exults over her. Miss Wade also chafes at what she considers the patronage of the children's mother, a pretty, young woman who wants to help her. When Miss Wade hands in her notice because she can no longer bear her jealousy of the other woman, her employer speaks to her as follows:

> 'Miss Wade, I fear you are unhappy, through causes over which I have not influence.'
> I smiled, thinking of the experience the word awakened, and said, 'I have an unhappy temper, I suppose.'
> 'I did not say that.'
> 'It is an easy way of accounting for anything,' said I.
> 'It may be; but I did not say so. What I wish to approach is something very different. My

husband and I have exchanged some remarks upon the subject, when we have observed with pain that you have not been easy with us.'

'Easy? Oh! You are such great people, my lady,' said I.

'I am unfortunate in using a word which may convey a meaning – and evidently does – quite opposite to my intention. ... I only mean, not happy with us. It is a difficult topic to enter on; but from one young woman to another, perhaps – in short, we have been apprehensive that you may allow some family circumstances of which no one can be more innocent than yourself, to prey upon your spirits. If so, let us entreat you not to make them a cause of grief. My husband himself ... formerly had a very dear sister who was not in law his sister, but who was universally beloved and respected –'

I saw directly that they had taken me in for the sake of the dead woman ... and to have the boast of me and advantage of me; (...) I left that house that night. (729-30)

After some similar experiences Miss Wade is employed by a rich family as the governess of a fifteen-year-old daughter. She becomes engaged to a nephew of this family but is tortured by her jealousy and her constant apprehension of being treated like a servant and relates that she "would have suffered anyone to kill me sooner than I would have laid myself out to bespeak their approval" (731). When her fiancé's aunt tells her several times how greatly her life will be changed after her marriage, she smarts with vexation.

Henry Gowan, who visits the family, understands her character and strengthens her in her feelings of wounded pride. It is therefore his company that she seeks, the more so, as she perceives her lover's jealousy and exults in the thought that he will suffer too.

When her fiancé's aunt hints that she should spend less time with Gowan, Miss Wade breaks out and asks her

how she knew that it was only necessary for her to make a suggestion to me, to have it obeyed? Did she presume on my birth, or on my hire? I was not bought, body and soul. She seemed to think that her distinguished nephew had gone into the slave-market and purchased a wife. (733)

She leaves the family at once. Gowan follows her and amuses himself "as long as it suited his inclinations" only to leave her afterwards for Pet Meagles (and, presumably, her money), an act which is the source of Miss Wade's deep resentment and hatred of Pet. In Pet's maid Tattycoram she sees herself and therefore comes to rescue her from "swollen patronage and selfishness, calling themselves kindness, protection, benevolence, and other fine names" (734).

In his number plans to *Little Dorrit* Dickens writes about the " 'Self-Tormentor Narrative': *Miss Wade's Story*. Unconsciously laying bare all her character."[1]

What Dickens has in mind seems evident. Miss Wade's character is laid bare indeed: she is full of jealousy, full of suspicion, full of hatred and disdain. Dickens manages to show to the reader as well that she is paranoiac when attributing base motives to people who really want to help her. Thus we feel that her friend Charlotte did not distribute pretty looks and smiles in order to pain Miss Wade but because she felt friendly towards them all and that the young lady employed her – as Miss Wade perceives – for the sake of her husband's dead sister but not – as she mistakenly thinks – in order to exult over her. Let us look more closely at the evidence that points to Miss Wade's guilt and her responsibility for her hard fate.

1 See Appendix B in Charles Dickens, *Little Dorrit,* ed. by Harvey Peter Sucksmith, Oxford 1979, p. 822; *Miss Wade's Story* underlined three times by Dickens.

This is how Dickens describes Miss Wade's face to the reader:

> It was dressed and trimmed into no ceremony of expression. Although not an open face, there was no pretence in it. 'I am self-contained and self-reliant; your opinion is nothing to me; I have no interest in you, care nothing for you, and see and hear you with indifference' – this it said plainly. It said so in the proud eyes, in the lifted nostril, in the handsome but compressed and even cruel mouth. Cover either two of those channels of expression, and the third would have said so still. Mask them all, and the mere turn of the head would have shown an unsubduable nature. (62)

From this quotation alone one can be fairly sure about Dickens's conscious attitude towards Miss Wade. She is extremely unfriendly, rejecting people's advances and she has a cruel mouth. Her pride is surely reprehensible in the author's eyes[2] and he also points out that she does not have the cardinal virtue of an open face. This is borne out later on when Miss Wade is described as Tattycoram's evil spirit (pp. 67, 378-79, 583, 880). She draws Tatty away from the Meagles family and is full of scorn regarding Mr. Meagles's attempt to redeem the lost child. She is rude towards Arthur and Mr. Meagles, sends back the letters Tattycoram gets and tells her young charge in no uncertain terms what a bad lot Mr. and Mrs. Meagles and their friends are:

> 'See here,' she said ... 'Here is your patron, your master. He is willing to take you back, my dear, if you are sensible of the favour and choose to go. You can be, again, a foil to his pretty daughter, a slave to her pleasant wilfulness, and a toy in the house showing the goodness of the family. You can have your droll name again, playfully pointing you out and set apart. (Your birth you know; you must not forget your birth.) You can again be shown to this gentleman's daughter, Harriet, and kept before her, as a living reminder of her own superiority and her gracious condescension. You can recover all these advantages and many more of the same kind which I dare say start up in your memory while I speak, and which you lose in taking refuge with me – you can recover them all by telling these gentlemen how humbled and penitent you are, and by going back to them to be forgiven.' (377)

Obviously Dickens wants to show us that Miss Wade is mistaken. Thus he talks about "Poor Mr. Meagles's inexpressible consternation in hearing his motives and actions so perverted" (377) and makes Tattycoram seek refuge with the Meagleses when she discovers Miss Wade's baseness. Miss Wade, then, is an evil woman. The people who surround her are wicked. Gowan, her former lover, is extremely heartless, and even Blandois, the personification of the devil in the story, is seen in her company. She is also observed to enter the house of the bloodsucking Patriarch, Mr. Casby. Miss Wade cannot accept the fact that she does not know her parents, that she is probably an illegitimate child. This, Dickens tells us, is quite wrong. Look at Little Dorrit, the heroine of the story! She was even born in prison and see what an angel she has become! Dickens drives this point home when Tattycoram recovers Mrs. Clennam's lost papers and takes them back to Mr. Meagles. This is how he moralizes for Tatty's benefit:

---

2 Dickens, who engaged in charity work on behalf of fallen women, selected the girls who were taken up at Urania Cottage. He writes to Miss Burdett-Coutts about a candidate: "The two best things I observed in her were her trembling very much while I was talking to her, and her being extremely grateful when I gave her hope" (*Letters from Charles Dickens to Angela Burdett-Coutts 1841–1865,* ed. by Edgar Johnson, London 1953, p. 200). Miss Wade defies this image of femininity, whereas Little Dorrit complies with it.

'You see that young lady who was here just now – that little, fragile figure passing along there, Tatty? Look. The people stand out of the way to let her go by. (...) I have heard tell, Tatty, that she was once regularly called the child of this place. She was born here and lived here many years. I can't breathe here. A doleful place to be born and bred in, Tattycoram?' 'Yes indeed, sir!' 'If she had constantly thought of herself, and settled with herself that everybody visited this place upon her ... she would have led an irritable and probably useless existence. Yet I have heard tell, Tattycoram, that her young life has been one of active resignation, goodness, and noble service. Shall I tell you what I consider those eyes of hers, that were here just now, to have always looked at, to get that expression?' 'Yes, if you please, sir.' 'Duty, Tattycoram.' (881-82)

It is curious to hear this message from Dickens, who was always wounded in his pride because his father was no longer a gentleman so that he, Charles Dickens, had to work in the company of "*common* men and boys"[3], as he tells us in the autobiographical fragment. Dickens hastens to add that

Though perfectly familiar with them, my conduct and manners were different enough from theirs to place a space between us. They, and the men, always spoke of me as 'the young gentleman.' ("AF", 25-26)

It is not surprising, then, to become aware of the fact that in Little Dorrit Dickens is of a divided mind. The interpolated story, which, according to the author, contains the message that is spelt out in the novel as a whole, does not put the blame on the child only. It is easier to see this if we look at the relation between the child-figure Tattycoram – obviously Miss Wade's double[4] – and the parent-figure Mr. Meagles. The question Dickens raises is whether Tattycoram's difficult temper or her bad treatment from the Meagleses is to blame for her outbursts. Obviously Dickens again wants to show to the reader that Mr. Meagles is all goodness – trying to understand Tattycoram's difficult character by "making allowances", i.e. by being aware of the fact that her temper has its source in her unhappy childhood. At the same time the reader feels the author's sympathy and empathy for the unhappy girl.[5] In her first outbreak Tatty starts by complaining about the "selfish brutes", i.e. the Meagles family, thus:

'Not caring what becomes of me! Leaving me here hungry and thirsty and tired, to starve, for anything they care! Beasts! Devils! Wretches!' (64)

While verbally abusing the parental figures and thus directing her aggression outwards, she at the same time has an "unsparing hand" which pinches her neck that is "freshly disfigured with great scarlet blots" (64) and thus she becomes a self-tormentor as well. Tattycoram, then, is torn by Dickens's own conflict when the author tells us that

3 "AF", 25, emphasis mine.
4 Tattycoram tells Miss Wade: "You seem to come like my own anger, my own malice, my own – whatever it is – I don't know what it is" (65) and the two of them almost always appear together in the novel. Dickens also remarks in his notes "Then shew Tattycoram like her" (Charles Dickens, *Little Dorrit*, ed. by Harvey Peter Sucksmith, p. 822).
5 Dickens's judgement of the candidate for Urania Cottage has been mentioned. We may add that Dickens also had surprising insight when he wrote, for instance, of girls who left the house in anger, "This sudden dashing down of all the building up of months upon months, is, to my thinking, so distinctly a Disease with the persons under consideration that I would pay particular attention to it, and treat it with particular gentleness and anxiety" (*Letters from Charles Dickens to Angela Burdett-Coutts 1841–1865,* ed. by Edgar Johnson, p. 81).

It was wonderful to see the fury of the contest in the girl, and the bodily struggle she made as if she were rent by the Demons of old. (65)

At the end of the scene, however, Tatty takes the blame upon herself:

> 'When my temper comes upon me, I am mad. I know I might keep it off if only I tried hard enough, and sometimes I do try hard enough, and at other times I don't and won't. What have I said! I knew when I said it, it was all lies. They think I am being taken care of somewhere, and have all I want. They are nothing but good to me. I love them dearly; no people could ever be kinder to a thankless creature than they are always to me.' (65-67)

The sentence "They think I am being taken care of somewhere" does not sound very convincing to me – wherever could Tattycoram possibly go in quarantine to be taken care of? – and is never taken up later in the novel. As the story continues and Tattycoram stays with Miss Wade, she resolves her conflict by putting the blame on the others. Towards the end of the novel she gives us the opposite solution by returning to Father and Mother Meagles and repeatedly accusing herself of being "bad" (880). It seems that indeed her temper is accountable for her difficulties. Yet in our ears there reverberates Miss Wade's sentence about people with a bad temper: "It is an easy way of accounting for anything" (730). Mr. Meagles frequently refers to Tatty's stormy temper. He attributes all her outbursts to it and his unfailing advice to her is to count five and twenty before speaking. He encourages her, in other words, to control her violent feelings and to suppress her complaints. Never does he think of possible reasons for Tattycoram's dissatisfaction *in the present*. And yet, as Lionel Trilling points out

> No reader of *Little Dorrit* can possibly conclude that the rage of envy which Tattycoram feels is not justified in some degree, or that Miss Wade is wholly wrong in pointing out to her the insupportable ambiguity of her position as the daughter-servant of Mr. and Mrs. Meagles and the sister-servant of Pet Meagles.[6]

As Miss Wade was employed for the sake of her employer's dead sister, so Tattycoram was brought to Twickenham in order to replace Pet's dead twin sister. Pet is fondled by her parents while Tattycoram has to look on, although – as she points out – she is younger than Pet and just as pretty as she is.[7] She is given food, clothes, shelter and protection but she always has to stand in her mistress's shadow. She is her obedient servant and she is often reminded of her position. (Miss Wade, we remember, tells her "you must not forget your birth".) A few quotations may illustrate Tattycoram's place in the family. When Tatty mentions to the Meagleses that she has recently seen Miss Wade, Pet tells her to take her hands away from her because she feels as if Miss Wade were touching her. Dickens then comments:

> She [i.e. Pet] said it in a quick involuntary way, but half playfully and not more petulantly or disagreeably than a favourite child might have done, who laughed next moment. (240)

On the following page Pet continues:

> 'Miss Wade almost frightened me when we parted, and I scarcely like to think of her just now of having been so near me without my knowing it. Tatty dear.' (241)

---

6 Lionel Trilling, "Introduction" in Charles Dickens, *Little Dorrit*, OID, xi.
7 Originally Dickens meant to call Pet Meagles "Baby". See his notes in the edition by Harvey Peter Sucksmith.

When Tatty does not at once comply with Pet's plea for reconciliation, she is admonished by Mr. Meagles to "count five-and-twenty", i.e. to come to her better senses. Dickens then goes on:

> She might have counted a dozen, when she bent and put her lips to the caressing hand. It patted her cheek, as it touched the owner's beautiful curls, and Tattycoram went away. (241)

Dickens simultaneously shows the inherent equality of the two girls (we might at first hesitate to say whether "the owner of the beautiful curls" is Tattycoram or Pet) and Pet's condescension. It is only a hand that caresses Tatty, not Pet as a person, and the hand pats Tatty's cheek just as it might pat a dog. When Tattycoram later returns to Mr. and Mrs. Meagles, her self-abasement – which Dickens meant to be so virtuous – is embarrassing to the reader:

> 'For I am not so bad as I was,' pleaded Tattycoram; 'I am bad enough, but not so bad as I was, indeed. I have had Miss Wade before me all this time, as if it was my own self grown ripe – turning everything the wrong way, and twisting all good into evil. (...) I was as bad as bad could be. I only mean to say, that, after what I have gone through, I hope I shall never be quite so bad again, and that I shall get better by very slow degrees. I'll try very hard. I won't stop at five-and-twenty, sir, I'll count five-and-twenty hundred, five-and-twenty thousand!' (880)

Dickens's admiration, on the other hand, for Miss Wade's "unsubduable nature" and for Tatty's fierce outbreaks comes through very clearly. Thus he mentions once of Tatty that "the bolts and bars of the old Bastille couldn't keep her" (369). We know that Dickens himself wanted to break prison doors and remember how vividly he describes the destruction of the Newgate Prison in *Barnaby Rudge* and of the Bastille – whose fall became a symbol for the breaking of crippling chains[8] – in *A Tale of Two Cities*. If he chooses this symbol for Tatty's revolt, he implies that she rightly objects to her prison.

We also realize that Dickens puts some blame onto the paternal figure if we have a closer look at Mr. Meagles. Mr. Meagles, it is true, is good-natured and amiable. He is always ready to help his friends, Daniel Doyce and Arthur Clennam, and he loves his daughter dearly. Mr. Meagles, like Mrs. Meagles, is "comely and healthy, with a pleasant English face" (54) and he often calls himself "practical". "If the people who are usually called practical, were practical in your direction –" (59) says Arthur admiringly; "practical" is an understatement for "warm-hearted". Like Dickens himself[9] Mr. Meagles knows that unhappy childhood experiences may have a lasting effect on a person's character. But was it not also "practical" in the real sense of the term to find a maid for Pet who would be bound to them by gratitude? Our attitude towards the good-natured Mr. Meagles changes a little, when we become aware of his double standards. He himself frets and chafes under quarantine. To him it is absurd that they are kept there. It is unacceptable to him that his pretty Pet could be the bearer of the plague and he feels ill-treated. This is how he feels in his temporary imprisonment:

> 'I have had the plague continually, ever since I have been here. I am like a sane man shut up in a madhouse; I can't stand the suspicion of the thing. I came here as well as ever I was in my life; but to suspect me of the plague is to give me the plague.' (54)

8 See Lionel Trilling, "Introduction", pp. vi-vii.
9 See note 5, p. 100.

We can sympathize with him here and later on, when he cannot stand the air of the Marshalsea prison. However, when other people than himself are talked about, Mr. Meagles feels differently. He is convinced that a prisoner should forgive his prison as soon as he is let out, because "it's not natural to bear malice" (61) and he marvels at Miss Wade, who tells us

> 'If I had been shut up in any place to pine and suffer, I should always hate that place and wish to burn it down, or raze it to the ground.' (61)

Dickens always introduces his characters carefully and our first meeting with Mr. Meagles and Arthur Clennam is described as follows:

> 'No more of yesterday's howling over yonder to-day sir, is there?'
> 'I have heard none.'
> 'Then you may be sure there *is* none. When these people howl, they howl to be heard.'
> 'Most people do, I suppose.'
> 'Ah! but these people are always howling. Never happy otherwise.' (53)

Mr. Meagles sweepingly condemns the French nation, who – according to him – "are always at it". We cannot help feeling, then, that he takes his own discomforts seriously, but lightly dismisses those of others as non-existing. He must not be put into prison – others may. Pet must be loved – Tattycoram need not. He and his family are comfortably off – others who are in want and complain about it are "always howling". Mr. Meagles changed Harriet Beadle's name into Tattycoram without thinking much about the effect it might have on the girl. It is at the end only, that he confesses that "perhaps if I had thought twice about it, I might never have given her the jingling name" (878). There is no doubt about Dickens's censuring Mrs. Gowan's haughtiness when she cannot remember the name of her daughter-in-law and speaks of "the Miggles people". Similarly, Mr. Meagles's lack of concern about Tatty's name might indicate an equal condescension on his part.

There is one more hint given by the author that Mr. Meagles is not altogether the admirable figure he first seems to be. It is his refusal to learn any foreign languages. When he tries to recover Mrs. Clennam's papers, he goes about his business "with an unshaken confidence that the English tongue was somehow the mother-tongue of the whole world, only the people were too stupid to know it" (875). Dickens was to criticize this attitude in more detail in the formidable Mr. Podsnap in *Our Mutual Friend*. In the chapter "Podsnappery" Mr. Podsnap "clears the world of its most difficult problems, by sweeping them behind him" (*OMF*, 174) much as Mr. Meagles rattles his money at the disparaged Marseille (p. 53). Mr. Podsnap's similarity to Mr. Meagles is evident:

> Beginning with a good inheritance, he had married a good inheritance, and had thriven exceedingly in the Marine Insurance way, and was quite satisfied. He never could make out why everybody was not quite satisfied ... (*OMF*, 174)

Dickens, who himself spoke French and Italian quite well, parodies at length Mr. Podsnap's attitude, by making him endlessly correct a French gentleman at a dinner-party whenever he makes a mistake in English. Mr. Podsnap's prejudices are summarized in the following sentence:

> Mr. Podsnap's world was not a very large world ... he considered other countries ... a mistake, and of their manners and customs would conclusively observe, 'Not English!' (*OMF*, 174)

Thus I cannot agree with Stanley Tick, who says that "The Sad End of Mr. Meagles"[10] is not in keeping with the goodness of his character. Mr. Tick contends that Mr. Meagles is a thoroughly admirable man who, according to Dickensian morals, ought to be rewarded at the end of the book. He argues that Mr. Meagles's unhappiness about his daughter's marriage is an unjust punishment and is not in keeping with what he deserves to get. He feels that the sad end of Mr. Meagles shows us Dickens's inconsistency, his lack of art.

Mr. Meagles's sad fate could also be used as an argument for showing Dickens's subtle art of portraying a good character with some blemishes. It is because he is not perfect that he is not fully rewarded at the end of the novel. Mr. Meagles is downcast when he thinks of his daughter and tells Little Dorrit

> 'she [i.e. Pet] is very fond of him, and hides his faults, and thinks that no one can see them – and he certainly is well connected, and of a very good family!'
> It was the only comfort he had in the loss of his daughter, and if he made the most of it, who could blame him? (883)

Certainly nobody can blame him, but all the same it is no coincidence that Dickens, who was to caricature condescension and snobbery, makes Mr. Meagles patronize Daniel Doyce on the one hand and admire the Barnacles on the other. He adores them although he knows that they have harassed Daniel Doyce most unfairly and that they are parasitic and useless people. Therefore his daughter's marriage to one of them seems a just punishment, although, of course, Pet is the main sufferer.

In Miss Wade's story, then, Dickens is out to depict how suffering is self-inflicted. Miss Wade torments herself – she is to blame. At the same time Dickens also conveys to the reader that the "unhappy temper" is not an explanation for everything. In a novel that abounds in inadequate parents, Father and Mother Meagles seem at first an exception. However, they cannot mother and father Tattycoram well enough. If she breaks out, it is partly because of the treatment she gets. On the other hand there is another figure in our novel, Little Dorrit, who never complains or flies into a rage. As Edmund Bergler has shown, Little Dorrit could well be looked upon as a self-tormentor. Miss Wade utters her anger, Little Dorrit never seems to feel any.[11] Let us have a closer look at how the various "children" in this book grow up and how they are affected by their upbringing.

## 3.2 The Child of Circumstances

There are quite a few characters in our novel that are seen as children of particular parents, shaped by a particular upbringing. In the situation of the parent-child relationship the following "children" are mentioned: Arthur Clennam, Edward, Fanny and Amy Dorrit, Maggy, Young John, Edmund Sparkler, Henry Gowan, Flora Finching, Pet Meagles and, as we have seen, Miss Wade and Tattycoram.

10 Stanley Tick, "The Sad End of Mr. Meagles", *Dickens Studies Annual,* vol. 3 (1974), ed. by Robert B. Partlow, pp. 87-99.
11 Edmund Bergler, "*Little Dorrit* and Dickens' Intuitive Knowledge of Psychic Masochism," *American Imago,* vol. 14 (1957), pp. 371-88.

The influence of a person's environment and upbringing on her/his later development is in some cases denied and sometimes described in detail and with great empathy. Thus Dickens depicts Arthur's sad childhood and its consequences but makes the reader feel that Young John and Edmund Sparkler are naturally foolish, whereas Henry Gowan and Blandois are naturally wicked and Little Dorrit naturally good. According to Dickens, then, there are children who are impervious to the influence of their surroundings and there are others who are the product of their upbringing.

Let us first turn to the author's careful description of the stunted emotional growth of two rather important characters, Arthur Clennam and Fanny Dorrit, and afterwards look at Little Dorrit and Blandois as examples of inherent goodness or wickedness.

### 3.2.1 Stunted Growth

*Arthur*'s childhood is described not only by himself. His subjective tale is supported by what we get to know from Mrs. Clennam later in the book. When she confesses her life to Blandois, Flintwinch and Affery she says that she has endeavoured

> 'to bring him up in fear and trembling and in a life of practical contrition for the sins that were heavy on his head before his entrance into this condemned world' (846)

and later, when she seeks Little Dorrit's forgiveness, she adds,

> 'I was stern with him, knowing that the transgressions of the parents are visited on their offspring, and that there was an angry mark upon him at his birth. I have sat with him and his father, seeing the weakness of his father yearning to unbend to him; and forcing it back, that the child might work out his release in bondage and hardship. I have seen him, with his mother's face, looking up at me in awe from his little books, and trying to soften me with his mother's ways that hardened me.' (859)

In fact, we are given the whole tragedy of his early life. We hear that his father had loved his real mother and that they had been secretly married, although after a manner that was not accepted by the law. His father was then forced by his uncle to renounce his love and to marry Mrs. Clennam. Arthur's father, so Affery tells us, "had everything but his orphan life scared out of him when he was young" (840) by his uncle. He therefore could not rebel against his uncle's dictum and married a woman he did not love. This woman, Mrs. Clennam, is a passionate person. She tells us that she herself has been brought up in "wholesome repression, punishment, and fear" (843) and that she was told that her future husband's life had been like hers "one of severe restraint" (843). When she discovers that her husband has preferred another woman to her, her rage is not to be appeased. His transgression is insupportable to her. She deceives herself in veiling her vindictiveness with her religion; she is convinced that she is appointed by the Lord to punish the sinners:

> 'Was I to dismiss in a moment – not my own wrongs – what was I! but all the rejection of sin, and all the war against it, in which I had been bred?' (844)

Her revenge is terrible. She crushes her rival, who first goes mad and later dies. She deprives her of her child and justifies this action as follows:

'If the presence of Arthur was a daily reproach to his father, and if the absence of Arthur was a daily agony to his mother, that was the just dispensation of Jehovah.' (846)

Dickens shows us how stern, how cold, how unforgiving her religion is. If Dickens himself repeatedly stressed that he admired the teachings of Christ and wrote a *Life of Our Lord* for his children, he also made it quite clear that he abhorred the religion described in the Old Testament. And it is this doctrine that Mrs. Clennam follows. Thus she talks of Jehova, the jealous God, who is as jealous as she is.[12] She prays

> that her enemies ... might be put to the edge of the sword, consumed by fire, smitten by plagues and leprosy, that their bones might be ground to dust, and that they might be utterly exterminated. (75)

It is not surprising that Arthur hates the ringing of church bells as they remind him of "a long train of miserable Sundays" (69). Dickens makes it quite clear that Mrs. Clennam's "slow, fierce, wrathful" disposition is deadly and that she renounces life, sitting "on a black bier-like sofa" (73) in a black dress, with a black picture of the plagues of Egypt on the wall. For fifteen years she has not left her room, as she is stricken with a hysterical paralysis and the daily routine of her life is always exactly the same. But underneath her cold shell there is a burning and passionate spirit like fire under dead embers. Only once does she admit that she has suffered from the lack of love on the part of Arthur's father. It is when she confesses her guilt to Little Dorrit:

> What Arthur's father was to me, she made him. From our marriage day I was his dread, and that she made me. I was the scourge of both, and that is referable to her. (859)

It is striking that she temporarily regains her power of movement when her repression of her (sexual) desire for her husband and her guilt feelings about her dreadful revenge are lifted. It seems that she punishes herself for feeling forbidden passions – love and hatred – by being a cripple who is confined to her room and totally dependent on her servants:

> 'I endure without murmuring, because it is appointed that I shall so make reparation for my sins. Reparation! Is there none in this room? Has there been none here this [sic] fifteen years?'
> Thus was she always balancing her bargains with the Majesty of heaven ... (89)

Many of Arthur's character traits can be accounted for by this bleak childhood and his tragic relationship with his parents. We first meet Arthur in the novel in a conversation with Mr. Meagles. While Mr. and Mrs. Meagles, Pet and Tattycoram are called by their names, there are almost six pages of text before we get to know Arthur's name. In the conversation he is called "Mr. Meagles's companion", "the other", "the second speaker" and we hear that he has a dark, grave face. Mr. Meagles finally addresses him and asks him about his plans for the future. This is Arthur's answer to the question:

> 'I am such a waif and stray everywhere, that I am liable to be drifted where any current may set' and
> 'I have no will. That is to say,' – he coloured a little – 'next to none that I can put in

---

12 She sticks to "for I the Lord thy God am a jealous God, visiting the iniquity of the fathers upon the children unto the third and fourth generation of them that hate me" and forgets the end of the sentence: "and shewing mercy unto thousands of them that love me, and keep my commandments" (*Exodus* 20: 5-6).

action now. Trained by main force; broken, not bent; heavily ironed with an object on which I was never consulted and which was never mine; shipped away to the other end of the world before I was of age, and exiled there until my father's death there, a year ago; always grinding in a mill I always hated; what is to be expected from *me* in middle life? Will, purpose, hope? All those lights were extinguished before I could sound the words.' (59)

Arthur is shy, restrained, subdued. At forty he has no friends, no family, no occupation that satisfies him, and he cannot believe that a woman could love him. In Arthur's life "so much was wanting ... to think about, so much that might have been better directed and happier to speculate upon" (80) that he has become a dreamer. Thus he imagines a beautiful young Flora who still loves him and is downcast when his daydream is shattered. He is not the sailor Frederick Dorrit takes him for, his face is not sunburnt from working in the open and he is not what Dorrit associates with "sailor", someone who is master of the tempestuous sea, who is free and in the fresh air, a lover of women. Arthur is simply "a brown, grave gentleman" (208). When he realizes that he has fallen in love with Pet Meagles, he never endeavours to win her but renounces his love at once:

> Arthur Clennam was a retiring man, with a sense of many deficiencies; and he so exalted the merits of the beautiful Minnie in his mind, and depressed his own, that when he pinned himself to this point, his hopes began to fail him. (239)

Arthur talks of himself as of "a diffident man, from the circumstances of his youth" (244). Dickens emphasizes Arthur's self-effacement by the titles of the chapters dealing with his love of Pet Meagles: "Nobody's Weakness" (chapter 16), "Nobody's Rival" (chapter 17), "Nobody's State of Mind" (chapter 26), "Nobody's Disappearance" (chapter 28). His self-imprisonment[13], his neurotic shying away from getting too much involved, does not seem to help him, though. This is Dickens's comment on Arthur's situation after he has heard of Pet's engagement to Henry Gowan:

> The rain fell heavily on the roof, and pattered on the ground, and dripped among the evergreens and the leafless branches of the trees. The rain fell heavily, drearily. It was a night of tears.
> If Clennam had not decided against falling in love with Pet if he had had the weakness to do it; if he had had, little by little, persuaded himself to set all the earnestness of his nature, all the might of his hope, and all the wealth of his mature character, on that cast; if he had done this and found that all was lost; he would have been, that night, unutterably miserable. As it was –
> As it was, the rain fell heavily, drearily. (254)

As Douglas Hewitt has aptly pointed out, Arthur can only love the asexual Little Dorrit, who is as much his daughter as his wife, and it is therefore no coincidence that on the eve of their wedding they burn, without reading it, Mrs. Clennam's confession, a confession of sexual passion in Mrs. Clennam as well as in Arthur's mother and father.[14] This inheritance must be destroyed – already after the loss of Pet's love Arthur became in his own eyes "a very much older man who had done with that part of life" (383) and he does not strike us as having turned younger again when he marries Little Dorrit.

---

13 Cp. T. N. Grove, "The Psychological Prison of Arthur Clennam in Dickens's 'Little Dorrit' ", *Modern Language Review*, vol. 68 (1973), pp. 750-755.
14 Douglas Hewitt, *The approach to fiction*, London 1972, p. 101.

A passionate sexual love between a man and a woman marked Arthur's beginnings. This same love was "visited upon him" by his step-mother in such a way that he cannot mature and love a woman. He is and remains to the end of the novel partly dead.

On the other hand we could expect a child who grew up like him to be emotionally much more crippled than Arthur is. He could easily have become antisocial, incapable of loving kindness, an egotist, a person full of hatred, even a criminal. Arthur's comparative "goodness" derives partly from a suppression of "bad" thoughts. Thus he resolves, for instance, to keep a "high, unenvious course" (367) in his feelings for, and actions towards, Henry Gowan. After Pet has confessed to him that she loves Gowan and is going to marry him, Arthur does not show his wound but soon enters her parents' house:

> The lights were bright within doors when he entered, and the faces on which they shone his own face not excepted were soon quietly cheerful. (387)

And yet it is love which has saved Arthur from a harder lot. Dickens quite clearly maintains that – much as with Oliver Twist – the unknown mother's love has had a benign influence on her son's life, although she has not been near him in person. "I had a mother who loved me", is a phrase that Mrs. Ebbs keeps repeating in Susan Hill's "Missy",[15] in order to regain her self-respect. Similarly, the Dickensian hero gains worth by a mother's love, albeit the love of an absent or even dead parent. The very fact that there once existed a loving mother proves that the child is lovable. that it is due to adverse circumstances and not to his inherent wickedness that this love cannot endure.

*Fanny Dorrit* is also one of the realistic characters of this novel whose fate is determined by her childhood.

Her father is first described when newly imprisoned and worrying about the effect this imprisonment might have on his "delicate and unexperienced wife" (98). When he tells the turnkey that he has two children

> The turnkey followed him with his eyes. 'And you another,' he observed to himself, 'which makes three on you. And your wife another, I'll lay a crown. Which makes four on you. And another coming, I'll lay half-a-crown. Which'll make five on you. And I'll go another sixpence to name which is the helplessest, the unborn baby or you!'
> He was right in all particulars. She came next day with a little boy of three years old, and a little girl of two, and he stood entirely corroborated. (99)

When Fanny's mother is actually in labour, the Dorrits are in a panic and the filthy doctor and his assistant, Mrs. Bangham,

> took possession of the poor helpless pair, as everybody else and anybody else had always done. (102)

We do not hear anything else of Mrs. Dorrit but that she died when Amy was eight years old "of her own inherent weakness" (104). We are then told that her father got used to living in prison, that he

> languidly slipped into his smooth descent, and never more took one step upward (103)

and that Little Dorrit soon recognizes that

15 Susan Hill, "Missy" in: *A Bit of Singing and Dancing,* Penguin Books 1975, pp. 140-154.

a man so broken as to be the Father of the Marshalsea, could be no father to his own children. (112)

Time and again he is presented to us accepting money from others, shutting his eyes to the fact that his daughter supports him, but always displaying "a wonderful air of benignity and patronage" (122). He proudly stresses that occasionally more than fifty people a day have been introduced to him:

> On a fine Sunday in term time, it is quite a Levee – quite a Levee (123)[16],

but he is neither ashamed to eat his daughter's well-earned dinner, nor to sell her to Young John for a few extra cigars. Chapter 3.3 will deal in greater detail with Mr. Dorrit's gentility, but what has been said so far will suffice to show that he is at best an indifferent parent. Nor does Fanny have any parent substitute. Her uncle, who is called "Dirty Dick" and is supposed to take care of her,

> accepted the task of serving as her escort and guardian, just as he would have accepted an illness, a legacy, a feast, starvation – anything but soap. (114)

Fanny works as a dancer in a third-rate theatre, her uncle playing the clarionet in its orchestra. We hear that the

> carpenters had a joke to the effect that he was dead without being aware of it

(and that)

> Though expecting now to be summoned by his niece, he did not hear her until she had spoken to him three or four times; nor was he at all surprised at the presence of two nieces instead of one, but merely said in his tremulous voice, 'I am coming, I am coming!' and crept forth by some underground way which emitted a cellarous smell. (232)

He is, of course, no fit guardian to look after his niece but rather a cumbersome piece of luggage she wants to get rid of. Fanny, just as Mr. Dorrit, has "the jail-rot" (273) upon her. Dickens repeatedly likens her to Mr. Dorrit and calls her "the Daughter of the Father of the Marshalsea" (283). Like her father she has to stress the family dignity all the time in order to be able to forget the lowliness of their station. Whenever Dickens describes concrete situations, Fanny behaves just like her father. This is the case when the family leave the prison and forget Amy, which was "perhaps the very first action of their joint lives that they had got through without her" (480) and which recalls an earlier scene in the novel: Mr. Plornish's father, "old Nandy" is a protégé of Mr. Dorrit's. The Father of the Marshalsea usually receives him with great affability and condescension. When Little Dorrit walks arm in arm with old Nandy towards the prison and is seen by Fanny, the latter explodes in "burning indignation":

> 'Well! I could have believed a great deal of you ... but I don't think even I could have believed this even of you!'
> 'Fanny!' cried Little Dorrit, wounded and astonished.
> 'Oh! Don't Fanny me, you mean little thing, don't! The idea of coming along the open streets, in the broad light of day, with a Pauper!' (418)

16 Dickens writes on March 22, 1842 from America to Daniel Maclise: "Imagine Kate and I – a kind of Queen and Albert – holding a Levee every day (proclaimed and placarded in newspapers) and receiving all who choose to come." (*PE*, vol. III, 1974, p. 154.) The Mackenzies also refer to this letter in the title of chapter 7 of their recent Dickens biography: "A Kind of Queen and Albert". (See Norman and Jeanne Mackenzie, *Dickens. A Life,* 1979, p. 109).

Mr. Dorrit bursts into tears when he sees the two together because, as he tells Little Dorrit, he was spared humiliation until seeing his own daughter with old Nandy, when he "keenly felt it" (420). Fanny, like the rest of the family, finds "a low tendency ... at the bottom of her [Amy's] heart" from which she must be "roused" (763). This low tendency is nothing else but her absence of snobbery in Book I and her unwillingness and inability to forget their life in prison and "adapt" to their new station in Book II. Fanny has obviously suffered much under the family's earlier descent into poverty and shame. Already in Book I she adopted her father's way of warding off unpleasant feelings about their situation by displaying "spirit" (see chapter 31) and pride. When they have turned wealthy, the Dorrits (except Amy) make up for their past humiliation by being haughty towards their servants and always stressing the family dignity. Thus, when one of their rooms at a hotel in Martigny is given to a "very genteel lady", Mr. Dorrit is enraged and cannot be appeased and "Miss Fanny ... supported her father with great bitterness" (512).

Finally, Fanny as well as her father behave peevishly when they feel guilty, throwing things about and accusing the person who causes their guilt feelings, Little Dorrit. Thus Mr. Dorrit begins by

> laying down his knife and fork with a noise, taking things up sharply, biting at his bread as if he were offended with it, and in other similar ways showing that he was out of sorts (272)

and continues by accusing Little Dorrit of not caring whether he has enough to eat or must starve, yet he is actually ashamed of himself for having asked her by means of a thinly veiled story to "lead him [i.e. Chivery] on" for her father's sake.

Similarly, Fanny, who has accepted Mrs. Merdle's bribery and is secretly ashamed of this act, jumps at Little Dorrit:

> 'You little Fool!' ... 'Have you no spirit at all? But that's just the way! You have no self-respect, you have no becoming pride ... you would let your family be trodden on, and never turn.' (289)

Little Dorrit then prepares the meal and

> When at last Fanny sat down to eat and drink, she threw the table implements about and was angry with her bread, much as her father had been last night. (290)

Fanny indeed has suffered so much under the family's disgrace that she has one great need, that is to come topmost in any situation of rivalry. She marries Mr. Sparkler because she wants to take revenge on her future mother-in-law for having humbled her and because she does not want to be ousted by Mrs. General, who aspires to become Mr. Dorrit's second wife. When Little Dorrit, "upon whom a kind of terror had been stealing as she perceived what her sister meant" (648), asks her,

> 'My dear sister, would you condemn yourself to an unhapy life for this?'

Fanny answers,

> 'It wouldn't be an unhappy life, Amy. It would be the life I am fitted for. Whether by disposition, or whether by circumstances, is no matter; I am better fitted for such a life than for almost any other.'
>
> There was something of a desolate tone in these words; but with a short proud laugh she took another walk ... (650)

Dickens surely means to tell the reader here that Fanny is a victim. Her later unhappy life can be explained by what she has experienced in her childhood. Fanny explains to her sister that

'Other girls, differently reared and differently circumstanced altogether, might wonder at what I say or may do. Let them. They are driven by their lives and characters; I am driven by mine.' (649)

The reader is not left in doubt as to the unhappiness of Fanny's marriage. Towards the end of the novel we meet Fanny and her husband together at their house. Fanny, who is pregnant and can therefore no longer play off her good figure against that of her mother-in-law, is intensely bored and irritable. The day which has just gone seems the longest day she has ever lived through. She is determined not to see such another, that is, never to spend another day in the company of her husband alone. Edmund Sparkler is a good-natured simpleton who constantly gets on Fanny's nerves and is reproached for his very existence. Dickens shows us Fanny's unpleasant nagging at him while at the same time making it very understandable that her husband's silliness[17] might drive anyone crazy. The situation is described in a masterly way:

'It's like lying in a well,' said Mrs Sparkler, changing her position fretfully. 'Dear me, Edmund, if you have anything to say, why don't you say it?'
Mr Sparkler might have replied with ingeniousness, 'My life, I have nothing to say.' But as the repartee did not occur to him, he contented himself with coming in from the balcony and standing at the side of his wife's couch. 'Good gracious, Edmund!' said Mrs Sparkler more fretfully still, 'you are absolutely putting mignonette up your nose! Pray don't!' (…)
'Is that your fan, my love?' asked Mr Sparkler, picking up one, and presenting it.
'Edmund,' returned his wife, more wearily yet, 'don't ask weak questions, I entreat you not. Whose can it be but mine?'
'Yes, I thought it was yours,' said Mr. Sparkler. (758)

We have seen, then, in what way two characters, Arthur Clennam and Fanny Dorrit, are blighted by their childhood experiences. Arthur is saved by Little Dorrit's love, but Fanny's suffering remains unrelieved. It is only in keeping with her fate that she cannot look after her own children and is going to leave them in Little Dorrit's care. However, Fanny is not a cold woman. She loves her sister and her outbursts are made quite understandable by the author. Dickens feels a lot of sympathy for Fanny. However, his old preoccupation with the question of who should bear the blame shows in a sentence such as the following:

Here was Fanny, proud, fitful, whimsical, further advanced in that disqualified state for going into society … resolved always to want comfort, resolved not to be comforted, resolved to be deeply wronged, and resolved that nobody should have the audacity to think her so. (872)

This description, which is true to life in that we often feel that something is owed to us, that others ought to give it to us while at the same time resenting any pity as condescension, is typical of Dickens. On the one hand he shows great empathy for Fanny's predicament. On the other hand, however, he implies that she could change her situation if she only wanted to by using the verb *resolve* four times. It seems as if

17 Dickens, who called himself "the National Sparkler", ridicules his own passion for Maria Beadnell in Edmund's unrequited love of a capricious lady.

the author said: "Let nobody suppose that I excuse Fanny by pointing at her upbringing and by depicting her tragic situation. Her sister Amy had the same childhood and turned out differently because she *resolved*[18] to be good. If Fanny had an unhappy life, she had only herself to blame. The fault is entirely the child's not the father's." In Fanny's resolution that nobody should have the audacity to think her wronged there is a shade of the widespread mistaken belief that if people suffer they have somehow asked for it, that they are at least partly responsible for what they endure. Fanny is ashamed of being wronged but is entitled to be furious about it. Dickens could not have told us the tales of Miss Wade and of Fanny Dorrit if he had not felt their suffering with them. He is thus the child's advocate. However, he superimposes on their stories his moral beliefs: There are good feelings and bad feelings. Good people endeavour to feel only good feelings. They are not downcast but cheerful and grateful. They are full of loving kindness and not of hatred or envy or jealousy. They are self-effacing, feel no aggression, always want to serve the other and to help. The embodiment of this ideal is our heroine, Little Dorrit.


## 3.2.2 Inborn Nobility Versus Inborn Wickedness

When Amy Dorrit visits Arthur Clennam in the Marshalsea, she insists upon being called "Little Dorrit" by him (826) and when Arthur later refers to her as "Amy", she whispers "Little Dorrit. Never any other name." (890) She remains a Dorrit, her father's daughter to the end and she stresses her littleness. She is, indeed, a small creature with a child-like figure, small features and small, slight hands with nimble fingers. Dickens calls her "diminutive", "fragile", "delicate", "defenceless", "slender", "little", "slight". She is Arthur's "poor child". Her sister Fanny calls her "my child", "best and dearest little mouse", "my precious child", "little owl", "little tortoise", "such a little oddity" and "the best of small creatures". When she walks in the streets with Maggy, she is taken for a child by a prostitute until she sees Little Dorrit's face. It seems as if even her slight figure ought to be less prominent, less space-consuming. Little Dorrit, in other words, always tries to be as small as possible. She is often hidden in dark corners, she is described as "timid", "shrinking", "bashful". She is shy and often she trembles. She is very quiet and has a soft, gentle voice – it would be too assertive for her to speak in an ordinary, let alone in a loud voice. It is her chief desire

> To pass in and out of the prison unnoticed, and elsewhere to be overlooked and forgotten. (337)

She goes so far in her self-effacement as to write from Italy "We are all fond of the life here (except me), and there are no plans for our return" (610). We may think of Esther Summerson and of Zwerdling's interpretation of Esther's character[19], but

---

18 We cannot but feel that Dickens's cheerfulness, which is praised by so many of his contemporaries, is the result of a conscious effort. People may find him full of spirits and yet Dickens writes at the same time in his letters of his despondency and depression. See *Dickens: Interviews and Recollections,* ed. by Philp Collins, 2 volumes, London and Basingstoke 1981. Cp. for example pp. 216, 295, 305, 315.

19 See Alex Zwerdling, "Esther Summerson Rehabilitated", *PMLA,* vol. 88 (1973), pp. 429-439.

Dickens calls Little Dorrit "a slender child in body, a strong heroine in soul" (433). In her, Dickens wants to portray a heroism that could grow against all possible odds. She is

> born and bred in a social condition, false even with a reference to the falsest condition outside the walls; drinking from infancy of a well whose waters had their own peculiar stain, their own unwholesome and unnatural taste. (111)

And yet, she can be her whole family's great stay and comfort. Dickens tells us about her childhood:

> What her pitiful look saw, at that early time, in her father, in her sister, in her brother, in the jail; how much, or how little of the wretched truth it pleased God to make visible to her; lies hidden with many mysteries. It is enough that she was inspired to be something which was not what the rest were, and to be that something, different and laborious, for the sake of the rest. Inspired? Yes. Shall we speak of the inspiration of a poet or a priest, and not of the heart impelled by love and self-devotion to the lowliest work in the lowliest way of life! (111)

According to Dickens, her heroism consists in her self-sacrifice for her father, her brother and sister, and later for Arthur Clennam. She is wholly devoted, has a pitying and loving heart, accepts the others with all their imperfections and never asks for anything on her own behalf. She is, indeed, everyone's mother but her own. She sees to it that her brother and sister get as much of an education as possible and that they can find a job or learn a trade. She provides her father with food and drink. She is Maggy's "Little Mother" and she is Arthur's mother, just as he is her father.[20] We could also call Little Dorrit everyone's nurse. Fanny, who is a far more lively character and who also comes much more to life in the author's descriptions of her, once says of Amy:

> There are times when my dear child is a little wearing to an active mind; but as a nurse, she is Perfection. (762)

Whenever someone falls ill, Amy appears and takes on the nursing of the sick person. This happens with Pet Meagles just as it does with her brother Tip and her uncle and – most important – with her father and with Arthur. The nurse is superfluous and useless when the Dorrits are well-off and travel in Italy. By her very existence she recalls earlier wounds, their former littleness and helplessness. As the

20 Dianne F. Sadoff thinks that Amy "appears to be Arthur Clennam's metaphorical mother, both by analogy to the Clennam family tree and because his revealed parentage makes him lack a mother. Clennam and Amy are metaphorical son and mother, just as they are father and daughter." ("Storytelling and the Figure of the Father in *Little Dorrit*", *PMLA* vol. 95, p. 242.) There are two instances in the novel which spell out Little Dorrit's maternity. The first occurs in the Marshalsea when Little Dorrit tries to soothe her father and is compared to Euphrasia who breastfed her father in prison. (See pp. 273-274.) Later, when Little Dorrit reads to Arthur, who occupies her father's former room, she is compared to "great Nature" at whose knees alone Arthur has "ever dwelt in his youth on hopeful promises, on playful fancies, on the harvests of tenderness and humility that lie hidden in the early-fostered seeds of the imagination; on the oaks of retreat from blighting winds, that have the germs of their strong roots in the nursery acorns. But, in the tones of the voice that read to him, there were memories of an old feeling of such things, and echoes of every merciful and loving whisper that had ever stolen to him in his life." (884) Unlike Sadoff, however, I think that Arthur's and Amy's mothering and fathering each other is not primarily an incestuous affair, but an attempt to make up for earlier wants.

family cannot bear to be reminded of their past, any remembrance of it is repressed. Therefore Amy is treated with much unkindness by her family. It is only with the return of the repressed in Mr. Dorrit's breakdown that she is allowed to come back and assume her former place:

> the child who had done so much for him and had been so poorly repaid was never out of his [i.e. Mr. Dorrit's] mind. Not that he spared her, or was fearful of her being spent by watching and fatigue; he was no more troubled on that score than he had usually been. No; he loved her in his old way. They were in jail and she tended him, and he had constant need of her; and he even told her sometimes, that he was content to have undergone a great deal for her sake. (710)

Mr. Dorrit is indeed a child who is mothered by his daughter. A child is at first not able to feel any concern for his mother. She must look after herself – the child can only demand that his needs be met. The expectation that these needs will be met by the mother and the preference for the mother is the kind of love the small child can give – it is the love Mr. Dorrit feels for his daughter, "he loved her in his old way".

We see that the images of nurse and mother fuse. Little Dorrit is the nursing mother, i.e. the mother who nurses others back to health as well as the mother who feeds the child with her milk. For Dickens, being a mother or a nurse requires self-denial, self-sacrifice and unbounded love and tenderness. However, with Fanny the reader may find that "our child is a little wearing" sometimes. Consider, for instance, the following description of Little Dorrit's visiting the sick Arthur in the Marshalsea:

> He roused himself, and cried out. And then he saw, in the loving, pitying, sorrowing, dear face, as in a mirror, how changed he was; and she came towards him; and with her hands laid on his breast to keep him in his chair, and with her knees upon the floor at his feet, and with her lips raised up to kiss him, and with her tears dropping on him as the rain from Heaven had dropped upon the flowers, Little Dorrit, a living presence, called him by his name. (825)

Dickens's propagation of selfless love, in other words, is insistent but not necessarily convincing. It is, as we have shown, the author's daydream and a comfort for his wounds to conceive of the existence of such women. Only a divine love, however, could heal the wounds of the past – the various shades of human love will not do. Thus Dickens uses a religious vocabulary to describe Little Dorrit. Dickens would have been indignant had he been accused of blasphemy, and yet he echoes the Old Testament when describing Little Dorrit:

> But now thus saith the LORD that created thee, O Jacob, and he that formed thee, O Israel, Fear not: for I have redeemed thee, I have called thee by thy name; thou art mine (*Isa.* 43:1),

and Little Dorrit's "living presence" recalls the "living Father" who sent Jesus Christ into this world (*John* 6:57).

Again, as with Miss Wade, Dickens's conscious efforts do not tally with his subconscious sympathies. Fanny commands the reader's interest – Little Dorrit does not. Her heroism seems insipid, her lack of self-assertion is embarrassing, she does not even seem to *be* in the world. Dickens tells us, however, that there is more to Amy Dorrit than the "Angelic comforter". When the Dorrits are in Italy, Little Dorrit writes a letter to Arthur Clennam and says

> 'Do you know that since the change in our fortunes, though I appear to myself to have dreamed more than before, I have always dreamed of myself as very young indeed! ... I

have always dreamed of myself as a child learning to do needlework ... always as that little child. I have dreamed of going down to Mrs. General, with the patches on my clothes in which I can first remember myself. I have over and over again dreamed of taking my place at dinner at Venice when we had a large company, in the mourning for my poor mother which I wore when I was eight years old, and wore long after it was threadbare and would mend no more. It has been a great distress to me to think how irreconcilable the company would consider it with my father's wealth, and how I should displease and disgrace him and Fanny and Edward by so plainly disclosing what they wished to keep secret. But I have not grown out of the little child in thinking of it ...' (609)

Little Dorrit finds herself in an embarrassing situation in her dream. She pictures herself as the small child in a worn, darned dress who confronts Mrs. General, who is always impeccably dressed. One can imagine how the lady who "ran over several people who came in the way of proprieties; but always in a high style and with composure" (499) would have scolded the little child Amy for appearing in such a dress and for being "stupid". The child has yet to learn the art of needlework in her dream, she feels weak and exposed. Little Dorrit does not like this dream. It recalls her past helplessness and it also recalls how little help she got from her relatives and this is why it "disgraces" her father and her sister and brother. But Little Dorrit in her dream is also true to herself. She has not "Grown out of the little child in thinking of it" because it is still part of her. She is still very small somehow, a child who needs mothering and can therefore not part from the clothes she wore after her mother's death because they are the link to that missing and most needed mother. Giving up the clothes would mean giving up the mother as well, accepting her death and not having any more expectations of her motherly love. And – unknown to herself – her dream may also be understood to express her wish to shame her father, to expose him publicly, to tell all the world that she was poor and starving at her father's dinner table and that he bought himself a new tie rather than shoes for his daughter.

She is clumsy in her dream just like Maggy, who spills the potatoes in the mud, and she is a small child, just like Maggy, who has not grown any older than ten years of age. Maggy is indeed Little Dorrit's double and expresses all the needs that are suppressed by our heroine. Maggy is the granddaughter of Amy's old nurse, who "was not so kind to her as she should have been" (143) because she was a drunkard. Maggy is always with Little Dorrit when the latter prepares meals for her father or tidies up his room. When the Dorrits become rich, William Dorrit does not only want a milliner to make new clothes for his daughters, but he also insists that "Something must be done with Maggy, too, who at present is – ha – barely respectable, barely respectable" (470). Little Dorrit and Maggy visit Clennam together, are shut out of the prison and spend the night in the streets where they are met by a prostitute, who at first takes Little Dorrit to be Maggy's child. They sleep together in the vestry. When the Dorrits leave England, Maggy stays behind, but she is always in Little Dorrit's mind, as we see in her letter:

I cannot quite keep back the tears from my eyes when I think of my poor Maggy, and of the blank she must have felt at first, however kind they all are to her, without her Little Mother. (521)

When Little Dorrit returns to England and visits Clennam in prison, sure enough Maggy is one of the party.

Maggy expresses all the needs Little Dorrit does not seem to feel any more. Maggy is voracious, whereas Little Dorrit hardly ever touches food. When the two of them visit Arthur Clennam, Amy, whose stunted growth stems from malnutrition, refuses food and drink, whereas Maggy is "gloating over the fruit and cake with chuckles of anticipation" (214). She is dirty – Little Dorrit is always clean. She is dependent – Litle Dorrit always looks after others. She is a child of ten years and will never grow any older – Little Dorrit had to be an adult very early in her life. Maggy is susceptible to slights – Little Dorrit is never hurt. Maggy complains in uncomfortable situations, for instance when they spend the night walking in the open – Little Dorrit never complains. Maggy is noisy and can laugh boisterously – Little Dorrit makes no noise at all. Maggy can fall asleep and wake up whenever and wherever she chooses – Little Dorrit allows herself no rest. Maggy thus enjoys the privileges of a child; she is taken care of in hospital. Little Dorrit is the nurse – Maggy is nursed. What Maggy enjoyed most in hospital is – significantly – food, she is still enraptured at the thought of the "chicking" she got there. It is thus psychologically sound that Maggy has to be with Little Dorrit whenever the latter lovingly tends others. It is as if Dickens knew that Little Dorrit could not give her love without her double, Maggy, by her side, who was given love by others. It is only in Italy that Maggy is absent, but, as we have seen, Little Dorrit is not allowed near her father in Italy until he dies.

Dickens, then, sets up the ideal of the pure, selfless heroine who does not seek her own well-being. However, the author also feels that a human being cannot exist with her basic needs constantly denied her. Maggy expresses Little Dorrit's feelings that are unfulfilled or even unfelt, because they are unacceptable. She wants food and drink and stories. She needs love and attention and the feeling that she is important to others. She expresses the basic needs of every child and by creating her, Dickens undermines his ideal of an entirely selfless child who needs no love and can miraculously give love to everyone all the same. In the creation of Maggy, Dickens follows his better knowledge, namely that every child needs to be loved and that no one can become a loving adult without having received love in the first place.

The figure of Little Dorrit condemns the child who cannot grow up into a loving adult. If Little Dorrit could become an angel under atrocious circumstances why could not the others as well? The creation of our heroine puts the blame on all the unangelic characters. But the existence of Maggy takes this blame away again. Maggy tells us that an angelic Little Dorrit is an impossibility, that Little Dorrit can only exist together with her other half. There is another side to the picture. There are repressed needs which must be met to enable a person to give love to others.

The opposite of Little Dorrit in our novel is the villain Rigaud/Lagnier/*Blandois,* the embodiment of evil. Dickens wants to tell us that – regardless of their upbringing – some people are evil, just as some are good. Blandois, who has murdered his wife, is acquitted because of a lack of evidence. The mob, however, is so enraged at him that it wants to tear him to pieces and speaks of "the devil ... set loose" (168). In an inn in France, where Blandois is going to put up for the night, the people are talking about this event. May he not have been the child of circumstances and have some hidden good in him? someone asks and the landlady then answers as follows:

'I tell you this, my friend, that there are people (men and women both, unfortunately) who have no good in them – none. That there are people whom it is necessary to detest without compromise. That there are people who must be dealt with as enemies of the human race. That there are people who have no human heart, and who must be crushed

like savage beasts and cleared out of the way. They are but few, I hope; but I have seen
... that there are such people. And I do not doubt that this man – whatever they call him,
I forget his name – is one of them.' (169)

Dickens obviouly agrees with the landlady and remarks that there are "amiable whitewashers" in Great Britain who might object to this reasoning. Let us have a look, then, at this devil in human shape. Blandois tells us that he is a "cosmopolitan gentleman" and a "citizen of the world". His father was Swiss, his mother was "French by blood, English by birth", he was born in Belgium. In the grandiose manner in which he talks about his origin he covers up the fact that he belongs nowhere, that he "own[s] no country" (48).[21] He tells us that society has wronged him and that he is going to turn the tables on society. When his wickedness is found out, he says "Add, always a gentleman, and it's no matter" (814). His main character traits are his ruthlessness (as shown in the murder of his wife) and his utter lack of consideration for others. When Blandois stays at a hotel

> His utter disregard of other people, as shown in his way of tossing the little womanly toys of furniture about, flinging favourite cushions under his boots for a softer rest, and crushing delicate coverings with his big body and his great black head, had ... [a] brute selfishness at the bottom of it. (402)

Unlike Little Dorrit, he takes up a lot of space and crushes the others. He has a loud voice and loud laughter, and it is his "character to govern" (174). Whereas Little Dorrit is defined in her doing service to others, Blandois is characterized by his arrogant demand to be served. Blandois has a "wicked head" (175) and when he smiles, his moustache goes up and his nose comes down, an "ugly play of nose and moustache" (409), which gives him an evil look. But Blandois also has exceptionally small, white hands, which he always displays to his advantage and which give him a gentlemanly air. They are unlike Little Dorrit's workworn hands and they are compared to snakes:

> There had been something dreadful in the noiseless skill of his cold, white hands, with the fingers lithely twisting about and twining one over another like serpents. Clennam could not prevent himself from shuddering inwardly, as if he had been looking on at a nest of those creatures. (818)

When Blandois wants to be served he is rude – be it to Cavaletto or to Flintwinch or Affery at Mrs. Clennam's house. He addresses Cavaletto as "contraband beast" or "pig" when he needs him. He is proud of his laziness for, as he explains to Cavaletto in prison, a gentleman never works. Since he has never done a scrap of work in his life, this proves him to be – in his opinion – a gentleman. The two innocent creatures, Little Dorrit and Pet, immediately feel his wickedness and find him repugnant and so does the noble dog Lion. In the end he is buried under the ruins of Mrs. Clennam's house, and is thus "crushed", as the French landlady hoped he would be. However, as has been pointed out by Dickens critics, Blandois is Clennam's darker self.[22] Clennam announces himself as "Blandois" to Miss Wade. Blandois greets Clennam in prison as

21 Dianne F. Sadoff argues that: "Rigaud's criminality ... originates in his confused lineage, the mysterious circumstances of his birth. Like Clennam, Rigaud is a metaphorical orphan, waif, and bastard through his indeterminate nationality ... Rigaud, however, imagines himself deprived of aristocratic birthright." (Dianne F. Sadoff, "Storytelling and the Figure of the Father in *Little Dorrit*, p. 237.)

22 Sadoff mentions Welsh, *The City of Dickens* (Oxford 1971, pp. 134-135); ibid., p. 244.

"fellow jail-bird" and "brother-bird" (810). Both of them want to be shown round Mrs. Clennam's old house when they are there on a visit. Clennam escapes his mother's wrath but Blandois is buried underneath Mrs. Clennam's house. Clennam gives Pet up and Blandois follows her to Rome. Clennam would like to express his hatred of his mother but dares not. Blandois blackmails Mrs. Clennam and makes her miserable. When Blandois disappears, it is Arthur who wants him found at all costs. Both Blandois and Arthur Clennam are likened to Cain by Dickens. When Blandois walks towards Chalons "Cain might have looked as lonely and avoided" (165). Clennam is described as working in Doyce's counting house and through some trap-doors there falls a shaft of light which

> brought to Clennam's mind the child's old picture-book, where similar rays were the witnesses of Abel's murder. (312-313)

When describing Blandois as "lonely" and "avoided", Dickens suddenly seems to feel pity with his wretch, who says of himself that he "treasures" in his breast "the wrongs society has heaped on him" (274). In the Bible the wicked son, Cain, slays Abel, but this murder is a reaction to the Lord's injustice in accepting Abel's offering but refusing Cain's. We see, then, that although Dickens clearly blames Blandois and with him the "wicked child", he also excuses them in likening them to Cain and in demonstrating that Arthur and Blandois really belong together.

The "good child", then, is just as one-sided a picture as the "bad child". Both of them are drawn as if there existed naturally angelic and naturally devilish creatures. However, their doubles, Maggy and Arthur, show us that there does not exist a human being who is entirely "good" nor one who is entirely "bad". Dickens's conscious message that we are master/mistress of our fate and are to blame if we do not turn out right is modified by his better psychological insight, which has its roots in his own childhood experiences. In his autobiographical fragment Dickens wrote

> I know that, but for the mercy of God, I might easily have been, for any care that was taken of me, a little robber or a little vagabond ("AF", 25),

and he also speaks of himself as of "small Cain that I was, except that I had never done any harm to anyone" ("AF", 23). In this fragment he puts the blame on his parents. Had he turned out a robber or a vagabond it would have been their fault, since they did not take care of him. But again things are not so simple as they seem. Had he not unconsciously feared he was responsible for his suffering, he would not have compared himself to Cain, nor would he have hastened to add that he had not really murdered anyone. In his description of good and bad children Dickens still tries to find an answer to his old question of who is to blame for the suffering of children.


## 3.3   Ladies and Gentlemen, or The Return of the Repressed

When the Dorrits get rich, Mr. Dorrit engages Mrs. General "to form the mind" of his two daughters. Mrs. General tells her charges that they must have no opinions of their own because a truly refined mind has none. They must not look at "vagrants", as she calls poor people in whom Amy gets interested. Anything shocking or unpleasant must never be mentioned in her presence. Dickens tells us that there was another of her ways of forming a mind – to cram all articles of difficulty into cupboards, lock them up, and say they had no existence, (503)

and that

Passion was to go to sleep in the presence of Mrs. General, and blood was to change to milk and water. The little that was left in the world, when all these deductions were made, it was Mrs. General's province to varnish. In that formation process of hers, she dipped the smallest of brushes into the largest of pots, and varnished the surface of every object that came under consideration. The more cracked it was, the more Mrs. General varnished it. (503)

Mrs. General is the female counterpart to Mr. Podsnap in *Our Mutual Friend,* who does not want to know about anything disagreeable:

'I don't want to know about it; I don't choose to discuss it; I don't admit it!' (*OMF,* 174)

In order to become a lady or a gentleman, in other words, you must follow Mrs. General's and Mr. Podsnap's doctrine of repression.[23] This is indeed what Mr. Dorrit and his two elder children do all along. As long as Mr. Dorrit is in the Marshalsea, he represses the knowledge of his dependent position and of his poverty. He is, in fact, the poorest of the prison's inhabitants, for he cannot get out for more than twenty years, but this fact is reversed into the opposite: Mr. Dorrit becomes a public character to whom homage is due. The money he gets from his fellow-prisoners and from visitors is called "testimonials" – it testifies to his greatness – and Mr. Dorrit always manages to behave in an even more distinguished way after receiving such gifts. Still, the money is most acceptable when it is given clandestinely, for instance in a cluster of bright red geraniums.[24] Similarly, it must never be mentioned to Mr. Dorrit that his daughters go out to earn a little money – he is too genteel to let his children work. Thus Mr. Dorrit feels infinitely superior to his "old pensioner", Edward John Nandy, Mrs. Plornish's father, who lives in the workhouse. Although Mr. Dorrit is in fact poorer than the old man, for he owes money to people, whereas Old Nandy just does not have any, his condescension is infinite:

Old Nandy had a patron: one patron. He had a patron who in a certain sumptuous way – an apologetic way, as if he constantly took an admiring audience to witness that he really could not help being more free with this old fellow than they might have expected, on account of his simplicity and poverty – was mightily good to him. (...) Mr. Dorrit was in the habit of receiving this old man as if the old man held of him in vassalage under some feudal tenure. He made little treats and teas for him, as if he came with his homage from some outlying district where the tenantry were in a primitive state. (415)

Mr. Nandy has to take his tea on the window-sill on which an old newspaper is spread, while the others are having theirs at the table. Whenever the Dorrits feel particularly shaken, they "air the miserably ragged old fiction of the family gentility" (257). What Mr. Dorrit has to offer to the inmates of the Marshalsea are "manners", "pomp", "polish", "bowed-down beneficence", "mild wisdom", "benevolence", "gracious condescension", "grace", "the amiable solicitude of a superior being", "magnanimity", "patronage", "general clemency", "infinite forbearance", "great

---

23 Mrs. General advises Amy to say words to herself that give a nice form to her lips, for instance when entering a room: "Papa, potatoes, poultry, prunes, and prism are all very good words for the lips: especially prunes and prism" (529). The assonance of *prism* to *prison* is obvious.

24 Scarlet geraniums were Dickens's favourite flowers and he had a large bed of them at Gad's Hill.

suavity". He is "graciously disposed", "in a bland temper", "courtly, condescending and benevolently conscious of a position" and he stands at his window "with the air of an affable and accessible Sovereign" who receives the salutes of his people as his due and can just about prevent himself from blessing them. In this way Mr. Dorrit manages a reversal into the opposite of his humiliating situation. His general bearing reminds us of Mr. Turveydrop's "deportment" in *Bleak House*. Mr. Turveydrop is "very gentlemanly", as is Mr. Dorrit, and works his son to death while doing nothing but deport himself, just as Mr. Dorrit employs Amy to get him the necessary food and clothes while graciously and benevolently looking on. In *Bleak House* there is an old lady at Turveydrop's dancing academy who is very indignant at the father's behaviour:

> 'Look at the son's dress!' It certainly was plain – threadbare – almost shabby. 'Yet the father must be garnished and tricked out,' said the old lady, 'because of his Deportment. I'd deport him! Transport him would be better!' (*BH*, 244.)

Just like Mr. Dorrit, Fanny and Edward also "systematically ... produce the family skeleton for the overawing of the College" (277).

However, as has been pointed out, their repression is endangered by the presence of Little Dorrit, who, for instance, walks arm in arm with Old Nandy. On seeing this, Fanny gets very angry and reproaches her sister with these words:

> The principal pleasure of your life is to remind your family of their misfortunes. And the next great pleasure of your existence is to keep low company. (418)

When the Dorrits come into their fortune, they let other people feel their power. Thus both Mr. Dorrit and Fanny fly at the unfortunate Mr. Rugg, who does his utmost to enable the Dorrits to leave the prison as soon as possible. When they do leave,

> Mr Dorrit, yielding to the vast speculation how the poor creatures were to get on without him, was great, and sad, but not absorbed. He patted children on the head like Sir Roger de Coverley going to church, he spoke to people in the background by their Christian names, he condescended to all present, and seemed for their consolation to walk encircled by the legend in golden characters, 'Be comforted, my people! Bear it!' (480)

It is in keeping with their attempt to forget the unpleasant prison life that they leave the unconscious Amy behind and that they have a lasting grudge against Arthur, who carries her to them in her old prison dress and in this way reminds them of their years spent there.

The Dorrits go abroad and create some distance between the place of their old suffering and themselves. This time they do not only try to cover up their humiliation while in prison but to forget this period of their lives altogether. As has been mentioned, the Dorrits – except for Amy and her uncle Frederick – are proud and arrogant and keep the servants "in their places". The incident at Martigny (see p. 110) makes Mr. Dorrit feel that "the family dignity was struck at by an assassin's hand" (511). When the lady appears in order to apologize for the incident, Fanny and Amy recognize her at once: it is Mrs. Merdle, who once bribed Fanny to discourage her son's attentions to her. At that time Fanny was a second-rate dancer in a third-rate theatre and poor enough to accept the dresses of Mrs. Merdle's maid. It is in keeping with the pretensions of ladies and gentlemen that neither Fanny nor Mrs. Merdle will ever allude to their former acquaintance. However, the humiliation

Fanny felt at that time rankles in her breast; she tries to overcome it by marrying Mr. Sparkler and giving Mrs. Merdle's maid on the eve of her wedding day "a trifling little keepsake ... about four times as valuable as the present formerly made by Mrs. Merdle to her" (672).

Fanny, Edward and William Dorrit quickly adapt to their new situation although they are apt to see "the whole Marshalsea and all its testimonials" (660) in their servants' behaviour towards them. Little Dorrit cannot easily learn "to preserve the rank of a lady" (516) and she tries "to escape from the attendance of [her] ... oppressive maid, who was her mistress, and a very hard one" (519). Little Dorrit, born in the Marshalsea prison, symbolises the time spent there. Therefore, she is no longer allowed near her father and whereas her brother and sister go into society, she is always alone. Her loneliness is relieved by the company of her uncle, who – unlike the others – treats Little Dorrit with "a marked respect, very rarely shown by age to youth" (510) and gets very angry when she is slighted in his presence.[25] A footman who does not help Little Dorrit to get off the mule is nearly trampled to death by him and he also surprises them all by bursting out unexpectedly when Amy is criticized for her lack of deportment:

'I protest against any one of us here who have known what we have known, and have seen what we have seen, setting up any pretension that puts Amy at a moment's disadvantage, or to the cost of a moment's pain.' (538)

It is no surprise for us that Fanny finds her uncle "altogether unpresentable" (647), if he reminds them of their past in such a way. However, in letting Frederick Dorrit visit the picture galleries together with his niece "silently presenting her to the noble Venetians" (534), Dickens implies where true rank and true nobility are to be found. This is spelt out in the chapter "Something Wrong Somewhere", in which Amy is blamed by Mrs. General for her lack of "force of character and self-reliance" (526). Dickens imagines what a grateful parent could answer to Mrs. General:

O Mrs General, ask the Marshalsea stones and bars ... O Mrs General, Mrs General, ask me, her father, what I owe her; and hear my testimonial touching the life of this slighted creature from her childhood up! (526)

Of course Mr. Dorrit, who wants to forget the Marshalsea, says nothing of the sort but assents to the lady's judgement of Amy's character. In this way Dickens exposes the seeming gentility of society, while stressing that the true ladies and gentlemen must be sought elsewhere.

Apart from their arrogance and their ability to repress, further characteristic traits of the false ladies and gentlemen are that they are idle and parasitic. Fanny, to whom her father declares that it is her duty to "assert its [the family's] dignity and – hum – maintain its importance" (691), will, like the other members of society, avoid doing any work and leave her children to the care of her sister, Little Dorrit. In genteel society work seems to be almost indecent.[26] Mr. Merdle is reproached by his wife for

25 When Arthur meets Little Dorrit at her uncle's flat, he notes that the street door is "extensively scribbled over in pencil" (132), for instance with the inscription "Dirty Dick". This is another example of Dickens's hidden self-representation. (Cp. above, pp. 38 ff.) It also implies that Mr. Dorrit's rage is Dickens's own.

26 See Dickens's pun on *industry* when he makes Blandois declare that he is a "Knight of Industry" (837), i.e. a chevalier d'industrie or – as the editor of the Penguin Edition explains – "a man who lives by his wits" (912) and by no means an industrious man.

showing the burden of his office in his preoccupied manner. As has been mentioned, Blandois prides himself on never having done any work in his life, which – to him – proves that he is a gentleman. His white hands, which are so unlike Little Dorrit's work-worn hands, are always displayed by him and give people the impression that he is, indeed, a gentleman. The Dorrits prove their gentility to themselves and to others by the fact that they have a lot of servants, and even Mrs. Clennam is not able to do any work, for she is reduced to immobility in her wheelchair by her hysteric illness. The social novel *Little Dorrit* savagely attacks such parasites.[27] The ladies and gentlemen who pride themselves on their laziness exploit the working population. Dickens gives the exploiters telling names: they are the Barnacles and the Stiltstalkings, who draw large salaries and keep their good positions while they always find ways of "how not to do it", i.e. how to avoid doing anything at all.[28] These people are called "such high company" (459) by Mr. Meagles at the wedding of his daughter. They are the snobbish high society of England, whose stupidity is sometimes amazing, as with the sprightly young Barnacle, who is preoccupied with tormenting his eye with an eye-glass and retrieving it from all kinds of impossible places.[29]

The links between this particular class of exploiters and the characters of our story are manifold. There is Mr. Henry Gowan, who is a "disappointed man" because he has not been given a sinecure by his distant relatives, the Barnacles; there is his mother, Mrs. Gowan, who lets her son's parents-in-law pay his debts but then chooses not to know them any longer; there is Mr. Merdle, the financier, who is courted by everyone and whose suicide and discovered fraud condemns thousands of people to poverty and hardship, while his wife and stepson never suffer any want; there is Flora's father, the Patriarch, who is part of the system and ruthlessly exploits his tenants while affecting benevolence. Our protagonists, Little Dorrit and Arthur Clennam, are linked with these high people. Little Dorrit's father and Arthur both entrust their money to the fatal care of Mr. Merdle and lose everything. Fanny has married Merdle's stepson. Mr. Merdle commits suicide with a penknife he borrowed from Fanny. The woman who passes for Arthur's mother has suppressed a codicil that

27 It would be interesting to investigate all the shades of condescension between the various characters of our novel and to demonstrate how Dickens propagates equality between people as a prerequisite for lasting good relations. The counterpart to the Barnacles and Stiltstakings is Daniel Doyce, who is "medalled and ribboned, and starred, and crossed ... like a born nobleman" (891) because of the work he has been doing. It could also be shown that – both in *Little Dorrit* and in private life Dickens sometimes falls victim to the very vice he so bitingly exposes, but this would lead me too far away from my theme.

28 Of Gowan's father we hear that he, "originally attached to a legation abroad, had been pensioned off as a Commissioner of nothing particular somewhere or other, and had died at his post with his drawn salary in his hand, nobly defending it to the last extremity" (250).

29 Shaw apparently called *Little Dorrit* Dickens's most "seditious" book because of its judgement of the nobility. (Cp. John Halloway, "Introduction", *Little Dorrit,* The Penguin Edition, p. 19). He spoke very highly of Dickens's later novels to his biographer Frank Harris: "Your ignorance of Dickens is a frightful gap in your literary education. He was by far the greatest man since Shakespeare that England has ever produced in that line. Read *Little Dorrit, Our Mutual Friend* and *Great Expectations.* Until you do, you will not have the faintest notion of what the name Dickens means. (...) He did not come of age until Ruskin and Carlyle probed his social conscience to the depth, and he made a beginning of his great period with *Hard Times.* But when it came, it *was* great." (Quoted in: Frank Harris, *Bernard Shaw,* Hamburg, Paris, Bologna 1932, p. 240.)

would have given some money to Little Dorrit. Arthur's real mother, the rival Mrs. Clennam crushed, was a former pupil of Frederick Dorrit's. Mrs. Clennam is blackmailed by Blandois (he has got hold of her secret history), who also spies on the Gowans on behalf of Miss Wade. Miss Wade was once Gowan's sweetheart. Her jealousy and hatred of Pet Meagles are due to her being replaced by the latter – mainly for reasons of money. Pet Meagles – now Mrs. Gowan – was loved by Arthur. Earlier still, Arthur had been in love with Flora, the Patriarch's daughter.

It seems to me that Dickens portrays his snobbish characters as utterly evil when he looks at them from the outside, as it were. The Barnacles and Stiltstakings are types just as are "Bar", "Bishop" and "Physician". We are asked to condemn them wholeheartedly. The embodiment of evil in the novel, Blandois, is "a gentleman" and nothing else. Mr. Gowan and his mother, as well as Mrs. Merdle, are superficial and heartless creatures. When Dickens tells us more about the motives of a character's superciliousness, however, he makes us understand why he/she has to adopt such a pose. This is the case with Fanny and William Dorrit as well as with Mrs. Clennam. Dickens does not spare them his moral judgement: he condemns their actions. But he understands rather than judges the persons themselves. It is as if he intuitively understood something of the nature of guiltless guilt. There is a softening touch to the portrait of Mr. Dorrit and Mrs. Clennam, the parental figures of our heroine and hero, just as there is understanding of the wayward child Fanny. In his treatment of these characters Dickens has been partly able to overcome his old quest for the culprit. Let us consider, for instance, his description of the return of the repressed past with Mr. Dorrit as well as with Mrs. Clennam.

When Mr. Dorrit wants to settle his affairs in England after Fanny's marriage, the fact that he visits London, the city in which his suffering took place, is already a threat to his defences. At first it seems as if he could counterbalance this by his proximity to Merdle:

> leaning on Mr Merdle's arm, did Mr Dorrit descend the staircase, seeing the worshippers on the steps, and feeling that the light of Mr Merdle shone by reflection in himself. Then the carriage, and the ride into the City; and the people who looked at them; and the hats that flew off grey heads; and the general bowing and crouching before this wonderful mortal the like of which prostration of spirit was not to be seen – no, by high Heaven, no! (...) It was a rapturous dream to Mr. Dorrit to find himself set aloft in this public car of triumph ... (677)[30]

However, this elation does not last. At Mr. Merdle's dinner table Mr. Dorrit is disturbed by the way the Chief Butler looks at him with a "glazed fixedness" (687). In this case Mr. Dorrit's apprehensions that the butler knows something about his past in the debtors' prison are not paranoic, for the Barnacles had discussed Mr. Dorrit's fate at the very same dinner table some time earlier and complained of the trouble he

---

30 Dickens may have identified with Mr. Dorrit here and felt with him, that even adulation of the people cannot lastingly give a person the self-esteem he lacks. The young Dickens, who was lionized not only in America but also at home, often felt embarrassed as well as thrilled when old people gave homage to the young man and the "hats that flew off grey heads" in our text echo this sentiment. However, it sounds a little strange in connection with Mr. Dorrit, who is himself old and probably grey, and therefore points to an unconscious connection between Dickens and Mr. Dorrit.

caused their office when he wanted to pay his old debts.[31]. When Mr. Dorrit dresses to visit Mr. Merdle for the second time and is already apprehensive of the Butler's behaviour towards him, Flora Finching's name is announced to him. She is, of course, another link to that fatal past he is not allowed to forget, even if it be only in the fact that she is wearing a dress Little Dorrit sewed for "daily compensations", something – Mr. Dorrit stresses – he would never have permitted her to do, had he known of it. When Flora mentions Mr. Clennam and Pancks, Mr. Dorrit is bound to react with hostility, for both of them remind him keenly of what he has gone through. She finally explains what she has come for: to ask whether Mr. Dorrit has any knowledge of the whereabouts of Blandois, who has disappeared. Blandois thus serves as a link between the past and the present as well as between our heroine and hero, between Little Dorrit and Arthur. When Mr. Dorrit visits Mrs. Clennam in order to obtain more information, the two families are brought together. Mrs. Clennam, too, represses something – not only the codicil to the will of Arthur's late uncle, but also the fact that she felt very much slighted by her husband and was unbearably jealous of her rival, Arthur's true mother.[32] Mr. Dorrit's house of cards, called "the proud structure of a family edifice" (662) by Mrs. General, will collapse, just as Mrs. Clennam's abode will "heave, surge outward, open asunder in fifty places, collapse, and fall" (862, tenses altered). Moreover, in Mrs. Clennam's house there is Affery, whose behaviour is like a pictorial description of the mechanism of repression. Affery is frightened to death of her "lord and master", who often threatens to give her "such a dose" (i.e. of beating) and she deals with this situation by "having dreams" whenever she sees something that troubles her. Very early in the novel she overhears a conversation between her husband and his twin-brother, Epharim Flintwinch, who "speculated unsuccessfully in lunatics" (852) and was chosen as the keeper of Arthur's mad mother by Mrs. Clennam. Into Ephraim's hands have fallen the documents which Blandois uses to blackmail Mrs. Clennam. When Flintwinch realises that Affery has witnessed the scene, he shakes her until she is black in the face, calling all the time: 'Why, Affery woman – Affery! ... What have you been dreaming of? Wake up, wake up!' (83) Affery no longer trusts her eyes and ears but takes everything she perceives to be a dream – what is real and threatening becomes unreal and less threatening. In order to ward off terrifying sights, Affery keeps her head constantly covered with her apron. She pays for thus blotting out her knowledge of what happens by blindness and her growing confusion. Mrs. Clennam is to call her "this piece of distraction" later on (836). Dickens also chooses Affery, this symbol of enforced repression, to hint at the future collapse of Mrs. Clennam's psychic structure. Affery's sound perception of slight noises, caused by vibrations in the walls of the house, are treated as madness, but her terror is contagious – Mr. Dorrit, Mr. Flintwinch, and Mrs. Clennam all feel it.

After having visited Mrs. Clennam, Mr. Dorrit's defences are even more shaken by the proximity of her house to the Marshalsea and his wavering doubt of whether or not to pass by its gate. However, when the coach-man wants to take a route which

---

31 Again Dickens's own past is present, for Mr. Barnacle says that Mr. Dorrit "was a partner in a business house in some large way – spirits, or buttons, or wine, or *blacking*, ..." (620, emphasis mine). Even here, however, the past is beautified, for Dickens's father was never a partner in a business house in *some large way!*

32 The oedipal triangle is of course very much a part of Mrs. Clennam's story. This is so obvious, however, that I have not enlarged upon it.

would have brought them close to the prison, Mr. Dorrit gets very angry with him. Mr. Dorrit is then invited to a farewell dinner at the Merdle's and is very much pleased with the company and with himself. When he returns to his hotel, this "grandeur" is "yet full upon" him (691), and he passes through the hotel hall with a "serene magnificence" when the repressed past returns with a vengeance:

> lo! a sight presented itself that struck him dumb and motionless. John Chivery, in his best clothes, with his tall hat under his arm, his ivory-handled cane genteelly embarrassing his deportment, and a bundle of cigars in his hand! (691)

Mr. Chivery flings the past back into Mr. Dorrit's face with his mock gentility, his "deportment" and the cigars he used to present to him, and as soon as they are alone together, Mr. Dorrit flies at him in an irrepressible rage and nearly chokes the young man. When Chivery tries to defend himself, saying that these were the very cigars Mr. Dorrit used to smoke, the latter is quite beside himself: "Tell me that again, ... and I'll take the poker to you" (692), he says. When Mr. Dorrit perceives John's shocked, white face, he feels guilty and apologizes:

> 'Young John, I am very sorry to have been hasty with you, but – ha – some remembrances are not happy remembrances, and – hum – you shouldn't have come.' (693)

Once more Mr. Dorrit tries to reverse the situation by presenting the cigars to his Courier as a "little offering from – ha – son of old tenant of mine" (695) although John Chivery is the turnkey's son, who has taken over his father's business now.

The old associations gain more and more power over Mr. Dorrit, who defends himself first by putting "the Channel between himself and John Chivery"[33] and by building castles in the air. To consolidate his position in society, he plans to marry that "very genteel lady", Mrs. General, for whom he buys a "love gift" and a "nuptial gift" in Paris. However, the chapter "The Storming of the Castle in the Air" makes us feel in the first paragraph that misfortune is to come:

> The sun had gone down full four hours, and it was later than most travellers would like it to be for finding themselves outside the walls of Rome, when Mr Dorrit's carriage, still on its last wearisome stage, rattled over the solitary Campagna. The savage herdsmen and the fierce-looking peasants who had chequered the way while the light lasted, had all gone down with the sun, and left the wilderness blank. At some turns of the road, a pale flare on the horizon, like an exhalation from the ruin-sown land, showed that the city was yet far off; but this poor relief was rare and short-lived. The carriage dipped down again into a hollow of the black dry sea, and for a long time there was nothing visible save its petrified swell and the gloomy sky. (697)

Indeed, the collapse of the castle is foreshadowed in the

> fragments of ruinous enclosure, yawning window-gap and crazy wall, deserted houses, leaking wells, broken water-tanks, spectral cypress-trees, patches of tangled vine, and the changing of the track to a long, irregular, disordered lane where everything was crumbling away, from the unsightly buildings to the jolting road (698)

near Rome. They meet a funeral procession on their way to Rome and the priest's chanting lips seem to threaten Mr. Dorrit. He arrives in his palace in Rome, only to

---

33 Dickens, too, tried to find relief by creating some distance between himself and the place of his suffering. In his autobiographical fragment he tells us that he never went near Warren's until the place was pulled down, and Dickens often escaped from his unsatisfactory marriage by going on shorter and longer excursions with his male friends, and he often went abroad when conflicts at home (for instance with his publishers) were too exasperating.

find Little Dorrit and his brother Frederick keeping each other company and making him jealous of their mutual affection:

> So had he sat many a night, over a coal fire far away; so had she sat, devoted to him. Yet surely there was nothing to be jealous of in the old miserable poverty. Whence, then, the pang in his heart? (699)

Mr. Dorrit seems to realize dimly that what he has given up in leaving the Marshalsea is not wholly bad, that his new life is in one respect much poorer than his existence in the Marshalsea where he could always feel his daughter's love for him.

Mr. Dorrit, who is exhausted, sends his brother Frederick to bed and claims that he does not feel at all tired. However, he repeatedly falls into brief heavy dozes. It is as if he could only escape from the crowding memories of former times by becoming oblivious to everything and everybody around him. The closeness of his daughter is dangerous to Mr. Dorrit, who twice has to reassure himself that he is not wearing his old prison cap. Both times he wards off old memories by

> immediately expatiating on the great riches and great company that had encompassed him in his absence, and on the lofty position he and his family had to sustain. (703)

Dickens once more stresses in this way that the snobbery of the Dorrit family is defensive in nature, is used as a weapon against unbearable suffering.[34] On the following day Mr. Dorrit hints to Mrs. General that he would like to marry her and she lets him know that she is by no means disinclined to accept his proposal. Mr. Dorrit's defences are once more strengthened, and he feels reassured when he is asked to Mrs. Merdle's dinner, for

> Mrs. Merdle received him with great distinction ... the dinner was very choice; and the company was very select. (707)

However, the repressed past can no longer be kept down and Mr. Dorrit suddenly surprises the illustrious crowd by addressing them in his pathetic Marshalsea speech:

> 'Ladies and gentlemen, the duty – ha – devolves upon me of – hum – welcoming you to the Marshalsea! Welcome to the Marshalsea! The space is – ha – limited – limited – the parade might be wider; but you will find it apparently grow larger after a time – a time, ladies and gentlemen – and the air is, all things considered, very good. (...) This is the Snuggery. Hum. Supported by a small subscription of the – ha – Collegiate body. In return for which – hot water – general kitchen – and little domestic advantages.
> Those who are habituated to the – ha – Marshalsea, are pleased to call me its Father. I am accustomed to be complimented by strangers as the – ha – Father of the Marshalsea. Certainly, if years of residence may establish a claim to so – ha – honourable a title, I may accept the – hum – conferred distinction. My child, ladies and gentlemen. My daughter. Born here!' (708-9)

Mr. Dorrit's imprisonment in the Marshalsea may (among other things) be looked upon as a symbol of neurosis. A neurotic person is restricted in his space of action

34 Sadoff contends that "William Dorrit dies because a different father-lover sits with Amy" ("Storytelling and the Figure of the Father in *Little Dorrit,* p. 240). The incestuous nature of the attachment between Mr. Dorrit and his youngest child is pretty obvious. Thus Mr. Dorrit pauses at a revealing place when he tells Little Dorrit before going to bed that day, "We must marry – ha – we must marry *you* now" (704). This incestuous love, however, may also be part of all the emotions and experiences Mr. Dorrit so desperately tries to forget, for it, too, has imprisoned him (as well as Amy) by not letting him give his love to another woman.

because he is locked in his past. The space is indeed limited. It is a marvel that he can breathe (survive): "all things considered, the air is very good". After a while he gets used to his prison and starts to embellish it with a "Snuggery", the space "apparently grows larger". And just as some people pride themselves on being more neurotic than anyone else, on having suffered most, on needing the longest treatment, so Mr. Dorrit derives a questionable distinction from being the prison's oldest inhabitant.

In the fate he assigns to Mr. Dorrit Dickens shows us his intuitive understanding of neurosis. Looked at from this angle, the question of guilt is no longer relevant. Dickens can now pity Mr. Dorrit and feel sympathy for his plight, while showing that his solution to his problems can only temporarily help him.

Similarly, Mrs. Clennam's self-righteousness and rigidity is shown as a defence against feelings of deep shame at having been slighted by her husband. Instead of being the loser in the battle between herself and Arthur's mother, she becomes powerful by preoccupying herself with her religion, which gives her the right to condemn other sinners while feeling superior to them. She speaks in the Pharisee's words "God, I thank thee, that I am not as other women are, unjust, adulteresses ..." (after *Luke* 18:11). She even proves her holiness to herself in her physical suffering, her handicap proves to her that she belongs to the Lord's elect.

On p. 106 a quotation was given in which Mrs. Clennam talks about her sins. What does she refer to apart from the sin of hating Arthur's true mother violently, to which feeling she openly confesses and which she does not at all repress? May it not be – not unlike Mr. Dorrit's sin – a sin of unlawful love? It cannot be the love for Arthur's father, for she neither loves him nor would it be unlawful if she did. Rather, it is incestuous in its nature once again: her love for little Arthur. She has wrenched this child from his real mother and has tried to obtain his love by sheer force. Again, the incestuous love between the generations springs up to cover a basic need of love that has never been fulfilled. Significantly, Mrs. Clennam can walk freely when her repression is temporarily lifted and when she discloses her deepest feelings to Little Dorrit:

> 'my enemy ... wronged me. (...) What Arthur's father was to me, she made him. From our marriage day I was his dread, and that she made me. I was the scourge of both, and that is referable to her.' (859)
> 'He [i.e. Arthur] never loved me, as I once half-hoped he might – so frail we are, and so do the corrupt affections of the flesh war with our trusts and tasks; but he always respected me.' (860)

> 'I would not, for any worldly recompense I can imagine, have him in a moment, however blindly, throw me down from the station I have ever held before him all his life, and change me altogether into something he would cast out of his respect, and think detected and exposed. Let him do it, if it must be done, when I am not here to see it. Let me never feel, while I am still alive, that I die before his face, and utterly perish away from him, like one consumed by lightning and swallowed by an earthquake.' (860)

Mrs. Clennam uses the vocabulary of a cosmic catastrophe here to give voice to her passionate love for Arthur. We can guess that it must have been very bitter for her that he never loved her, as she wished him to do with all her heart and did not only "half-hope" for, as she claims. She is ashamed of this need for his love and calls it frailty and corruption of the flesh! We can understand that it is preferable for Mrs. Clennam to be hysterically crippled rather than face her deeply hidden painful emotions.

Arthur's function of uncovering the past is similar to that of Little Dorrit. Mrs. Clennam is reminded of her suffering when she sees Arthur, "with his mother's face, looking up at me in awe from his little books" (859) – his very existence becomes a threat to her. It can be inferred that she has to be so stern and so cold with him and even has to send him abroad because she cannot bear feeling the pangs of unrequited love any longer.

Both Mr. Dorrit and Mrs. Clennam pay dearly for the temporary lifting of their repressions. They are forced to uncover their feelings but they can never recover from this shock. Mr. Dorrit dies soon after and Mrs. Clennam lives for another three years as a living statue that cannot move or speak.

# 4. Conclusion

Dickens's blacking warehouse trauma has become famous since Forster's biography. It was a tremendous surprise for Dickens's contemporaries to hear of his early sufferings, for Dickens had carefully hidden all traces of it, even from his wife. There can be no doubt that the period at Warren's was a very painful time for the boy Charles Dickens. However, I have argued that this traumatic experience was for us – and possibly also for Dickens himself – some sort of a blessing in disguise as well. As Dickens was twelve years old when he went to the blacking factory, the events happened late enough for him to remember them afterwards. And they also happened early enough for him to be strongly reminded of his still earlier childhood experiences. In this way Dickens did not lose contact with the child in himself. I believe this to be the key to much of the Dickensian charm. The Dickens world lives by atmosphere rather than by plot or characters. The emotions Dickens could set free in his novels and could make the reader feel are in their intensity those of a child. Dickens land is the child's land.

A child may be impressed, for instance, by particular idiosyncracies of the adults or by mannerisms of speech – Dickens characterizes his people in this way.[1] Just as a child is sometimes unable to distinguish between the living and the dead, the animate and the inanimate, Dickens is famous for his animation of concrete objects or things and for his reification of human beings.[2] And just as a small child has difficulty in integrating various facets of people as all belonging to the self-same persons, Dickens resorts to splitting mechanisms throughout his literary career.

I have argued in this study, however, that Dickens's way of dealing with his past does not remain the same from the beginning to the end of his writing life. Critics often talk of the sunny early Dickens and the gloomy late Dickens. Whereas it is true that the elder Dickens lost some of what Forster called "animal spirits", his sheer psychic energy, there is in my opinion much sadness, heaviness, fright, etc. in the early novels as well, but they are detached from the whole and not so well integrated as later. In his first novel, *The Pickwick Papers,* they are even separated from the main story and are only expressed in the gruesome interpolated stories. The change takes place gradually, but *David Copperfield* seems to be some sort of centre around which the other novels symmetrically group. All Dickens's writing is an attempt at

---

1 Examples are of course legion. To mention just a few: "Barkis is willin' ", "when found make a note of" (Captain Cuttle), "Put the bottle on the chimley piece and ... I'll put my lips to it when I'm so disposed" (Sarah Gamp); Blandois' smile, Mr. Merdle taking himself into custody.
2 As an example of reification we could mention Mrs. Merdle, who is reduced to a snow-cold bosom. The following letter shows Dickens's power to give life to the inanimate: "My dear Sir, Since my hall clock was sent to your establishment to be cleaned it has gone (as indeed it always has) perfectly well, but has struck the hours with great reluctance, and, after enduring internal agonies of a most distressing nature, it has now ceased striking altogether. Though a happy release for the clock, this is not convenient to the household. If you can send a confidential person with whom the clock can confer, I think it may have something on its works that it would be glad to make a clean breast of" (quoted in Sir Henry Dickens, *Memories of My Father,* London 1928, pp. 85-6). In Stefanie Meier's study, *Animation and Mechanization in the Novels of Charles Dickens,* Bern 1982, many other charming examples of this particular Dickensian gift are given.

dealing with the past, some sort of work of mourning. This seems to be especially true of his veiled autobiography, *David Ðopperfield*. If we read the letters Dickens wrote while working on it, we notice that his psyche was in turmoil. The acute distress he had to endure brought about some change in him. After *David Copperfield* Dickens was able to present a fictitious world to the reader with fewer illusions and fewer escapes into fantasy. I have tried to show Dickens's altered attitude by looking more closely at two corresponding novels, *The Old Curiosity Shop* and *Little Dorrit*.

It does not seem to me that *The Old Curiosity Shop* is any less heavy in atmosphere than the later *Little Dorrit*. Both books convey feelings of oppression, of being stifled and imprisoned, of isolation, loneliness, despair. The description of the Black Country in the earlier novel rivals that of the dilapidated houses and streets near Rome in *Little Dorrit* in its ghastly intensity. However, the artistic solution to these problems is not the same. In *The Old Curiosity Shop* Dickens controls these frightening feelings by finding a cause for them either in the "bad" child or in the "bad" adult. He makes use of extensive splitting mechanisms. To almost any bad person there is a corresponding good one. The wicked grandfather is contrasted with his benevolent brother, the sadistic spinster Sally Brass with the gentle and pretty Mrs. Quilp, the heartless Miss Monflathers with the motherly Mrs. Jarley, the exploiting Codlin with the benevolent Garlands, the bitter Mrs. Jiniwin with the always cheerful Mrs. Nubbles, the egotistical Mr. Vuffin with the charitable furnace-keeper, the bad child Quilp with the angel Nell, the law-abiding Kit with the lawless Tom Scott, the rebellious pony with the meek Abel Garland. Even the humanized fire of the furnace keeper, which gives warmth and protection, is contrasted with the dehumanized Brasses, the "sharks" that destroy people.

Often there is a pair of good child and bad parent (Nell – her grandfather, the Marchioness – Sally Brass, Miss Edwards – Miss Monflathers) or of a bad child and a good parent (Quilp – Mrs. Quilp, the pony – the Garlands, Dick and his aunt). The search for the culprit goes on throughout the book – villains must be found and punished, the innocent must be saved from contamination by the bad. Dickens escapes from this life in two ways. There is first the escape into death, which is looked upon as a peaceful happening, a reunion between loved child and loving parent (God). It preserves the good child from becoming corrupted by life and justly punishes the bad child. The escape into a glorified death is not convincing, for – using Marcus's definition – it is sentimental in that it covers up particular emotions and feelings while stressing others. Thus loneliness and fear are said not to exist and are replaced by tender affection and reunion with a loved person.

The other escape into fantasy in *The Old Curiosity Shop* is the relationship between Dick Swiveller and the Marchioness. The name "Marchioness" is a reversal of the child's position as a servant or almost a slave. Dick and the Marchioness can transcend exasperating reality by pretending that lemon peel and water make a delicious drink and that they live in spacious rooms. As we are fully aware that they are playing a game, "writing a book in company", as it were, the escape of Dick's and Sophronia Sphynx's fiction is a relief. Apparently Dickens was able to play this game not only with the boys at Warren's factory but also with his parents' maid, a little orphan girl who was the model for the Marchioness. Forster tells us that the twelve-year old Dickens used to tell her marvellous stories whenever he met her in front of the Marshalsea in order to lighten her life as well as his own. (*F*, I, 27)

130

Both the kinds of escape into fantasy we found in *The Old Curiosity Shop* are only marginally present in *Little Dorrit*. Although Clennam too wistfully thinks at one time of death as a peaceful end to his troubles, Dickens makes it quite clear that he does not regard this as a solution but lets his protagonists live a "modest life of usefulness and happiness", which, however, cannot change society at large:

> They went quietly down into the roaring streets, inseparable and blessed; and as they passed along in sunshine and shade, the noisy and the eager, and the arrogant and the froward and the vain, fretted and chafed, and made their usual uproar. (*LD*, 895)

Dickens now also admits to the "shade" as an essential element of human life. He can bear more suffering without having to undo it by wishful thinking and an escape into fantasy. There is a lot of resignation in *Little Dorrit* rather than a happy – albeit unconvincing – solution or a deus ex machina. On the whole the tempo of *Little Dorrit* is slower; Dickens seems to have become a much older man. There is a hilarity in *The Old Curiosity Shop*, a boisterous laughter that we miss in *Little Dorrit*. There is nothing comparable to the happy flight into poetry of a Dick Swiveller. The Plornish's "Happy Cottage", Little Dorrit's pathetic fairy tale, Mrs. Plornish's fiction of her being an adept in Italian, Edward Nandy's songs, Flora's feigned youthfulness are often more pathetic than truly amusing and do not offer the comic relief we get from Dick Swiveller. Dickens's release of aggression in his wit, however, is far more biting and sarcastic in the earlier novel. Sally Brass is relentlessly ridiculed, whereas the author makes good-natured fun of Flora. Her dialogues are the most amusing parts of the novel and are said to have inspired Joyce in his creation of Molly Bloom.[3]

In *Little Dorrit* Dickens can also integrate some of his conflicting attitudes towards parents and children. He gives us one of his most touching portraits in William Dorrit. Despite his exposing him in all his weakness, he has also a lot of affection for this character, who has a "poor, weak breast, so full of contradiction: vacillations, inconsistencies, the little peevish perplexities of this ignorant life" (*LD*, 699-700). Both William Dorrit and Mrs. Clennam are complex human beings, no longer just victims or victimizers, and Dickens condemns their actions rather than the characters themselves. Unlike the child figures Little Dorrit and Arthur Clennam, still preternaturally good, Fanny is not only a disobedient wicked child but is shown to have the author's sympathy for her wilfulness, her courage, her determination, her silent suffering, her pride. It is also a great achievement of Dickens's that Flora Finching is not painted all black but as a silly yet likeable and essentially good-natured woman.

Still, Dickens could not quite do without splitting mechanisms; this is borne out by his doubles (Blandois/Arthur – Little Dorrit/Maggy – Miss Wade/Pet/Tattycoram – William Dorrit/Frederick Dorrit) and by the existence of one of his eccentrics, Mr. F's Aunt. She expresses all the hatred of Arthur and Little Dorrit that we would expect Flora to feel because of her unrequited love.[4]

Dickens, then, could integrate some of his ambivalence in *Little Dorrit* although there are still some stock characters of good and evil. However, as has been shown,

---

3 See Fred Kaplan, "Dickens' Flora Finching and Joyce's Molly Bloom", *Nineteenth Century Fiction* 23 (1968), pp. 343-6.
4 Dickens often describes what one could see as innerpsychic relationships as relationships between two people. Thus Mr. F's Aunt, who constantly levels her animosity at Arthur and belittles him whenever she can, reveals the effects a sadistic superego can have on a person.

the author now realizes that people can bring suffering upon others without being wicked. The culprit is partly found in the structure of society (the Circumlocution Office) and partly in parental figures (Mr. Dorrit, the Patriarch, Mrs. Clennam, Mr. and Mrs. Meagles) and in child characters (Edward and Fanny Dorrit, Tattycoram and Miss Wade). However, he often describes people he outwardly disapproves of with concealed sympathy (Fanny, Miss Wade, Tatty, Mrs. Clennam, Mr. Dorrit).

We know that to the end of his days Dickens never forgot his humiliating experiences at Warren's. In his books, unexpected allusions to this time are common. Dickens's son Henry also tells us that at the last Christmas the novelist saw he joined in a memory game:

> One of the party started by giving a name, such as, for instance, Napoleon. The next person had to repeat this and add something of his own ... until the string of names began to get long und difficult to remember. My father, after many turns, had successfully gone through the long string of words, and finished up with his own contribution, "Warren's Blacking, 30, Strand." He gave this with an odd twinkle in his eye and a strange inflection in his voice which at once forcibly arrested my attention and left a vivid impression on my mind for some time afterwards. Why, I could not, for the life of me, understand. When, however, his tragic history appeared in Forster's Life, this game at Christmas 1869, flashed across my mind with extraordinary force, and the mystery was explained.[5]

How far, then, did Dickens succeed in dealing with the past? His constant reenactment of his childhood experiences in his books, his partial work of mourning in all of them and particularly in *David Copperfield,* his guiltless release of aggression in his wit, the admiring public that worshipped him, helped him to cope with his old feelings. John Gross maintains that Dickens felt a hatred for his mother "which he could never get out of his system".[6] Apparently this feeling frightened him and had to be kept down and counterbalanced by his host of sickly-sweet, saintly women, such as Rose Maylie, Kate Nickleby, Madeline Bray, Little Nell, Ruth Pinch, Dot, Milly, Florence Dombey, Agnes, Esther Summerson, Little Dorrit, and Lucie Manette. At the time of writing *Little Dorrit,* Dickens still needs this particular kind of defence, for his heroine is only slightly more real than the earlier comparable characters. It is possible that the appearance of a Bella Wilfer or a Rosa Bud in his last novel points to a further work of mourning and a coming to terms with his own parents, particularly with his mother. If she had given him cause for hatred, she had also given him a means of coping with it: it was Elizabeth Dickens who taught him to read and write. In his autobiographical fragment Dickens says in apparent though probably unconscious self-deception, "I do not write resentfully or angrily: for I know how all these things have worked together to make me what I am" ("AF", p. 32). It is easier for the reader to bear no resentment and to accept Dickens's blemishes along with his greatness as being deeply rooted in his psychic structure.

5 Sir Henry Dickens, *Memories of My Father,* London 1928, pp. 23-4.
6 John Gross in his review of Michael Slater, *Dickens and Women* in *The Observer,* 13 February 1983. As the book came out after the completion of this study, it has not been taken into account.

# Appendix

## Summary of *The Old Curiosity Shop*

The nearly fourteen-year-old Nelly Trent and her grandfather, a dealer in curiosities, live together in the latter's shop, a house full of "lumber and decay, and ugly age". Little Nell, as she is called, is an orphan. She has an older brother, Fred, a dissolute profligate who is trying to get at his grandfather's money. The old man wants to secure a fortune for his granddaughter. He pictures her to himself as a grand lady in rich dresses, riding in carriages. To attain this end he has started gambling and he has not only lost all their savings but has borrowed large sums of money from the malicious dwarf, Daniel Quilp, as well. Quilp cunningly contrives to overhear a conversation between his wife and Little Nell wherein Nell tells Mrs. Quilp how altered her grandfather is and that he is absent every night. From this Quilp gathers the old man's secret, namely his gambling mania, and he refuses to lend him any more money. Instead he gets hold of the house and of all the possessions of Nell's grandfather. (We never get to know his name.) The desperate and raging old man wants to know who has betrayed him. "Was it Kit?" he asks. Kit is his servant and Quilp bears him a grudge because he once said in a quarrel with Quilp's servant boy that Quilp was "an uglier dwarf than can be seen anywheres for a penny". So Quilp confirms the old man's suspicion that Kit has betrayed him. Nell's grandfather falls into a fit and then into a "raging fever". He is dangerously ill for many weeks and Kit must not come near him any more.

Meanwhile Fred, who is exasperated at the thought that Nell will inherit the great riches he supposes his grandfather to possess, urges his friend Richard (Dick) Swiveller to marry his sister and then to share the money with him.

When Nell's grandfather recovers, he is told by Quilp that he must leave the house in a few days. Nell and the old man decide to seek their fortunes in the country, to "travel afoot through fields and woods, and by the side of rivers, and trust ourselves to God in the places where He dwells." The story now divides into two strands: there are the wandering Nell and her grandfather and the people they meet, on the one hand, and the characters in London and their fate, on the other. The narrator skips back and forth between these two places of action. At the end of the book the two strands are knit together, the actors brought to play on one and the same stage.

## The experiences of Nell and her grandfather

At first they enjoy the lovely country-side and their mutual attachment. But – as the old man is flying from temptation and frightened of succumbing to it – he frequently urges Nell on, insisting that they must be "farther away, farther away". They are thus soon exhausted but the restlessness of the old man does not allow them to stop at a cottage where they are invited to rest. They meet two men, exhibitors of a Punch and Judy show, and decide to travel with them. However, the two players, who are called Codlin and Short, suspect that Nell and the old man are runaways and that they will be sought by rich relatives. They hope to be given a reward by these imaginary wealthy people and are determined to treat the two well. At the same time they want to keep an eye on them so that they cannot escape. Nell, however, notices their attempts and she and her grandfather decide to flee. They are now destitute and have to earn their bread by begging.

In their wanderings they also come to a small village and spend the night at the schoolmaster's house. He is very kind to them but he is also very sad – his favourite pupil and personal friend is ill. The schoolmaster attempts to ignore the danger signals but while Nell and her grandfather are staying at his house he is called for and the little boy dies. The schoolmaster seems to transfer his love from the boy to Little Nell, who was beside him at his dying pupil's bedside. Nell and her grandfather are obliged, however, to leave him and after a day's walking they suddenly come upon a caravan. There they meet Mrs. Jarley, "the comfortable proprietress" of a wax-work exhibition and the inhabitant of the caravan "who has not only a peculiar relish for being comfortable herself, but for making everybody about her comfortable also." Mrs. Jarley employs Nell, who has to explain the wax-work figures to the visitors of the exhibition. She is well treated and earns enough money to keep both her grandfather and herself. One day Nell and the old man return from a walk and are surprised on their way home by a fearful storm. They take shelter at a nearby inn where they put up for the night. There are people playing cards, however, and the old man is at once again in the grips of his gambling fever. He loses all the money Nell gives him and at night he robs her of every penny she possesses. Nell discovers the theft and surprises her grandfather, "his white face pinched and sharpened by the greediness which made his eyes unnaturally bright – counting the money of which his hands had robbed her."

During the following weeks, Nell hands over to her grandfather all the money she earns and he speedily loses it at cards. One day, again returning from a walk, Nell passes by a gypsies' tent and perceives her grandfather in a conversation with two of the gamblers she has previously seen at the inn. She overhears their talk – her grandfather pledges himself to rob Mrs. Jarley, their benefactress, and to stake the money at the gambling table. At night the horrfied Nell urges him to flee with her and they are once more cast upon the world without any money or any place to go to. They arrive at a crowded city where they feel more lonely than before in the midst of strange people who do not care for them, but they are also befriended by a man who is an outsider himself. His only friend in the world is a roaring fire in a furnace which he has to feed, and he offers them a rough but dry place to sleep at. On the following day they pass the slums of the industrialized city. Everywhere they find misery, the countryside is blighted – it seems like hell. When the child is about to succumb to her fatigue and her suffering, they suddenly meet the schoolmaster. Nell swoons at his feet. He takes care of them and when Nell is better they travel on together to a peaceful village where the schoolmaster has been appointed schoolmaster and parish clerk. They are given a place to live in, a dilapidated old house. Nell has to show the church to tourists from the city and to explain the various sights therein and she can thus earn enough for the two of them. However, she grows steadily weaker and finally, in the middle of winter, she dies. Her grandfather is wild with grief. Every day he sits by her grave waiting for her to return. He finally dies too and is buried beside her.

# What happens to the characters in London

They are all baffled by the unexpected flight of Nell and the old man. Kit is almost broken-hearted and cherishes a forlorn hope that the two will seek refuge at his home. Dick finds his plans to obtain money in an easy way suddenly thwarted. Quilp suspects the old man of having hidden some money from him and is furious at the thought. Kit – who has to find new employment – is given a post at the Garlands' house after having given proof of his honesty. The Garlands are an elderly couple with a twenty-eight-year-old son who is apprenticed to a notary, Mr. Witherden. They are very sedate and orderly people. At their house there is also a servant girl called Barbara who becomes friendly with Kit. Barbara's mother makes the acquaintance of Kit's mother and they get on well together. Kit is in charge of an untractable pony which also belongs to the Garland household. Quilp worms Dick's secret plans out of him by making him drunk. He encourages them, promising to help Dick find the fugitives. Secretly, however, he roars with laughter at the thought that Dick will marry Nell and find out that she is penniless after the wedding.[1]

The ever distrustful dwarf wants to spy on his lawyer, Sampson Brass, and on the latter's sister, Sarah (or Sally) Brass, and he therefore forces Brass to appoint Dick Swiveller as his clerk.

After a fitful time of exasperation with his boring work and with the presence of the "female dragon" Sally, during which Dick finds relief by flourishing his ruler about, he becomes friendly with her. She calls him "a funny chap". However, Dick also soon finds out the awful way in which she treats a small servant girl, who is remorselessly beaten and is on the verge of starvation.

The Brasses let a room to a single gentleman. He is of a peculiarly impatient and impetuous temper and later turns out to be the younger brother of Nell's grandfather. He wants to find them and as somebody has told him that they were seen with a Punch and Judy show, he invites all the Punches that are in town to play in front of the Brasses' establishment and later to share a glass of wine with him. Brass is exasperated with their noise but "as he could by no means afford to lose so profitable an inmate, deemed it prudent to pocket his lodger's affront along with his cash." The single gentleman finds out that Nell and the old man are staying at Jarley's wax-works and sets out to take them back to London. Kit's mother is to accompany him and to speak to them first and convince them of his friendly intentions. However, when they finally arrive at Mrs. Jarley's caravan, Nell and her grandfather have already departed. They return to London disappointed. Quilp, who has secretly followed them, returns by the same coach and nearly frightens Mrs. Nubbles out of her wits by his horrible grimaces and gymnastic exercises.

As Mr. Quilp has not informed his wife of his departure, he has been missed for a few days and is supposed drowned. When he returns home he surprises Brass, his wife, his hated mother-in-law and two watermen all happily drinking his punch and conjuring up a description of his body. He determines to punish Mrs. Quilp by being "a bachelor" henceforth, living on his own in an old hut by the riverside, only coming back to his old lodgings from time to time in order to spy on his wife and to worry her.

---

1 In a later novel, *Our Mutual Friend,* Dickens was to expand this idea. Alfred and Sophronia Lammle get married, each in the conviction that the other one possesses a fortune only to find out the mistake after the wedding.

Quilp is still nursing his grudge against Kit and he decides to destroy him. To this end he invites Sampson and Sally Brass to his dilapidated summer house and they plot Kit's downfall.

Meanwhile Dick discovers at the office that the little slipshod girl whom he is later to baptize "The Marchioness" is "looking through the keyhole for company." He feeds her and teaches her to play cribbage. Kit falls into Brass's trap. A five-pound note is found upon him. He is found guilty of theft and sentenced to transportation. Dick befriends him by sending a pot of beer to the jail every day.

Quilp – in his ecstasy about the sentence – demolishes and tortures a large figure-head which to him resembles his enemy.

Dick falls dangerously ill and is nursed back to life by the Marchioness, who has run away from the Brasses. She also tells him that she has overheard a conversation between Sampson and Sally Brass in which they discussed the details of how to entrap Kit. The truth is known – Kit is pardoned. Sampson is imprisoned but Sally manages to flee and to warn Quilp. In endeavouring to follow her advice and to flee, too, Quilp misses his way in the foggy starless night and is drowned in the river.

The single gentleman has found out where Nell and her grandfather are living. He travels there together with Kit and Mr. Garland. However, when they finally arrive they are once more too late. Nell has died two days earlier. The old man is half mad with grief. All his thoughts are bound up with the dead – he never grasps the idea that his younger brother has returned and means to share his wealth with him. After the old man's death the single gentleman travels in the steps of the two wanderers rewarding everybody who has helped them. Dick inherits a legacy and sends the Marchioness to school. They get married when she is about nineteen years old. Kit and Barabara get married, too, and have children. Kit often tells his children the story of Miss Nell and shows them where the old curiosity shop used to stand. "But he soon became uncertain of the spot, and could only say it was thereabouts... Such are the changes which a few years bring about, and so do things pass away, like a tale that is told."


## Summary of *Little Dorrit*

William Dorrit, an elderly gentleman, has been imprisoned for debt for more than twenty years. He has acquired a special standing in the prison. He is the "genteelest" of its inhabitants and is called the Father of the Marshalsea. Newcomers are presented to him and render him homage while at the same time supporting him with their "testimonials", i.e. little offerings of money. Mr. Dorrit has three children, Fanny, Edward and Amy or – as she is often called – Little Dorrit. His wife had died when Amy was still only a very small child. Little Dorrit was born in the Marshalsea and is called the Child of the Marshalsea. At the beginning of the story she is about twenty-two years old but of small stature and childlike appearance. She tenderly loves her father, whose every ill humour she patiently bears. She is also devoted to her brother and sister. Fanny is a dancer in a third-rate theatre and lives with her uncle, Frederick Dorrit, a slovenly but lovable clarinet-player. Tip or Edward Dorrit tries his hand at several occupations without success and invariably returns to the care of his sister Amy. Little Dorrit has been in charge of the family affairs for many years and goes out sewing to earn their living. She is unbelievably self-denying and modest. One of her employers is Mrs. Clennam, a sternly religious and gloomy woman who has been confined to her wheelchair for some fifteen years. Her husband has just died and her son, Arthur, has returned from China where he worked together with his father on behalf of the firm.

Arthur meets Little Dorrit at his mother's house and immediately takes an interest in her. He befriends her and Little Dorrit falls in love with him without his being aware of it. Clennam, for his part, loves Pet Meagles, the beautiful daughter of a friend of his. Pet, however, gets married to the flippant and heartless Henry Gowan. The Meagles have half adopted and half employed a young girl to whom they have given the name Tattycoram. She is a companion to Pet and is given to sudden outbursts of jealousy. Miss Wade, a single woman of a proud and revengeful character, witnesses some of these scenes and encourages Tattycoram to leave the Meagleses and to live with her. We also meet another employer of Little Dorrit, Flora Finching. She is Arthur's former love, now a rather talkative and stout woman of forty whose husband has died and has left her a legacy, "Mr. F.'s aunt", an old woman who conceives an apparently groundless hatred of Arthur. Flora's father is Mr. Casby, "the Patriarch", who conceals behind his benevolent appearance a stunning greediness. Thus he urges his grubber, Pancks, again and again, to "squeeze" the people of his slum-houses, when they are unable to pay their rents.

In Mrs. Clennam's house there live a couple, Mr. and Mrs. Jeremiah and Affery Flintwinch. He is Mrs. Clennam's business partner, she is her maid and is terrorized by "them two clever ones". Strange things happen in the house. There are inexplicable noises and mysterious visitors but whenever Affery hints at having seen or heard any such thing she is violently shaken by her husband who commands her to wake up from her dream so that she becomes more and more confused.

It is Pancks, who, with a great deal of energy and zest, discovers and is able to prove that William Dorrit is heir to a large fortune. Mr. Dorrit is released from prison and takes his family abroad. His daughters are chaperoned by one Mrs. General, the "eminent varnisher of surfaces". Whereas Mr. Dorrit and his children Edward and Fanny take on airs and behave very snobbishly, Little Dorrit cannot get used to her new life in which her careful planning and fretting for the family is no longer needed and in which she is kept apart from her father.

Clennam has found employment as the business partner of Daniel Doyce, a friend of the Meagleses'. Doyce has contrived a highly original invention but cannot put it to use since the Circumlocution Office (a satire on the dilatory methods of the English government) is bent on discouraging people from having any thoughts at all and smothers them in forms that must be filled in. Dickens's satire finds another target in the persons of Mr. and Mrs. Merdle. Mr. Merdle is a financier who is adored by everyone because of his immense wealth, whereas Mrs. Merdle, "the Bosom", is there to hang jewels upon and to personify the voice of society. Mrs. Merdle has a son, Edmund Sparkler, by her former husband. Mr. Sparkler met Fanny Dorrit when her father was still imprisoned and immediately fell in love with her. However, Mrs. Merdle put an end to any further relations between them. In Italy the Dorrits once more meet with him and Mrs. Merdle and he becomes Fanny's devoted suitor. Fanny at first toys with him but finally accepts him although she despises him for his stupidity. She wants to take revenge on Mrs. Merdle, who has treated her so contemptuously, by making her look old in comparison with herself.

Mr. Merdle turns out to be a fraud. He kills himself, and thousands of people who have invested their money in his business are reduced to poverty. Clennam and Pancks have speculated as well and lost all their money. Clennam has not only invested his own capital but also that of the firm and is inconsolable. He is put into the Marshalsea prison for debt. Happily Mr. William Dorrit dies before having learned of the disaster which has ruined his family as well, his brother Frederick having joined him in death. Arthur lies ill in the Marshalsea. The son of the turnkey, "Young John", who loves Little Dorrit but has not been accepted by her, tells Arthur that she loves him. Arthur can hardly believe it. Little Dorrit comes to visit him and nurses him back to health. However, since Arthur believes her to be still rich, he does not want to accept her love. The dénouement of the novel is best told in the words of the appendix to the Penguin edition of *Little Dorrit:*

> Many years ago, a Mr Gilbert Clennam put forward his orphan nephew (Arthur's father) as husband for the Mrs Clennam in the story. They were married. Later, this Mrs Clennam discovered that her husband had already gone through a form of marriage with another woman, who had born him a son. Mrs. Clennam, a woman of vindictively self-righteous religiosity, demanded that the child (Arthur) be given into her own custody: if not, she would expose her husband, and bring about that his uncle cut off his financial support. She got her way, taking possession of the child Arthur, while his true mother went mad and died, and his father went abroad and later died too.
>
> Meanwhile, Gilbert Clennam has heard of the existence of Arthur's true mother; but all he has heard is that she was a girl whom his nephew had loved, but had abandoned in order to marry as his uncle had wished, and that she had subsequently gone mad and died. He has felt remorse at this, and as a kind of recompense has left, in a codicil to his will, a thousand guineas *to the youngest daughter of the man who had at one time acted as patron to this girl* (i.e. Arthur's true mother); *or,* if that man had no daughter, *to his brother's youngest daughter.*
>
> This man who had acted as patron to Arthur's mother was Frederick Dorrit: he had helped her, in her youth, to be a professional singer. But Frederick Dorrit had had no daughter. The legacy therefore became due to the youngest daughter of his brother: that is to say, *to Little Dorrit herself.*
>
> But: Arthur's father had dictated the codicil making this change in his will, to Mrs Clennam; and it had been witnessed by herself and Jeremiah Flintwinch. Mrs. Clennam, however, had concealed the codicil, hiding it in her house in a place which she alone knew. But then she became paralysed and could not get to it. Later the prospect of Arthur's home-coming from his many years in China made her uneasy: she saw that he might find the paper she had hidden. Therefore, on the very day of his return, she at last revealed the hiding-place to Flintwinch, and told him to locate the paper and destroy it. But he did not destroy it. Instead, he gave it, with other papers (old letters, in fact, written by Arthur's true mother during her madness), in an iron box, to his twin brother Ephraim Flintwinch, who was at that time staying in the house. (...) Jeremiah did this either as giving him a chance to blackmail Mrs Clennam, or simply for the satisfaction of knowing that he had bested her. Ephraim Flintwinch later resided at Antwerp (apparently to be out of reach of his creditors, since he too was a 'Debtor'). Rigaud-Blandois became one of his drinking cronies there, and when he died (of a fit), got possession of the box and so of the suppressed codicil, and was therefore in a position to blackmail Mrs Clennam as she had blackmailed her husband and Arthur's mother long ago.[2]

When Blandois tells Mrs. Clennam that she has no choice but to pay him, since he has left an account of the story in the hands of Little Dorrit to be read if not reclaimed

2 Charles Dickens, *Little Dorrit,* ed. by John Holloway, Penguin Books, 1978, pp. 896-897; emphasis the editor's.

before sunset, Mrs. Clennam suddenly regains the power of her limbs and hurries to Little Dorrit. She tells her to read the documents and implores her to spare her and not to divulge the secret to Arthur before she, Mrs. Clennam, has died. This Little Dorrit promises. When she hurries back with Mrs. Clennam to the old house they witness its sudden collapse and see how Blandois is buried in its ruins. Flintwinch, however, is not found underneath the stones; he has disappeared. Mrs. Clennam is reduced to total paralysis and has even lost the power of speech. Affery remains her faithful servant.

Doyce returns and releases Arthur from prison. Since Arthur has heard of Little Dorrit's loss of wealth, there is no longer any obstacle to their marriage and they are united to lead "a modest life of usefulness and happiness".

# Bibliography

## 1) Primary Sources

- Charles Dickens, "Introduction to the Memories of Grimaldi", *Thalia* 1 (1978), pp. 57-73.

### Editions of the Works of Charles Dickens

#### a) Novels and Shorter Pieces

- *The New Oxford Illustrated Dickens,* 21 vols., Oxford 1947-58.
- *The Clarendon Edition,* Oxford 1966 – .
  Harvey Peter SUCKSMITH, ed., *Little Dorrit,* Oxford 1979.
  Kathleen TILLOTSON, ed., *Oliver Twist,* Oxford 1966.
- *The Penguin Edition,* Harmondsworth 1965-78.

#### b) Letters

- Walter DEXTER, ed., *The Letters of Charles Dickens (The Nonesuch Edition),* 3 vols., 1938.
- Madeline HOUSE, Graham STOREY and Kathleen TILLOTSON, ed., *The Letters of Charles Dickens (The Pilgrim Edition),* 5 vols. issued so far, Oxford 1965 – .
- Walter DEXTER, ed., *Mr. and Mrs. Charles Dickens. His Letters to Her,* London 1935. With a Foreword by Their Daughter, Kate DICKENS PERUGINI.
- – – –, ed., *The Love Romance of Charles Dickens.* Told in His Letters to Maria Beadnell (Mrs. Winter), London 1936.
- Laurence HUTTON, ed., *Letters of Charles Dickens to Wilkie Collins,* Kraus Reprint Co., New York 1969.
- Edgar JOHNSON, ed., *Letters from Charles Dickens to Angela Burdett-Coutts.* 1841-65, London 1953.

#### c) Speeches

- K. J. FIELDING, ed., *The Speeches of Charles Dickens,* Oxford 1960.

## 2) Dickens: The Man and His Life

- A. W. C. BRICE and K. J. FIELDING, "Dickens and the Tooting Disaster", *Victorian Studies* 12 (1968), pp. 227-244.
- W. H. BOWEN, *Charles Dickens and His Family.* A Sympathetic Study, Cambridge 1956.
- R. L. BRANNAN, ed., *Under the Management of Mr. Charles Dickens.* His Production of "The Frozen Deep", New York 1966.
- Katherine CAROLAN, "Dickens' Last Christmases", *Dalhousie Review* 52 (1972), pp. 373-383.
- Philip COLLINS, *Charles Dickens. The Public Readings,* Oxford 1975.
- – – –, ed., *Charles Dickens. Interviews and Recollections,* 2 vols., London and Basingstoke 1981.
- Henry Fielding DICKENS, *Memories of My Father,* London 1928.
- – – –, *The Recollections of Sir Henry Dickens, K. C.,* London 1934.

- Kate DICKENS PERUGINI, "My Father's Love for Children", *The Dickensian* 7 (1911), pp. 117-119.
- Mary DICKENS, *Charles Dickens by His Eldest Daughter,* London 1885.
- Angus EASSON, " 'I, Elizabeth Dickens'. Light on John Dickens's Legacy", *The Dickensian* 67 (1971), pp. 35-40.
- John FORSTER, *The Life of Charles Dickens,* 1872-74, reprinted in the Everyman's Library Edition, 2 vols., ed. by A. J. HOPPE, London 1966.
- "New Letters of Mary HOGARTH and Her Sister Catherine", *The Dickensian* 63 (1967), pp. 75-80.
- Edgar JOHNSON, *Charles Dickens: His Tragedy and Triumph,* 2 vols., New York 1952, revised and abridged edition, *Charles Dickens,* London 1976.
- Fred KAPLAN, *Dickens and Mesmerism.* The Hidden Springs of Fiction. Princeton 1975.
- J. Hillis MILLER and David BOROWITZ, *Charles Dickens and George Cruikshank,* Los Angeles 1971.
- Norman and Jeanne MACKENZIE, *Dickens. A Life,* Oxford 1979.
- Ada NISBET, *Dickens and Ellen Ternan,* Berkeley 1952.
- J. B. PRIESTLEY, *Charles Dickens and His World,* London 1978.
- Sheila M. SMITH, "John Overs to Charles Dickens: A Working-Man's Letter and Its Implication", *Victorian Studies* 18 (1974), pp. 195-217.
- Harry STONE, "Dickens and the Jews", *Victorian Studies* 3 (1959), pp. 223-253.
- Gladys STOREY, *Dickens and Daughter,* London 1939.
- J. A. SUTHERLAND, "Dickens as Publisher", in: *Victorian Novelists and Publishers,* London 1976, pp. 166-187.
- Angus WILSON, *The World of Charles Dickens,* Penguin Books Ltd., Harmondsworth 1972.

## 3) Criticism

### a) The Old Curiosity Shop

- Rachel BENNET, "Punch Versus Christian in *The Old Curiosity Shop*", *The Review of English Studies* 22 (1971), pp. 423-434.
- A. E. DYSON, "*The Old Curiosity Shop.* Innocence and the Grotesque" in: A. E. DYSON, ed., *Dickens. Modern Judgements,* London 1968, pp. 59-81.
- Angus EASSON, "Dickens's Marchioness Again", *Modern Language Review* 65 (1970), pp. 517-18.
- George H. FORD, "Little Nell: The Limits of Explanatory Criticism" in: George H. FORD, *Dickens and His Readers,* Princeton 1955, pp. 55-71.
- Aldous HUXLEY, "Vulgarity in Literature" in: *Collected Essays,* London 1960, pp. 103-115.
- James R. KINCAID, "Laughter and Pathos: *The Old Curiosity Shop*" in: Robert B. PARTLOW, Jr., ed., *Dickens the Craftsman.* Strategies of Presentation, Carbondale and Edwardsville 1970, pp. 65-94.
- John LUCAS, "*The Old Curiosity Shop*" in: John LUCAS, *The Melancholy Man.* A Study of Dickens's Novels, London 1970, pp. 73-92.
- Robert Simpson McLEAN, "Putting Quilp to Rest", *Victorian Newsletter* 34 (1968), pp. 29-33.

- Robert Simpson McLEAN, "Another Source for Quilp", *Nineteenth Century Fiction* 26 (1971), pp. 337-39.
- John W. NOFFSINGER, "Dream in *The Old Curiosity Shop*", *South Atlantic Bulletin* 42 (1977), pp. 23-33.
- Toby A. OLSHIN, " 'The Yellow Dwarf' and *The Old Curiosity Shop*", *Nineteenth Century Fiction* 25 (1970), pp. 96-99.
- Robert L. PATTEN, " 'The Story-Weaver at His Loom': Dickens and the Beginning of *The Old Curiosity Shop*" in: Robert B. PARTLOW, Jr., ed., *Dickens the Craftsman*. Strategies of Presentation, Carbondale and Edwardsville 1970, pp. 44-63.
- Gabriel PEARSON, *"The Old Curiosity Shop"* in: John GROSS and Gabriel PEARSON, ed., *Dickens and the Twentieth Century,* London 1962, pp. 77-90.
- Branwen PRATT, "Sympathy for the Devil: A Dissenting View of Quilp", *Hartford Studies in Literature* 6 (1974), pp. 129-145.
- Philip ROGERS, "The Dynamics of Time in *The Old Curiosity Shop*", *Nineteenth Century Fiction* 28 (1973), pp. 127-145.
- Michael STEIG, "The Central Action of *The Old Curiosity Shop,* or Little Nell Revisited Again", *Literature and Psychology* 15 (1963), pp. 163-170.
- – – –, "Phiz's Marchioness", *Dickens Studies* 2 (1966), pp. 141-46.
- Mark SPILKA, "Little Nell Revisited", *Papers of the Michigan Academy of Science, Arts, and Letters* 45 (1960), pp. 427-437.
- Joan STEVENS, " 'Woodcuts Dropped Into the Text': The Illustrations in *The Old Curiosity Shop* and *Barnaby Rudge*", *Studies in Bibliography* 20 (1967), pp. 113-133.
- Stanley TICK, "The Decline and Fall of Little Nell: Some Evidence from the Manuscripts", *Pacific Coast Philology* 9 (1976), pp. 62-72.

b) Little Dorrit

- Robert BARNARD, "The Imagery of *Little Dorrit*", *English Studies* 52 (1971), pp. 520-32.
- Edmund BERGLER, " 'Little Dorrit' and Dickens' Intuitive Knowledge of Psychic Masochism", *American Imago* 14 (1957), pp. 371-388.
- B. A. BOOTH, "Trollope and *Little Dorrit*", *Nineteenth Century Fiction: Trollopian* (1948), pp. 237-40.
- Peter CHRISTMAS, "Little Dorrit: The End of Good and Evil", *Dickens Studies Annual* 6 (1977), pp. 134-153.
- Ross H. DABNEY, *"Little Dorrit"* in: Ross H. DABNEY, *Love and Property in the Novels of Dickens,* London 1967, pp. 93-124.
- Robert GARIS, *"Little Dorrit"* in: Robert GARIS, *The Dickens Theatre,* Oxford 1965, pp. 164-188.
- T. N. GROVE, "The Psychological Prison of Arthur Clennam in Dickens's *Little Dorrit*", *Modern Language Review* 68 (1973), pp. 750-755.
- Paul D. HERRING, "Dickens' Monthly Number Plans for *Little Dorrit*", *Modern Philology* (1966), pp. 22-63.
- George HOLOCH, "Consciousness and Society in 'Little Dorrit' ", *Victorian Studies* 21 (1978), pp. 335-351.
- Fred KAPLAN, "Dickens' Flora Finching and Joyce's Molly Bloom", *Nineteenth Century Fiction* 23 (1968), pp. 343-46.

– F. R. and Q. D. LEAVIS, "Dickens and Blake: 'Little Dorrit' ", in F. R. and Q. D. LEAVIS, *Dickens the Novelist,* London 1970, pp. 213-76.
– Ronald S. LIBRACH, "The Burdens of Self and Society: Release and Redemption in *Little Dorrit",* *Studies in the Novel* 7 (1975), pp. 538-51.
– John LUCAS, *"Little Dorrit"* in: John LUCAS, *The Melancholy Man: A Study of Dickens's Novels,* London 1970, pp. 244-286.
– R. D. McMASTER, *"Little Dorrit:* Experience and Design", *Queens Quarterly* 67 (1961), pp. 530-38.
– William MYERS, "The Radicalism of 'Little Dorrit' ", in: John LUCAS, ed., *Literature & Politics in the Nineteenth Century,* London 1975, pp. 77-104.
– Dianne F. SADOFF, "Storytelling and the Figure of the Father in *Little Dorrit",* *PMLA* 95 (1980), pp. 234-245.
– J. G. SCHIPPERS, "So Many Characters, So Many Words: Some Aspects of the Language of *Little Dorrit",* *Dutch Quarterly Review* 8 (1978), pp. 242-265.
– Randolph SPLITTER, "Guilt and the Trappings of Melodrama in *Little Dorrit",* *Dickens Studies Annual* 6 (1977), 119-33.
– Richard STANG, *"Little Dorrit:* A World in Reverse", in: Robert B. PARTLOW, Jr., ed., *Dickens the Craftsman.* Strategies of Presentation, Carbondale and Edwardsville 1970, pp. 140-164.
– Stanley TICK, "The Sad End of Mr. Meagles", *Dickens Studies Annual* 3 (1974), pp. 87-99.
– John WAIN, *"Little Dorrit"* in: John GROSS and Gabriel PEARSON, ed., *Dickens and the Twentieth Century,* London 1962, pp. 175-186.
– Alan WILDE, "Mr. F's Aunt and the Analogical Structure of *Little Dorrit",* *Nineteenth Century Fiction* 19 (1964), pp. 33-44.
– George WING, "Mr. F's Aunt: A Laughing Matter", *English Studies in Canada* 3 (1977), pp. 207-15.

c) The Other Works and General Criticism

– Richard J. ARNESON, "Benthamite Utilitarianism and *Hard Times",* *Philosophy and Literature* 2 (1978), pp. 60-75.
– Richard BARICKMAN, "The Comedy of Survival in Dickens' Novels", *Novel: A Forum on Fiction* 2 (1978), pp. 128-143.
– John BAYLEY, *"Oliver Twist:* 'Things as they really are' " in: John GROSS and Gabriel PEARSON, ed., *Dickens and the Twentieth Century,* London 1962, pp. 49-64.
– Jonathan BISHOP, "The Hero-Villain of *Oliver Twist",* *Victorian Newsletter* 15 (1959), pp. 14-16.
– John BUTT and Kathleen TILLOTSON, *Dickens at Work,* New York 1958.
– John CAREY, *The Violent Effigy.* A Study of Dickens' Imagination, London 1973.
– Philip COLLINS, *Dickens and Crime,* London 1962.
– – – –, *Dickens and Education,* London 1965.
– – – –, "Dickens' Self-Estimate: Some New Evidence" in: Robert B. PARTLOW, Jr., ed., *Dickens the Craftsman.* Strategies of Presentation, Carbondale and Edwardsville 1970, pp. 21-43.
– – – –, ed., *Dickens. The Critical Heritage,* London 1971.
– – – –, "Charles Dickens" in: *Victorian Fiction. A Second Guide to Research,* ed. by George H. FORD, New York 1978, pp. 34-113.

- R. G. COLLINS, "Dickens and Grimaldi", *Thalia* 1 (1978), pp. 55-56.
- Katherine CAROLAN, " 'The Battle of Life', A Love Story", *The Dickensian* 69 (1973), pp. 105-110.
- R. J. CRUIKSHANK, *The Humour of Charles Dickens,* London 1952.
- Peter COVENAY, *Poor Monkey.* The Child in Literature, London 1957.
- James A. DAVIES, "Forster and Dickens: The Making of Podsnap", *The Dickensian* 70 (1974), pp. 145-58.
- Joseph M. DUFFY, Jr., "Another Version of Pastoral: *Oliver Twist*", Journal of English Literary History 35 (1968), pp. 403-421.
- Leslie A. FIEDLER, "What Can We Do About Fagin? The Jew-Villain in Western Tradition", *Commentary* 8 (1949), pp. 411-18.
- George H. FORD, *Dickens and His Readers.* Aspects of Novel-Criticism Since 1836, Princeton 1955.
- E. M. FORSTER, *Aspects of the Novel,* first published 1927, Pelican Books 1971.
- Elliot L. GILBERT, "The Ceremony of Innocence: Charles Dickens' *A Christmas Carol*", *PMLA* 90 (1975), pp. 22-31.
- Russell M. GOLDFARB, "The Menu of *Great Expectations*", *Victorian Newsletter* 21 (1962), pp. 18-19.
- – – –, "Charles Dickens; Orphans, Incest, and Repression", in: GOLDFARB, *Sexual Repression and Victorian Literature,* Lewisburg 1970, pp. 114-138.
- Graham GREENE, "The Young Dickens", in: *Collected Essays,* London 1969, pp. 101-111.
- – – –, "The Lost Childhood", in: *Collected Essays,* London 1969, pp. 13-19.
- Albert J. GUERARD, *The Triumph of the Novel: Dickens, Dostoevsky, Faulkner,* New York 1976.
- Eiichi HARA, "Name and No Name: The Identity of Dickensian Heroes" *Studies in English Literature,* English Number, 1982, pp. 21-42.
- Douglas HEWITT, *The approach to fiction,* Bristol 1972.
- Keith HOLLINGSWORTH, *The Newgate Novel.* 1830-1847, Detroit 1963.
- Humphry HOUSE, *The Dickens World,* Oxford 1960.
- Edward HURLEY, "A Missing Childhood in *Hard Times*", *Victorian Newsletter* 42 (1972), pp. 11-16.
- Edgar JOHNSON, "Dickens, Fagin, and Mr. Riah. The Intention of the Novelist", *Commentary* 9 (1950), pp. 47-50.
- James R. KINCAID, "Laughter and *Oliver Twist*", *PMLA* 83 (1968), pp. 63-70.
- – – –, *Dickens and the Rhetoric of Laughter,* Oxford 1971.
- F. R. LEAVIS, *"Hard Times",* in: LEAVIS, *The Great Tradition,* London 1973, 227-48.
- Barbara LECKER, "The Split Characters of Charles Dickens", *English Studies* 62 (1981), pp. 429-41.
- Alec LUCAS, *"Oliver Twist* and the Newgate Novel", *Dalhousie Review* 34 (1954), pp. 381-87.
- Sylvia MANNING, "Masking and Self-Revelation: Dickens's Three Autobiographies", *Dickens Studies Newsletter* 7 (1976), pp. 69-74.
- Mordecai MARCUS, "The Pattern of Self-Alienation in *Great Expectations*", *Victorian Newsletter* 26 (1964), pp. 9-12.
- Steven MARCUS, *Dickens: From Pickwick to Dombey,* London and New York 1964.

- Stefanie MEIER, *Animation and Mechanization in the Novels of Charles Dickens,* Bern 1982.
- J. Hillis MILLER, *Charles Dickens: The World of His Novels,* Bloomington and London ²1973.
- Ada NISBET, "The Autobiographical Matrix of *Great Expectations*", *Victorian Newsletter* 15 (1959), pp. 10-13.
- Norman PAGE, " 'A language fit for heroes'. Speech in *Oliver Twist* and *Our Mutual Friend",* *The Dickensian* 65 (1969), pp. 100-107.
- William J. PALMER, "*Hard Times:* A Dickens Fable of Personal Salvation", *Dalhousie Review* 52 (1972), pp. 67-77.
- Robert L. PATTEN, "Autobiography Into Autobiography: The Evolution of *David Copperfield*", in: George P. LANDOW, ed., *Approaches to Victorian Autobiography,* Athens, Ohio 1979, pp. 269-91.
- Randolph QUIRK, "Some Observations on the Language of Dickens", *Review of English Literature* 2 (1961), pp. 19-28.
- John R. REED, "Confinement and Character in Dickens' Novels", *Dickens Studies Annual* 1 (1970), 41-54.
- J. C. REID, *The Hidden World of Charles Dickens,* Auckland 1962.
- Emil STAIGER, *Gipfel der Zeit.* Studien zur Weltliteratur, Zürich 1979.
- Michael STEIG, "Dickens, Hablôt Browne, and the Tradition of English Caricature", *Criticism* 11 (1969), pp. 219-33.
- – – –, "Cruikshank's Peacock Feathers in *Oliver Twist*", *Ariel* 4 (1973), pp. 49-53.
- Henri TALON, "On Some Aspects of the Comic in *Great Expectations*", *Victorian Newsletter* 42 (1972), pp. 6-11.
- J. J. TOBIAS, "Ikey Solomons – a Real-life Fagin", *The Dickensian* 69 (1972), pp. 171-75.
- Michael A. ULLMAN, "Where George Stopped Growing: Dickens's *George Silverman's Explanation*", *Ariel* 10 (1979), pp. 11-23.
- Angus WILSON, "Dickens on Children and Childhood", in: M. SLATER, ed., *Dickens,* New York 1970, pp. 195-227.
- Edmund WILSON, "Dickens: the Two Scrooges", in: *The Wound and the Bow,* first published 1941, revised edition, London 1952, pp. 1-93.
- Warrington WINTERS, "Charles Dickens: The Pursuer and the Pursued", *Victorian Newsletter* 23 (1963), pp. 23-24.
- – – –, "Dickens' *Hard Times:* The Lost Childhood", *Dickens Studies Annual* 2 (1972), pp. 217-36.
- Alex ZWERDLING, "Esther Summerson Rehabilitated", *PMLA* 88 (1973), pp. 429-439.

### d) Psychoanalytic Criticism

- Sharon BASSETT, "The Practice of Psychoanalytic Criticism" *Literature and Psychology* 27 (1977), pp. 43-48.
- Arthur Washburn BROWN, *Sexual Analysis of Dickens' Props,* New York 1971.
- Steven COHAN, " 'They Are All Secret': The Fantasy Content of *Bleak House",* *Literature and Psychology* 26 (1976), pp. 79-91.
- Lawrence Jay DESSNER, "*Great Expectations:* 'the ghost of a man's own father' ", *PMLA* 91 (1976), pp. 436-449.

- Sander L. GILMAN, "On the Use and Abuse of the History of Psychiatry for Literary Studies", *Deutsche Vierteljahresschrift für Literaturwissenschaft und Geistesgeschichte* 52 (1978), pp. 381-99.
- Sebastian GOEPPERT, "Vom Nutzen der Psychoanalyse für die Literaturkritik", *Neue Zürcher Zeitung,* 12./13. März 1977.
- Phyllis GREENACRE, *Swift and Carroll.* A Psychoanalytic Study of Two Lives, New York 1955.
- Dominick E. GRUNDY, "Growing Up Dickensian", *Literature and Psychology* 22 (1972), pp. 99-106.
- Gordon D. HIRSCH, "Charles Dickens' Nurse's Stories", *The Psychoanalytic Review* 62 (1975), pp. 173-79.
- Norman N. HOLLAND, *5 Readers Reading,* New Haven 1975.
- – – –, "Unity Identity Text Self", *PMLA* 90 (1975), pp. 813-22.
- Albert D. HUTTER, "Nation and Generation in *A Tale of Two Cities*", *PMLA* 93 (1978), pp. 448-62.
- Mark KANZER, "Autobiographical Aspects of the Writer's Imagery", *International Journal of Psychoanalysis* 40 (1959), pp. 52-58.
- Charles KLIGERMAN, "The Dream of Charles Dickens", *Journal of the American Psychoanalytic Association* 18 (1970), pp. 783-99.
- Ernst KRIS, *Psychoanalytic Explorations in Art,* New York 1965.
- Leonard F. MANHEIM, "The Law as 'Father' ", *American Imago* 12 (1955), pp. 17-23.
- – – –, "The Dickens Hero as Child", *Studies in the Novel* 1 (1969), pp. 189-95.
- – – –, "The Personal History of David Copperfield", in: Leonard TENNENHOUSE, ed., *The Practice of Psychoanalytic Criticism,* Detroit 1976, pp. 75-94.
- Steven MARCUS, "Who is Fagin?", in: MARCUS, *Dickens: From Pickwick to Dombey,* London and New York 1964, pp. 358-378.
- Peter von MATT, "Die Opus-Phantasie", *Psyche* 33 (1979), pp. 193-212.
- Adolf MUSCHG, *Gottfried Keller,* München 1977.
- William NIEDERLAND, "Psychoanalytic Approaches to Creativity", *The Psychoanalytic Quarterly* 14 (1976), pp. 185-212.
- Pinchas NOY, "Form Creation in Art: An Ego Psychological Approach to Creativity", *The Psychoanalytic Quarterly* 48 (1979), pp. 229-56.
- E. PEARLMAN, "David Copperfield Dreams of Drowning", in: Leonard TENNENHOUSE, ed., *The Practice of Psychoanalytic Criticism,·*Detroit 1976, pp. 105-117.
- Branwen Bailey PRATT, "Fred Kaplan, Dickens, and Mesmerism: The Hidden Springs of Fiction", *Literature and Psychology* 27 (1977), pp. 35-42.
- Gail Simon REED, "Dr. Greenacre and Captain Gulliver: Notes on Conventions of Interpretation and Reading", *Literature and Psychology* 26 (1976), pp. 185-190.
- Alan ROLAND, "Toward a Reorientation of Psychoanalytic Literary Criticism", *The Psychoanalytic Review* 65 (1978), pp. 391-414.
- Harry SLOCHOWER, "The Psychoanalytic Approach to Literature: Some Pitfalls and Promises", *Literature and Psychology* 21 (1971), pp. 107-111.
- Michael STEIG, "Dickens' Excremental Vision", *Victorian Studies* 13 (1970), pp. 339-54.
- Taylor STOEHR, *Charles Dickens: The Dreamer's Stance,* New York 1965.

– Harry STONE, "The Love Pattern in Dickens' Novels", in: Robert B. PART-
LOW, Jr., ed., *Dickens the Craftsman*. Strategies of Presentation, Carbondale and
Edwardsville 1970, pp. 1-20.
– Lionel TRILLING, "Freud and Literature", in: TRILLING, *The Liberal Imagina-
tion*. Essays on Literature and Society, New York 1953, pp. 44-64.
– David WERMAN, "Methodological Problems in the Psychoanalytic Interpretation
of Literature: A Review of Studies on Sophocles' *Antigone*", *Journal of the
American Psychoanalytic Association* 27 (1979), pp. 451-78.
– Warrington WINTERS, "*The Death Hug in Charles Dickens*", *Literature and
Psychology* 16 (1966), pp. 109-115.

## 4) Psychology – Psychoanalysis

– Karl ABRAHAM, "Versuch einer Entwicklungsgeschichte der Libido auf Grund
der Psychoanalyse seelischer Störungen" (1924), in: *Psychoanalytische Studien I*,
Frankfurt a. Main ²1971, pp. 113-83.
– Hermann ARGELANDER, *Der Flieger*. Eine charakteranalytische Fallstudie,
Frankfurt a. Main 1972.
– Thomas AUCHTER, "Trauer und Kreativität", *Psyche* 32 (1978), pp. 52-77.
– Virginia M. AXLINE, *Dibs in Search of Self*, first published 1964, Ballantine
Books 1977.
– Alice BALINT, *Die Urformen der Liebe und die Technik der Psychoanalyse*,
Stuttgart and Bern 1966, pp. 116-35.
– Therese BENEDEK, "Parenthood as a Developmental Phase", *Journal of the
American Psychoanalytic Association* 7 (1959), pp. 389-417.
– David BERES, "Psycho-Analysis and the Biography of the Artist", *International
Journal of Psychoanalysis* 40 (1959), pp. 26-37.
– Henri BERGSON, "Le rire", in: BERGSON, *Œuvres*, Paris 1959, pp. 387-483.
– Bruno BETTELHEIM, *The Uses of Enchantment*. The Meaning and Importance
of Fairy Tales, New York 1976.
– Harold P. BLUM, "On the Concept and Consequences of the Primal Scene", *The
Psychoanalytic Quarterly* 48 (1979), pp. 27-47.
– Janine CHASSEGUET-SMIRGEL, "Letztes Jahr in Marienbad. Zur Methodolo-
gie der psychoanalytischen Erschliessung des Kunstwerks", in: Alexander MIT-
SCHERLICH, ed., *Psychopathographien I: Schriftsteller und Psychoanalyse*,
Frankfurt a. Main 1972, pp. 182-213.
– Edwin I. CORBIN, "The Autonomous Ego Functions in Creativity", *Journal of
the American Psychoanalytic Association* 22 (1974), pp. 568-587.
– Martha EICKE-SPENGLER, "Zur Entwicklung der psychoanalytischen Theorie
der Depression", *Psyche* 31 (1977), pp. 1079-1125.
– Paula ELKISCH, "The Psychological Significance of the Mirror", *Journal of the
American Psychoanalytic Association* 5 (1957), pp. 235-44.
– Joan FLEMING and Sol ALTSCHUL, "Activation of Mourning and Growth by
Psychoanalysis", *International Journal of Psychoanalysis* 44 (1963), pp. 419-31.
– Victor E. FRANKL, *The Doctor and the Soul*. From Psychotherapy to Logother-
apy, first published in Vienna 1946 as *Ärztliche Seelsorge*, Penguin Books 1973.

– Anna FREUD, *Das Ich und die Abwehrmechanismen,* Wien 1936, München Kindler Taschenbücher No. 2001 (7th edition).

– – – –, *Wege und Irrwege in der Kinderentwicklung,* Bern und Stuttgart ²1971.

– Sigmund FREUD, *Aus den Anfängen der Psychoanalyse.* Briefe an Wilhelm Fliess, Abhandlungen und Notizen aus den Jahren 1887-1902. Ed. by Marie BONA-PARTE, Anna FREUD, Ernst KRIS, Frankfurt a. Main 1975.

– – – –, *Studienausgabe,* 10 vols. and suppl. vol., ed. by Alexander MITSCHER-LICH, Angela RICHARDS, James STRACHEY, Frankfurt a. Main 1969-75.

– Sigmund FREUD / C. G. JUNG, *Briefwechsel,* ed. by William McGUIRE and Wolfgang SAUERLÄNDER, Frankfurt a. Main 1974.

– Phyllis GREENACRE, "The Childhood of the Artist: Libidinal Phase Development and Giftedness", *The Psychoanalytic Study of the Chid* 12 (1957), pp. 27-72.

– – – –, "Play in Relation to Creative Imagination", *The Psychoanalytic Study of the Child* 14 (1959), pp. 61-80.

– Martin GROTJAHN, *Beyond Laughter,* New York 1957.

– Béla GRUNBERGER, *Vom Narzissmus zum Objekt,* Frankfurt a. Main 1976.

– Ursula GRUNERT, "Narzisstische Restitutionsversuche im Traum", *Psyche* 31 (1977), pp. 1057-1078.

– Heinz HENSELER, *Narzisstische Krisen.* Zur Psychodynamik des Selbstmords, Hamburg 1974.

– – – –, "Die Suizidhandlung unter dem Aspekt der psychoanalytischen Narzissmus-theorie", *Psyche* 29 (1975), pp. 191-207.

– Edith JACOBSON, "Contribution to the Metapsychology of Psychotic Identifica-tions", *Journal of the American Psychoanalytic Association* 2 (1954), pp. 239-262.

– – – –, *The Self and the Object World,* New York 1964.

– Otto F. KERNBERG, "Normal and Pathological Narcissism in Middle Age", unpublished paper, read at the Ausbildungszentrum der Schweizerischen Gesell-schaft für Psychoanalyse Zürich in June 1979.

– Charles KLIGERMAN, "Panel on 'Creativity' ", *International Journal of Psycho-analysis* 53 (1972), pp. 21-30.

– Heinz KOHUT, *The Analysis of the Self,* New York 1971.

– – – –, "Thoughts on Narcissism and Narcissistic Rage", *Psychoanalytic Study of the Child* 27 (1972), pp. 360-400.

– – – –, *The Restoration of the Self,* New York 1977.

– Heinz KOHUT and Ernest S. WOLF, "The Disorders of the Self and Their Treatment: An Outline", *International Journal of Psychoanalysis* 59 (1978), pp. 413-25.

– Marianne KRÜLL, *Freud und sein Vater.* Die Entstehung der Psychoanalyse und Freuds ungelöste Vaterbindung, München 1979.

– R. D. LAING, *The Divided Self.* An Existential Study in Sanity and Madness, first published 1960, Penguin Books 1976.

– Henry LOWENFELD, "Psychic Trauma and Productive Experience in the Artist", *The Psychoanalytic Quarterly* 10 (1941), pp. 116-130.

– Margaret S. MAHLER, Fred PINE, and Anni BERGMAN, *The Psychological Birth of the Human Infant.* Symbiosis and Individuation, London 1975.

– Alice MILLER, *Das Drama des begabten Kindes* und die Suche nach dem wahren Selbst, Frankfurt a. Main 1979.

– – – –, *Am Anfang war Erziehung,* Frankfurt a. Main 1980.

- Alice MILLER, *Du sollst nicht merken*. Variationen über das Paradies Thema, Frankfurt a. Main 1981.
- Hans MUELLER-BRAUNSCHWEIG, "Aspekte einer psychoanalytischen Kreativitätstheorie", *Psyche* 31 (1977), pp. 821-43.
- Wayne A. MYERS, "Imaginary Companions in Childhood and Adult Creativity", *The Psychoanalytic Quarterly* 48 (1979), pp. 292-307.
- – – –, "Clinical Consequences of Chronic Primal Scene Exposure", *The Psychoanalytic Quarterly* 48 (1979), pp. 1-20.
- Karin OBHOLZER, *Gespräche mit dem Wolfsmann*. Eine Psychoanalyse und die Folgen, Reinbek bei Hamburg 1980.
- Joshua M. PERMAN, "The .Search for the Mother: Narcissistic Regression as a Pathway of Mourning in Childhood", *The Psychoanalytic Quarterly* 48 (1979), pp. 448-464.
- George H. POLLOCK, "On Mourning, Immortality, and Utopia", *Journal of the American Psychoanalytic Association* 23 (1975), pp. 334-62.
- – – –, "The Mourning Process and Creative Organizational Change", *Journal of the American Psychoanalytic Association* 25 (1977), pp. 3-34.
- Horst Eberhard RICHTER, *Der Gotteskomplex*. Die Geburt und die Krise des Glaubens an die Allmacht des Menschen, Reinbek bei Hamburg 1979.
- Rose Maria ROSENKÖTTER, "Das Märchen – eine vorwissenschaftliche Entwicklungspsychologie", *Psyche* 43 (1980), pp. 168-207.
- Morton SCHATZMAN, *Soul Murder*. Persecution in the Family, first published 1973, Pelican Books 1976.
- Max SCHUR, *Freud: Living and Dying,* London 1972.
- Philip M. SPIELMAN, "Envy and Jealousy. An Attempt at Clarification", *The Psychoanalytic Quarterly* 40 (1971), pp. 59-81.
- René A. SPITZ, and Godfrey W. COBLINER, *The First Year of Life*. A Psychoanalytic Study of Normal and Deviant Development of Object Relations, New York 1965.
- René A. SPITZ, *No and Yes: On the Beginnings of Human Communication*, New York 1957.
- – – –, "The Derailment of Dialogue: Stimulus Overload, Action Cycles, and the Completion Gradient", *Journal of the American Psychoanalytic Association* 12 (1964), pp. 752-75.
- D. W. WINNICOTT, *Playing and Reality*, Penguin Books Ltd., Harmondsworth 1971.
- – – –, *The Piggle*. An Account of the Psycho-Analytic Treatment of a Little Girl, London 1978.
- Warrington WINTERS, "Dickens and the Psychology of Dreams", *PMLA* 43 (1948), pp. 948-1006.
- Martha WOLFENSTEIN, "How Is Mourning Possible?", *The Psychoanalytic Study of the Child* 21 (1966), pp. 93-123.